WALKING
in the
DUST *of* RABBI
JESUS

HOW THE JEWISH WORDS *of* JESUS CAN CHANGE YOUR LIFE

LOIS TVERBERG

FOREWORD BY RAY VANDER LAAN
AFTERWORD BY ANN SPANGLER

ZONDERVAN
BOOKS

ZONDERVAN BOOKS

Walking in the Dust of Rabbi Jesus
Copyright © 2012 by Lois Tverberg

Published in Grand Rapids, Michigan, by Zondervan. Zondervan is a registered trademark of The Zondervan Corporation, L.L.C., a wholly owned subsidiary of HarperCollins Christian Publishing, Inc.

Requests for information should be addressed to customercare@harpercollins.com.

ISBN 978-0-310-33000-4 (softcover)
ISBN 978-0-310-41222-9 (audio)
ISBN 978-0-310-41220-5 (ebook)

Library of Congress Cataloging-in-Publication Data

Tverberg, Lois.
    Walking in the dust of Rabbi Jesus : how the Jewish words of Jesus can change your life/ Lois Tverberg.
      p. cm.
    Includes bibliographical references and index [if applicable].
    ISBN 978-0-310-28420-8 (hardcover)
    1. Jesus Christ — Jewishness. 2. Jesus Christ — Words. I. Title.
BT590.J8T84   2011
232.9'06 — dc23   2011035954

Published in association with the literary agency of Ann Spangler and Company, 1420 Pontiac Road SE, Grand Rapids, MI 49506.

Cover photography: iStockphoto®
Interior illustration: iStockphoto®
Interior design: Beth Shagene

Printed in the United States of America

24 25 26 27 28 LBC 64 63 62 61 60

To the Meshugenah Ladies:
Shirley, Kathleen, and Hillari,
wonderful haverot, *faithful friends.*

Contents

III STUDYING *the* WORD *with* RABBI JESUS | 143

Foreword

As an author, Bible teacher, and study tour leader, I have had the privilege of walking the lands of the Bible with thousands of Jesus' followers who came to see where Abraham, Ruth, David, and Jesus lived. I enjoyed watching group after group slowly come to realize that the Bible's stories are set in real times and real places. As they learned more about the land, the people, and the culture of the Bible, these believers saw that the context God chose for his redemptive plan could help them apply the Word to their own lives. At the end of their travels, I often heard people say, "I will never read the Bible the same way again."

Many returned home from Israel or Turkey or Greece with their faith in Jesus deepened but hungry for more — much more. The pilgrim excitement of "walking where Jesus walked" became a growing thirst for a deeper understanding of God's story — a thirst as palpable as their need for bottled water in the hot, dry climate of Israel.

I know their experience well — that was my journey too. I began to explore the Jewish world of Jesus with a desire to deepen my faith *in* Jesus. I was familiar with the accounts of his life and believed them to be true. I accepted his claims to be the Messiah and believed in his redemptive death. But as I entered the world of Jewish thought, I began to wonder about the faith *of* Jesus. I struggled to understand what I should learn from the accounts of how he *lived*. Was it simply to explain why he must die? Or was his life a pattern to be understood and emulated? And what did it mean to imitate him in my walk with God?

As I explored the lands and cultures of the Bible, I realized that I did indeed need to have not only faith *in* Jesus, but also to develop the faith *of* Jesus. To be a disciple of Jesus I needed to know why and how he lived out his faith, so that I could follow him more closely.

This insight seems so obvious now that I cannot imagine that I had not considered it before. I grew up in a Christian community, lived in a Christian home where the Bible was often read, attended Christian schools through college, and received an advanced degree at an outstanding seminary. I believed the Bible to be the inspired Word of God and from my childhood was committed to Jesus as Savior and Lord. Yet I had not even considered the implications of the fact that Jesus lived among us as a Jewish man in a first-century Jewish culture. Jesus was Jewish! What a radical thought!

From the beginning, God chose to speak and act within the context of human culture, so it is no surprise that his Son would do the same. Jesus lived like a Jew, talked like a Jew, and worshiped like a Jew. His words, actions, and teaching methods were in keeping with the customs, traditions, and practices of the Semitic culture into which he was born. He wasn't born in northwestern Iowa among nineteenth-century Dutch immigrants. He was born in Judea, a land that was a hotbed of political and religious turmoil, a country that had been the crossroads of the ancient world for centuries. He grew up among the Jews, a people chosen by God to bear his name to the world. And he ministered under the mighty empire of Rome. While God's message was and is timeless, it was first revealed to a real people in a real place and at a real time. Understanding this ancient world is critical to interpreting and applying the biblical story to our own lives.

In a sense, as we study the Bible, we must temporarily leave our twenty-first-century culture and our Western attitudes and go back to another time and place ... to the land of Israel, the birthplace and home of Jesus. We must enter an Eastern culture that was passionately religious and that longed for God's great redemption. The Jews of Jesus' time knew their story and fiercely debated how God wanted them to live it out. The Hebrew Bible was their daily bread, and discussion of it dominated their lives, as it would Jesus' life. Paradoxically, stepping back into that setting makes the Bible even more relevant to our own culture and time.

That was my journey from faith *in* Jesus to learning to live out the faith *of* Jesus. What I had been taught from the Bible was not wrong. Few, if any, doctrines changed for me as I studied the Bible's ancient Jewish context. And after thirty-six years of intensive cultural study, I still believe God is our Creator, Jesus is our Savior, and the Bible is his inspired Word. But there are more riches in the Word than I had ever imagined. To view Scripture through the perspective of an ancient Near Eastern culture is to gain additional insights, as certainly as reading the Bible in the original languages deepens one's grasp of the text.

Somewhere on the journey of studying the context and culture of the Bible, I met Lois Tverberg. Just like so many others I had known, her first experience of the ancient world of the Bible produced an ever-growing thirst for greater understanding of its story in context. She was as intense and intentional in her search as any student I had ever met, bringing her training and skill as a scientist to her pursuit of deeper understanding of the biblical text. Her tenacity in learning the ancient languages, in studying the land of Israel, in exploring Jewish thought, and in investigating archaeological discoveries provide her with a unique set of tools to explore the text in context. Soon I was learning from her, as her insights gave me a new understanding of the Bible and particularly the life of Jesus—the One we both knew as Savior and Lord, for we share a faith *in* Jesus. Through her insights Lois has deepened my understanding of the faith *of* Jesus and encouraged me to "walk ... as [Jesus] walked" (1 John 2:6 NASB).

Lois's earlier work (with Ann Spangler), *Sitting at the Feet of Rabbi Jesus*, was an entry step into Jesus' world. The Jewish context into which Jesus came and the implications of that setting for understanding him better are powerfully presented and have guided many believers as they seek a greater understanding of the Teacher from Nazareth. I believe the present work will have even greater impact on those who desire to be disciples of Jesus. Readers will be deeply challenged as they discover the implications of Jesus' teaching for their daily walk.

While each chapter is supported with careful analysis of contemporary scholarship, ancient sources, and recent archaeological discovery, as you read you will feel as if you are on a journey back to the world of Jesus. You will see the beauty of the silvery green olive trees on the Galilean hills, feel the rocky path under your feet, and smell the dust as you follow the Rabbi. You will hear the sages discussing the Torah as their disciples listen and will discover the greatest interpreter of all ... Jesus the Messiah. For he is not only God incarnate, but also the Word incarnate. His life is in a real sense the Word — the Bible — in living flesh. And you will be challenged to become ever more passionate about being his disciple — having the faith *of* Jesus. So come along with us and follow in the dust of Jesus — the Jewish Rabbi — of Scripture.

Ray Vander Laan

PART I

HEARING OUR RABBI'S WORDS *with* NEW EARS

What would it be like to listen to Jesus' earth-shattering words through the ears of a first-century disciple? The first thing you'd notice is how Jewish they are. His greatest commandments begin with the *Shema*, the core statement of Jewish faith. For over two millennia, each morning and evening, Jews have committed themselves to loving their one and only God with all of their heart, soul, and strength. Learning more about Jesus' language, his Scriptures, and his people will deepen our understanding of his most important words.

CHAPTER 1

Brushing Away the Dust of the Ages

*Just as rain water comes down in drops and forms rivers,
so with the Scriptures: one studies a bit today
and some more tomorrow, until in time the understanding
becomes like a flowing stream.*
— Song of Songs Midrash Rabbah 2:8

In 1977, Pinin Barcilon won the assignment of a lifetime when she was asked to lead the restoration of Leonardo da Vinci's *Last Supper*, one of the most well-known images of all time. But the renowned Italian art conservator could hardly imagine how nerve-wracking the next twenty-three years would be.

The centuries hadn't been kind to the mural that da Vinci completed on a monastery wall in Milan, Italy, in 1498. Always the experimenter, Leonardo had reformulated his paints in a way that proved to be unstable, so that the paint began flaking off even before his death. And even though his mural was immediately hailed as a masterpiece, it was left unprotected from pollution and humidity. When Barcilon began her restoration, five hundred years of dust, mold, and candle soot had darkened the iconic work almost to the point of invisibility.

The real challenge for her team, however, was to undo the disastrous attempts at restoration that had begun back in the 1700s. Heavy coats of varnish, glue, and wax had been brushed on, each of them hastening the darkening process. Worst of all, hack amateurs had painted over da Vinci's work time and again, rendering its images distorted, brushing out details they didn't understand, and filling in gaps with their own interpretations.

After months of photographing every square centimeter of the painting's surface and analyzing it using state-of-the-art technology, Barcilon's team members finally began their work. Then, for over twenty years they hunched over microscopes, painstakingly scraping away five hundred years of grime and overpainting. On a good day, one postage stamp's worth of the image would emerge. In 1999, when da Vinci's brushstrokes were finally revealed, her team's meticulous, mind-numbing labor found its reward. Barcilon called it a "slow, severe conquest, which, flake after flake, day after day, millimeter after millimeter, fragment after fragment, gave back a reading of the dimensions, of the expressive and chromatic intensity that we thought was lost forever."[1]

Gloomy shadows banished; a well-lit banquet hall emerged. Peter's beard and nose were free of the clumsy weight that later retouchings had given them. Matthew sported blond hair, not black. Thomas gained a left hand. Andrew's expression was transformed — he was no longer sullen, but astonished. And Jesus' face glowed with new light after the dingy repaintings had been removed.

The essence of the scene remained unchanged. Da Vinci had depicted the fateful scene at the moment Jesus revealed one of his disciples would soon betray him. But after centuries of murky obscurity, restoration had brought to light the original beauty of the artist's masterful portrayal of the facial expressions and body language of Christ and his disciples.[2]

Unearthing Jesus' World

Just as modern technology enabled Barcilon to reveal da Vinci's original strokes, in recent decades scholars have gained new tools to restore the picture of Jesus that the gospel writers first gave us. In just the past fifty years, we have seen more advances in biblical archaeology and in the discovery of ancient texts than in all the centuries since the time of Jesus. As dingy accretions of history are cleared away, vivid details of Jesus' life and culture are emerging.

The same year that the *Last Supper* was newly unveiled, I took my first study trip to Israel. One of the scarier highlights of our tour was exploring the water tunnel that King Hezekiah built under Jerusalem in 701 BC. Half terrified, our group peered into the dark, stone-hewn shaft before us and stepped down into the icy, rushing waters of the Gihon spring. After groping our way through the cramped blackness by flashlight for a third of a mile, waist-high water sweeping us along, we heaved a sigh of relief when we finally glimpsed the exit.

Adding to the thrill, we were emerging at the site of the famous Pool of Siloam, where a blind man miraculously recovered his vision after Jesus sent him there to wash (John 9:7). The puddle-deep pool was, admittedly, unimpressive—only a few feet wide and a few more yards long. But this was the famous site, according to Christian tradition that went back to the fourth century AD.

Or so we thought.

In 2004, five years after our visit, a sewage pipe broke underneath a nearby Jerusalem street. Massive earth-moving equipment rumbled in to make the repair. Pushing into the soil, a bulldozer blade collided with a submerged object and came to a grinding halt. An ancient plastered step emerged as the dirt was brushed away. Within minutes prominent archaeologists had rushed over, the word "bulldozer" hurrying them to the scene. Excavation revealed several more steps down one side of an enormous rectangular pool. Within weeks this monumental reservoir (about 160 feet wide by 200 feet long) was identified as the *real* Pool of Siloam, the main source of fresh water within Jerusalem's walls. Coins embedded in the plaster confirmed that it was in use during Jesus' time.[3]

As they excavated the Pool of Siloam archaeologists also discovered a wide, stepped first-century street that leads from the pool up to the Temple. This was one of the main Jerusalem thoroughfares in the first century, and it would have been the final steps of ascent for pilgrims after days or weeks of journeying to celebrate the feasts. The Pool of Siloam was one of the places where they could have stopped to purify themselves before entering the Temple.

And reading John's gospel again, we discover that the Pool of Siloam played a part in another scene in Jesus' ministry. Each night of the joyous weeklong Feast of Tabernacles (Sukkot), the high priest would parade down this street amid great fanfare and fill a golden pitcher with *living water* from the Pool of Siloam for the water libation on the Temple's altar. On the last day of the feast, the high priest would process around the altar seven times as the crowds chanted fervent prayers for *living water*, rain for the next year's crops. The roar grew ever more thunderous until the priest finally approached the altar. A hush would descend as he filled a silver bowl and then ceremoniously poured the *living water* onto the sacrificial pyre. It was then when Jesus stood up and shouted, "Let anyone who is thirsty come to me and drink. Whoever believes in me, as Scripture has said, rivers of *living water* will flow from within them" (John 7:37–38, italics added).

Details That Connect the Dots

My first exposure to this field of study was about fifteen years ago when I signed up for a class at my church called "The Land, the Culture, and the Book." Having grown up in a devout Lutheran family, I figured that learning some historical background would be good for my Bible study. My grandparents had been missionaries in Madagascar, and several uncles and cousins were pastors. My own world was the sciences, so I was more used to facts and lectures. My graduate degree was in biology, and I was teaching human physiology and molecular biology at a nearby college.

I admit that I cringed a little before starting the class, bracing myself for what I thought would be a weekly dose of dusty, dry archaeological information. I didn't know much about the presenter except that he had taught high school for twenty-five years and had been leading study trips to Israel for twenty-five years—mentally I calculated his age at about eighty-seven. How appropriate to learn about the Old Testament from an octogenarian, I thought.[4] (Not catching that the presenter, Ray Vander Laan, had being doing these things *concurrently*, I was off by about forty years.)

But from the first session the class was like drinking from a fire hose. Everywhere the Bible started greening up, sprouting with new life. It was there that I first heard of the biblical idea of *living water* and learned about its association with the Feast of Tabernacles and with the outpouring of the Spirit during the messianic age (Ezekiel 47; Joel 2:23–29; Zechariah 14:8–18).

As I started to see how important history, geography, language, and culture were for unlocking the biblical text, my curiosity led me to study in the land of Israel, to learn from scholars there about first-century Jewish culture, and to study Hebrew and Greek.[5] A few years later I left the world of teaching biology to write and teach about this subject full-time.

You might think that you need to master whole textbooks before this kind of study starts to enrich your Bible reading, but I've been amazed at how the smallest details can help connect the dots. It's like when you're stumped doing a crossword puzzle but then finally decipher one word. Suddenly an adjoining word falls into place, which yields clues to unlock yet more words, and then the rest of the grid starts to fill in.

The simplest cultural details can unravel knotty mysteries, sometimes with powerful theological implications. For instance, how much would the firewood weigh for an average burnt offering? You might think that minutiae like this isn't worth studying, but this obscure detail casts light on one of the Bible's most difficult chapters.

After reading the account in Genesis 22 about God's asking Abraham to sacrifice Isaac, many people ask, "How old was Isaac?" Was he a toddler, a teen, or an adult? Most paintings picture Isaac as a child toting a bundle of sticks under his arm as he walks beside his elderly father. This is because Genesis 22:6 says that Abraham carried the knife while Isaac carried the wood for the sacrifice.

But a sacrifice was offered by roasting an animal as a whole burnt offering, which took several hours over a full fire.[6] The large logs needed for fuel would require the strength of a full-grown man to carry them. There was no way the elderly Abraham could lift them (remember, he was one hundred already when Isaac was born), so he carried the knife while Isaac carried the wood. In fact, for most of the journey, two donkeys bore the massive burden (verse 3).

Once you envision an adult Isaac bearing the heavy wood, the story takes on an entirely different tone. Now we see that the story is not just about Abraham's unshakeable faith in God; it's about Isaac's willing, heroic obedience to submit to his father's will. And suddenly the scene of Christ carrying his cross comes starkly into view.

Hearing Jesus through a Disciple's Ears

What does it mean that Jesus lived as a Jewish rabbi who called and trained disciples? And how does learning about his teachings in their original context enable us to better live out our calling? Jesus' first followers responded to his words with actions that astound us. They left home, family, and comfort behind to follow him, risking their lives to change the world. As life-changing as his teachings were in their original context, modern readers often struggle to see what provoked such a radical response. More than twenty centuries separate us. Could it be that the debris of time and cultural change have taken the edge off Jesus' earth-shattering words?

What if we could scrub off the dust and dirt of the ages to see the original Jesus in the Gospels? What if we allowed the scenery around him to come to life, so that we could visualize him once again in his native context? Jesus' words would not change, but they would burst with new meaning when understood in their original setting. We would see Jesus with new clarity as we bring into focus the fuzzy backdrop around him that is so foreign to our modern world—a place of rabbis and synagogues, nomads, farmers, kings, and shepherds.

> *The world stands on three things: on Torah, worship, and loving deeds of kindness.*
> —Mishnah, *Avot* 1:2

It's hard not to wonder if the early Jerusalem church might have had a few advantages in understanding Jesus that can help us as disciples today. In the first chapters in Acts we read of their amazing passion—their Spirit-filled prayers, their joyful gatherings, their loving generosity, and their dynamic witness to their neighbors.

Until a few years ago, it never occurred to me that the first believers of the infant Jerusalem church in Acts were all observant Jews, men and women who continued to study the Torah and worship in the Temple, even after they came to faith in Christ. In fact, for the first half of Acts, the rapidly expanding church was almost entirely

Jewish. It was only after God pushed Peter out of his comfort zone to witness to the Gentile centurion Cornelius that the church considered the possibility that the gospel was for Gentiles too (Acts 10).

We Christians often neglect this as we retell the stories of the early believers' joyful fellowship. We assume that the remarkable success of the Jerusalem church came from the fact that believers were freshly filled with the Holy Spirit. But Paul's Gentile church at Corinth had experienced the same outpouring, yet it struggled with immaturity, division, and sexual immorality. Why the difference? As wonderful as it was that the Corinthians found Christ, most had come out of a pagan reality, and their lives had not been saturated by the Scriptures that Jesus read, our Old Testament. They lacked the Torah's training in moral laws that Christ built upon. They had a lot of catching up to do.

Moreover, while the Gentiles worshiped Jesus as their Savior and God, the Jewish believers also knew him as their *rabbi*. As Jesus' disciples, they knew their obligation was to memorize his words and live according his *halakhah*, his interpretation of how God's Word teaches us to live.

Why Haven't We Known?

Nowadays, it seems only natural to wonder about Jesus' Jewish cultural setting. Why haven't we asked those questions in the past? A stroll through the aisles of my local grocery store suggests one answer: Sushi. Gyros. Kimchi. Tahini. Fifty years ago my mother had never even heard of these ethnic specialties; it wasn't until the late sixties that she even tried making a new-fangled dish called "pizza." Until only a few decades ago, a startlingly short list of bland foods comprised my family's entire culinary world. Creamed beef on toast. Macaroni and Spam. Ground beef over rice. In my white-bread world, I simply never thought to ask.

On my kitchen table is a little clay sculpture of Jesus healing a blind man, with a sticker on the bottom that says it was handcrafted in Peru. But you hardly need the label to guess where it came from when you see the dark braids, the ponchos, the Peruvian faces. Of course its creator imagined Jesus within his or her own reality, just as white Americans have cast Jesus as a blue-eyed Caucasian. As the gospel has gone out around the world, people have, by default, pictured Jesus through their own cultural lenses.

You might be surprised that Leonardo da Vinci's *Last Supper* does the same thing. This masterpiece has influenced the Christian imagination of Jesus' fateful last evening more than any other, yet it is culturally wrong in every detail. In the background are windows looking out on a sunny mid-afternoon scene, whereas the Passover meal always took place at night. And of course the faces of Jesus and the disciples are pale-faced Europeans, not Semitic. Most telling is what is on the table. Lacking are the essential elements of the Passover celebration, including the lamb and unleavened bread. In their place is a puffy loaf of bread, when leavening is strictly forbidden during the week of Passover, and a shockingly unkosher plate of grilled eels garnished with orange slices![8]

Of course da Vinci's goal was to portray the disciples' reactions at that critical moment, and he does so with brilliant technique and emotive depth. But by not including the elements of Passover, a feast that celebrated God's redemption and brimmed over with messianic expectations, we miss the fact that Jesus was powerfully proclaiming himself as the fulfillment of God's ancient promises. Jesus uses the symbols of Passover to point toward his coming atonement to redeem those who believed in him and to inaugurate a "new covenant" for the forgiveness of sin.[9]

Certainly much of the reason that we Christians have missed these details is simply out of ignorance. But it also comes out of how we've read our Bibles. As I was growing up, what I usually heard about Jesus' Jewish context was how much he opposed it and was bringing it to an end. Unfortunately, that attitude is not just a relic of the past. Just a few months ago I happened to tune my car radio to hear a popular pastor put it this way:

> When Jesus came, everything changed, everything changed.... He didn't just want to clean up the people's attitudes as they gave their sacrifices, He obliterated the sacrificial system

because He brought an end to Judaism with all its ceremonies, all its rituals, all its sacrifices, all of its external trappings, the Temple, the Holy of Holies, all of it.[10]

If this were what Jesus taught, his first passionate followers in Acts certainly didn't catch his drift. Peter and the other early Christians continued to participate daily in Temple worship (Acts 3:1; 21:23–26). Jesus did, of course, speak against corruption within the priesthood and prophesy the Temple's destruction forty years later. Other Jewish groups, like the Essenes, also denounced its corruption and sought to purify their worship. But while the Essenes abandoned the Temple,[11] Jesus' disciples never did, implying that Jesus did not preach against the Temple's ceremonies. And even though the Jerusalem church ruled that Gentiles did not need to observe Jewish law, Jewish believers in Jesus continued to carefully observe the Torah and were even known for their avid observance (see Acts 21:20, 25).[12]

When I used to read the passages in the New Testament about "the Jews" as those who opposed the church and rejected Jesus, I didn't realize that the people writing those words were *also* Jews. Often they used the phrase "the Jews" to refer to the Jewish leadership who opposed them. Acts tells us that thousands of Jews actually *did* believe in Christ (Acts 2:41; 5:14; 6:7; 21:20). So the issue to Paul in Romans 9–11 was not that *none* of the Jews had believed in Christ, but that not *all* of them did. (Have all of us Gentiles, for that matter, embraced him?)

Scholar Luke Timothy Johnson notes that many first-century documents show a cultural habit of referring to one's opponents with harsh epithets such as "hypocrites," "blind," or "demon-possessed." By our standards, every debate sounds overcharged and full of slander. When you hear John the Baptist calling his listeners a "brood of vipers" (Matthew 3:7), and Paul wishing that his opponents would emasculate themselves (Galatians 5:12), their comments should be heard in this light. Within its wider cultural setting, the New Testament's rebukes don't sound quite so harsh.[13]

The Jews were strongly divided over Jesus in the New Testament, and this within-the-family debate became heated. But it wasn't until centuries later when the church became overwhelmingly Gentile that the New Testament was understood as being hostile toward Jews as a whole. This has strongly contributed to anti-Semitism over the ages, and for many Christians has led to a disinterest in the Jewish setting of the Bible and our faith.

I was hardly aware of this attitude myself until a stunning encounter I had before my first study trip in Israel. I was chatting with a neighbor down the block and mentioned my upcoming travels. Since he was active in his church, I thought he might be interested. But he grimaced and blurted out, "Why on earth would you want to go there? Those Jews never did nothing good, except give us Jesus."[14]

Wouldn't that be enough?

New Tools to Know

Never before have we been more profoundly aware of the diverse mosaic of peoples that blanket our planet. With such heightened sensitivity, it seems only natural to ask about Jesus' Jewish setting. But ironically, as our world has become more sensitive to embracing ethnic differences, some have done exactly the opposite with Jesus. In 1999 the *National Catholic Reporter* magazine sponsored a "Jesus 2000" competition, searching for a new "image" of Jesus for the next millennium. The prize-winning painting, called "The Jesus of the People," portrayed Jesus as dark-skinned, thick-lipped, and feminine.[15] It's understandable that this Jesus is not white. But what about the fact that he's also not in any way *Jewish*?

This was the approach that the *Last Supper* caretakers took in former centuries. Each time da Vinci's scene grew dingy, the faces were "brightened" by repainting right over the top of them, touching them up in whatever way the current painter saw fit. In a similar way, the Christ we often encounter has been "repainted" to blend into everyone else's culture rather than his own. Each artist adds another layer to suit their tastes.

It's hard not to wonder if this is why each new book of the "Jesus reimagined" genre wildly disagrees with the previous one. In one Jesus is a wandering guru, in the next a subversive rebel, in the next a business CEO, in the next a dreamy mystic.[16] Instead of photoshopping Jesus into yet another improbable reality, a helpful corrective would be to restore Jesus to his original setting. And now we are gaining more and more tools to do so, with the discovery of ancient texts and archaeological remains of his day.

What would it look like to peel back the layers of time and to see the real Jesus? Obviously, it would be a mistake to project on him Jewish realities of later centuries. If we picture him with a bagel in one hand and a dreidel in the other, we'd be guilty of distorting his reality too, because both things are from later centuries and practices. But Jesus did eat *matzah* (unleavened bread) and celebrate Hanukkah, traditions that go back to before his time.[17]

How much can we know about the world of Jesus anyhow? A wealth of literature actually exists that preserves Jewish thought from the centuries before and after Christ. Best known are the Mishnah and the Talmud, two compendiums of discussion on the laws of the Torah, which contain teachings preserved orally from about 200 BC until AD 200 (Mishnah) or AD 400–500 (Talmud, in two editions).[18] Orthodox Jews still study these writings today. Of course Christians don't read these texts as authoritative, but they reveal an ancient river of thought that flowed through Jesus' world, which can fill in gaps in our understanding. Other first-century documents like the writings of Josephus and the Dead Sea Scrolls shed light on Jesus' world too.

You might be surprised to learn that some of Judaism's most influential thinkers, including Hillel and Shammai (30 BC to AD 10), lived in the decades right around Jesus' time. Hillel's grandson, Gamaliel, was Paul's teacher, who came to the defense of the early church in Acts 5:33–39. The words of these and other early rabbis allow us to reconstruct the conversations going on around Jesus. They used the same kind of logic to answer questions, interpret Scriptures, and weave parables, which yields fascinating clues to Jesus' words.

Of course, scholars disagree about the exact details of Jesus' reality, and Judaism is known for its wide diversity of opinion. My thoughts will hardly provide the last and best word. But as a Christian, I grew up without knowing the most basic details of Jesus' Jewish world, aspects of his reality that have persisted in Judaism from the first century until today. What I've chosen to share in this book are a few core concepts that Christians have hardly known about, yet shed light on Jesus' teachings. Often this Hebraic perspective unlocks biblical wisdom that our culture has forgotten over time.

Ken Bailey has spent decades traveling in the Middle East to study Arab peoples, showing how traditional societies there preserve the Bible's cultural perspective in ways that Western societies have not. He comments, "For us as Westerners the cultural distance 'over' to the Middle East is greater than the distance 'back' to the first century. The cultural gulf between the West and the East is deeper and wider than the gulf between the first century (in the Middle East) and the contemporary conservative Middle Eastern village."[19]

Christians may also be surprised at how Jewish traditions have preserved biblical attitudes. To catch the emotional power of Jesus' claim to be the source of "living water" in John 7, you can go to the parched Middle East and ask an Arab about how precious rain is to him. Or, go to the synagogue in your own hometown, where you'll hear passionate prayers for "living water" each day during the weeklong feast of Sukkot. (In one Jewish prayer book, these go on for over fifty pages.) Some liturgies preserve cultural memories that go back thousands of years.[20]

Why is God allowing us to discover these insights now? Perhaps it's because we need them now more than ever. Indeed, for much of the world, the culture of the Bible makes more sense than it does to us. Eugene Nida, a pioneer in Bible translation, has commented:

> In a sense, the Bible is the most translatable religious book that has ever been written.... If one were to make a comparison of the culture traits of the Bible with those of all the existing cultures of today, one would find that in certain respects the Bible is surprisingly closer to many of them than to the technological culture of the Western world. It is this "Western" culture that is the aberrant one in the world. And it is precisely in the Western world ... that the Scriptures have seemingly the least acceptance.[21]

Throughout history people have lived in extended families, practiced subsistence farming, and lived under the shadow of slavery and war. And around the world, many traditional cultures focus their children's training on sacred stories and order their lives around religious practices. With our individualism, secularism, materialism, and biblical illiteracy, we in the Western world are the ones who have moved farthest away from Jesus' world. Could it be that we're the ones who have the most to learn?

Not *Just* a Rabbi

One thing I don't want you to misunderstand. You might think that by calling Jesus "rabbi" I'm implying that he was just an innovative teacher trying to promote a new idea, like Edison with a light bulb or Bill Gates with a new operating system. We're so used to thinking this way that we assume that Jesus' goal was to compete in the realm of thought. We mistakenly hear Jesus' message about the "kingdom of God" as if he's trying to sell an exciting new plan for establishing world peace. But to Jesus' Jewish audience, to proclaim the kingdom of God was to make a shocking announcement that God's promised Messiah had arrived, because the task of the Messiah was to establish God's kingdom on earth. Jesus was making an earth-shattering claim that he was the Christ, and that God's redemption of the world would come through him.[22]

The reason I point this out is because it allows us to release Jesus from the age-old competitive game of "Jesus vs. Judaism," where his ideas can only be right if everyone else's are wrong, and vice versa. If, as a Christian, you start out by assuming that Jesus is the Messiah and the Son of God, he simply doesn't need to compete. He speaks with divine authority whether he disagrees with the Jewish thought of his day or affirms it. We can grow as his disciples when we hear his words in their Jewish context and learn how to better live them out.

Bearing this in mind, it is still appropriate to speak of Jesus as "rabbi," because part of his mission was to teach his redeemed people how God wanted them to live.[23] He did so by using the methods that other early Jewish sages used for teaching and raising disciples.

Throughout the Gospels Jesus was called "teacher" and "rabbi" by those around him, and members of the early church universally called themselves "disciples." They were *mathetai* (Greek for "students"), followers of the "Way" that Jesus had taught them for living.

Walking in His Dust

The way Jesus taught his first disciples was not unique but part of a wider tradition in Judaism that began a few centuries before his time. Jesus didn't hand his disciples a textbook or give them a course syllabus. He asked each one of them to follow him — literally, to "walk after" him. He invited them to trek the byways at his side, living life beside him to learn from him as they journeyed. His disciples would engage in life's activities along with him, observing his responses and imitating how he lived by God's Word.

Out of this unusual teaching method arose a well-known saying: you should learn from a rabbi by "covering yourself in his dust." You should follow so closely behind him as he traveled from town to town teaching that billows of sandy granules would cling to your clothes.[24] As you walked after your rabbi, your heart would change. This will be our task in this book, to stroll through Jesus' ancient world at his side, listening to his words with the ears of a disciple.

> *I did not go to the rabbi to learn interpretations of the Torah from him but to note his way of tying his shoelaces and taking off his shoes. . . . In his actions, in his speech, in his bearing, and his faithfulness to the Lord, man must make the Torah manifest.*
>
> — Aryeh Leib Sarahs

But in Hebrew, the word for *halakh*, "walk," encompasses so much more. Your "walk" in life refers to your overall lifestyle, how you conduct yourself morally. A rabbi's interpretation of the Torah was called *halakhah*, how to "walk" by God's Word. When Jesus called his disciples to "walk after" him, he meant the word in both ways. First they would follow in his literal footsteps; later they would follow in his teachings, taking his message out to the world.

Closely related was the word *derekh*, meaning "road," "path," or "way." The imagery was not of four-laned freeways that are paved for permanence, but the track left behind by people's footprints. Some paths led to good places, and some to dangerous, evil places. Your "way" was a spiritual metaphor for how you lived. This is still true today, as Jesus lovingly walks before us in the way we ought to live. And then he bids us to put our feet in his own footprints to follow after him, to become part of his "Way," as his early followers once did.

In *Sitting at the Feet of Rabbi Jesus*, my coauthor Ann Spangler and I began by looking at another first-century idiom, that to "sit at the feet" of a rabbi meant to study with him. We pondered what Jesus' words might have sounded like if we had gathered in Martha's house and sat alongside Mary at Jesus' feet, enjoying an after-dinner discussion with his disciples. Ann and I examined basic aspects of Jesus' Jewish reality like the yearly feasts, the daily prayers, and the way rabbis trained disciples. Through them we discovered many new insights on Jesus' life and mission.

In this book, I will be looking more closely at Jesus' words and teachings in their Jewish context. We'll push beyond externals to explore the world of Jewish thought. We'll contemplate some of the cultural ideas and biblical images that gave meaning and depth to Jesus' words. And, we'll discover some of the wisdom that Jewish culture has preserved over the ages that reveals ways we can become more like Rabbi Jesus.

We'll look at some key Hebrew words that Jesus knew from his Scriptures and discover how their deeper meanings cast light on our faith. We will listen with new ears to Jesus' interpretation of how to live out the *Shema*—the daily pledge to love God with all your heart that formed the very center of Jewish commitment from ancient times until today. As we do, we'll hear our Savior's calling in ways that will transform our lives today.

Wisdom for the Walk

1. Reflect on your own cultural and spiritual heritage. How may it have distorted your view of Jesus and his teachings? In what ways do you feel it portrays Jesus accurately?

2. Why have we lost an understanding of the Hebrew culture and context of Jesus? How might those things still affect our thinking today?

3. Read John 7, keeping in mind that Jesus' followers as well as his opponents were all Jews, and often the words "the Jews" refers to Jewish leaders who opposed him. How does that cast light on your reading?

4. The chapter points out the contrast between the maturity of the Jewish believers in Acts and the Gentile believers of Corinth, who were plagued with sins and scandals. Consider your own life and the life of your church. Do you exhibit signs of maturity, or do you have a long way to go, like the Corinthians? How can you and your church pursue spiritual maturity?

5. How does understanding Jesus' culture help us to better interpret and live out his words?

CHAPTER 2

Shema:
Living Out What You Hear

The word *Shema* itself means "listen,"
and the recital of the Shema is a supreme act of faith-as-listening:
to the voice that brought the universe into being,
created us in love and guides us through our lives.
— Rabbi Jonathan Sacks[1]

In 1945, Rabbi Eliezer Silver headed up the search for thousands of displaced Jewish children across Europe. They had been hidden from the clutches of the Nazis on farms and in convents and monasteries, and now he sought to return them to their families if at all possible.

The rabbi had a promising lead with a report that a monastery in southern France had taken in Jewish children. But the priest in charge was of little help, declaring that to his knowledge, all of their children were Christians. And Rabbi Silver could produce no records.

Schwartz ... Kaufmann ... Schneider. These family names were obviously German, but they could be either Jewish or Gentile. He scanned their small faces—many had lived there since they were toddlers. How could he know if any of them were from Jewish families?

He asked if he could visit the wards. In front of the children he began singing in Hebrew, "*Shema Israel, Adonai elohenu, Adonai echad.*" ("Hear, O Israel, the LORD our God, the LORD is one.") A handful of faces lit up, and tiny voices from around the room joined in. They recognized these ancient words from their bedtime prayers and from their earliest memories of their mothers and fathers reciting them each morning and evening during their own prayers.[2]

These six words begin the *Shema* (pronounced "shmah"), three sections of Scripture repeated twice daily to remind each Jewish person of his or her commitment to God (Deuteronomy 6:4–9; 11:13–21; Numbers 15:37–41; see pages 195–96 for the text). For thousands of years, observant Jewish parents have taught their children the words of the *Shema* as soon as they could speak. Jesus likely learned it on Joseph's knee when he was a youngster too. These same lines have been central to Jewish prayer life since centuries before Jesus was born.[3]

Before I started learning about Jesus' Jewish context, I, like most Christians, had never even heard of the *Shema*. But it was so central to Jesus' own faith that when a lawyer asked him what he believed was the greatest commandment, his answer began by quoting from the *Shema*:

> One of the teachers of the law came and heard them debating. Noticing that Jesus had given them a good answer, he asked him, "Of all the commandments, which is the most important?"
>
> "The most important one," answered Jesus, "is this: 'Hear, O Israel; the Lord our God, the Lord is one. Love the Lord your God with all your heart and with all your soul and with all your mind and with all your strength.' The second is this: 'Love your neighbor as yourself.' There is no commandment greater than these." (Mark 12:28–31)

Like many Christians, if you asked me to summarize this famous story, I'd rattle off Jesus' words about loving God and neighbor. But I'd skip over this mysterious preamble about God being "one," the very words that those Jewish children knew by heart. The line I had never heard of was the cornerstone of their faith.

Why did Jesus quote this line about the Lord being one? Because it is the opening line of the *Shema*. Immediately following it is the great command: "Love the Lord your God with all of your heart and with all your soul and with all your mind and with all your strength." Every morning and evening for thousands of years, the Jewish people have promised to love God wholeheartedly when they've said the *Shema*.

Believe it or not, Jesus' next command, "love your neighbor as yourself," comes straight from Leviticus 19:18. I used to think that the scribe's question was a legalistic quiz and that Jesus' talk of love rather than law would have shocked and scandalized his audience. Imagine my surprise to discover that every word of Jesus' answer came straight out of the *Torah*—from Leviticus and Deuteronomy—the Old Testament two books I had read the least.

The lawyer's query was not foolish either. Rather, it was an invitation to participate in a fascinating debate among the rabbinic teachers of his day. Most likely his words were: *Mah klal gadol ba'torah?* What is the great essence of God's Law? What overriding principle encapsulates all of God's instruction? (*Torah*, which we translate "law," actually means "teaching." Technically, the term "Torah" only refers to the first five books of the Hebrew Bible, what Christians call the Pentateuch. But often the word is used to refer to the Scriptures as a whole.) The goal of answering this classic question was not to summarize the Bible in one's own words, but to choose one key verse that distilled all the rest, focusing its light down to a single brilliant point. Jesus was being asked to give his opinion on an intriguing discussion that sought to get at the very heart of God's will.[4]

When we hear the lawyer's question in light of its Jewish context, we can see how profound it was. And Jesus' answer is all the more penetrating when we meditate on it in its original setting too. Let's begin to uncover some of the richness of God's greatest command by examining this first line of the *Shema*, which has been so central in Jewish thought for many centuries. In later chapters, we'll examine the rest of Jesus' words.

Shema—Hear and Obey

The Hebrew words that Jesus quoted from Deuteronomy overflow with great wisdom. Looking more closely, this is how the first line of the *Shema* is translated:

Shema (Hear)
Israel,
Adonai (the Lord)
elohenu (our God)

Adonai (the Lord)
echad! (one/alone)

The first word, *shema*, we usually translate "hear." But the word *shema* has a much wider, deeper meaning than "to perceive sound." It encompasses a whole spectrum of ideas that includes listening, taking heed, and responding with action to what one has heard.

I discovered the wideness of the word *shema* in my first Hebrew class. One classmate had a smattering of Hebrew knowledge gleaned from other places, and he let us all know it. He'd come late, leave early, and goof around during class. The teacher would pose a question to someone else, and he'd blurt out the answer before they could respond. Annoyed, one classmate pointedly inquired, "How do you tell someone to *obey*?"

"*Shema*," responded my instructor.

Later that afternoon, curiosity prodded me to search for verses that contained "obey" in my computer Bible program. In almost every case, the Hebrew behind "obey" was *shema*!

For instance, in English we read Deuteronomy 11:13 as, "So if you faithfully *obey* the commands I am giving you today. . . ." Literally, though, this verse reads, "And it will be if *hearing*, you will *hear*. . . ." And after Moses recited the covenant to the people of Israel, they responded, "We will do everything the LORD has said; we will obey" (Exodus 24:7). But the Hebrew here actually reads, "All that the Lord had said we will *do* and we will *hear*." The two verbs here are really synonymous — to hear *is* to do, to be obedient.

This became even clearer one sticky summer evening when I was visiting an old college friend. As we chatted together in her front yard, we could hear squealing and laughter coming from behind her house. Her kids were drenching each other in a water fight, a duel between the garden hose and a big squirt gun. As the sun sank below the horizon, it was getting past their bedtimes, so we paused our conversation so that she could call them inside. "It's getting late — time to go in," she announced. But the giggling and chasing didn't even slow down. She repeated her command, louder and louder. No effect.

"My kids seem to have a hearing problem, Lois," she sighed, wearily.

Since I knew that she had studied some Hebrew, I commented, "You know, actually, what I think your kids have is a *shema*-ing problem." Her words were vibrating their eardrums, but not actually moving their bodies toward the door to her house. She could have been talking in Klingon for all their response. She knew as well as I did that the natural outcome of listening *should* be response.

Grasping the wider meaning of *shema* yields insights to other biblical mysteries. In the psalms, David pleads, "O Lord, please *hear* my prayer." But he wasn't accusing God of being deaf or disinterested. Rather, he was calling on God to take action, not just listen to his words. When the angel appeared to Zechariah to announce that his wife Elizabeth was pregnant with John, he declared that their prayer had been *heard*—that God was answering the barren couple's prayerful longings to have a child (Luke 1:13).

How does this help us unlock the words of the *Shema*? In this line, it is saying in effect, "Hearken, take heed, Israel—the LORD is your God." Often God uses *shema* to call the Israelites to obey him, to trust him, and to follow in his ways. You can hear God saying this very thing in Psalm 81. Listen to it in light of the wider meaning of the word *shema*:

> *Hear* me, my people, and I will warn you—
> if you would only *listen* to me, Israel!...
> But my people would not *listen* to me;
> Israel would not submit to me.
> So I gave them over to their stubborn hearts
> to follow their own devices.
> If my people would only *listen* to me,
> if Israel would only follow my ways,
> how quickly would I subdue their enemies
> and turn my hand against their foes!...
> You would be fed with the finest of wheat;
> with honey from the rock I would satisfy you.
> (Psalm 81:8, 11–14, 16, italics added)

Having Ears to Hear

Understanding the word *shema* also helps us see why Jesus often concluded his teaching with the words, "Whoever has ears to hear, let them hear" (e.g., Mark 4:9). What he really meant was, "You have heard my teaching, now take it to heart and obey it!" He wants us to be doers of his words, not hearers only (James 1:22).

You see this especially in Jesus' parable of the sower, which concludes with his saying about having "ears to hear." He tells about a farmer who sows seed all over his land. But much of the ground is poor, so the seed bounces off the hardened pathway, withers in the rocks, and is choked by weeds (Mark 4:3–20). Only what lands in the good soil really grows.

In Jesus' parable, our hearts are the soil, and we "hear" by receiving his words with faith and obedience. His words are a call to examine ourselves as to which type of listener we are. Are our hearts hard to God's Word? Or are we shallow, distracted by wealth or daily living?[5] It's easy to insult Jesus' original audience by assuming that they were especially unwilling to respond. But are we so different than them? Who of us isn't choked by weeds in our lives? How many of us truly follow wherever Christ leads?

As tough as this parable is to hear, it makes a potent promise. God is like a farmer who sows a field, knowing that much of the land is poor. But the seed he is sowing is supercharged. When Christ's kingdom takes hold of the few who will *shema*,[6] hear and obey, what an amazing impact it will have—a huge, hundredfold yield, the very limits of ancient productivity. Through an obedient disciple God can do truly miraculous things to expand his kingdom, far beyond human imagination.

Wise Hebrew Words

The reason that *shema* has such a breadth of meaning is because Hebrew is a "word-poor" language. Biblical Hebrew includes only about 8,000 words, far fewer than the 400,000 or more we have in English.[7] Paradoxically, the richness of Hebrew comes from its poverty. Because this ancient language has so few words, each one is like an overstuffed suitcase, bulging with extra meanings that it must carry in order for the language to fully describe reality. Unpacking each word is a delightful exercise in seeing how the ancient authors organized ideas, sometimes grouping concepts together in very different ways than we do.

Many verbs in Hebrew that we think of as only mental activities often encompass their expected physical result. For instance, to "remember" can mean "to act on someone's behalf." In Genesis 8:1 it says that "God remembered Noah ... and he sent a wind over the earth, and the waters receded." But God didn't just wake up one morning and suddenly recall that an ark was out bobbing around somewhere. He "remembered" Noah by coming to his rescue. And to "know" another person is to have a relationship with them, to care about them, even to be intimate with them. When Adam "knew" Eve, she conceived Cain (Genesis 4:1).

> *The Hebrew tongue, above other languages, is very plain, but withal it is majestic and glorious: it contains much in few and simple words, and therein surpasses all other languages.*
> — Martin Luther

Hebrew verbs stress action and effect rather than just mental activity. This isn't unique to Hebrew. Lorrie Anderson, a New Testament translator in Peru, searched for months to find a word for "believe" in the Candoshi language. No direct equivalent existed for that all-important term in Bible translation. What she finally discovered was that "hear" in that language also can mean "believe" and also "obey." Anderson writes:

> The question, "Don't you hear His Word?" in Candoshi means "Don't you believe-obey His Word?" In their way of thinking, if you "hear" you believe what you hear, and if you believe, you obey. These are not separate ideas as in English.

She and other Bible translators share the same observation. They often struggle to find words for mental activities we see as all-important, but simply don't exist in indigenous languages where thought is tied to its expected outcome.[8]

Part of why this seems strange to us is because of our Western perspective. Many of our Greek cultural ancestors, including Plato, considered the mental world all-important and physical reality worthless. As a result, our culture tends to exalt our intellect as critical and discount our actions. Some of us Christians even see actions as "dead works" that are irrelevant, even opposed to faith.

You often see this unhappy disconnect online, when Christians respond to what they consider theological error with rude, ugly insults, feeling innocent of wrongdoing as long as they are outing a "heretic." *Knowing* the right thing is paramount; *obeying* Christ's command to "love your neighbor" is irrelevant. But Jesus said that we'll be held accountable on judgment day for every careless word we speak (Matthew 12:36). Just imagine what he'll read off from his heavenly computer monitor as he scrolls through our online comments.

The logic of Hebrew (and other languages) realizes that an action should result from what is in our minds. If you "remember" someone, you will act on their behalf. If you "hear" someone, you will obey their words. If you "know" someone, you will have a close relationship with them. Hebrew realizes that the longest twelve inches that your faith has to move is from your head to your heart. And once your faith makes that move, it naturally comes out through your hands and feet.

Echad — The One and Only

The other key word in the first line of the *Shema* is *echad* (ech-HAHD). Its most common meaning is simply "one," but it can also encompass related ideas, like being single, alone, unique, or unified. The multiple shades of meaning of *echad* and the difficult wording of the rest of the line have made the *Shema* a topic of debate for millennia.

Part of the problem is that Deuteronomy 6:4 doesn't even have verbs. It literally reads: "YHWH ... our God ... YHWH ... one."[9] The verse can be read either as saying "The Lord is our God, the Lord alone," or "The Lord our God, the Lord is one." Of these two readings, the more common reading is the second, that "the Lord is one" in the sense that God is unique. There is only one God, the God of Israel. So this line is usually understood as a statement of belief in monotheism.

The word *echad* has been a sticking point between Jews and Christians. Often Jews point to the fact that it means "one" as a reason that they cannot believe in the Trinity or in the deity of Christ. And Christians respond that *echad* can refer to a compound unity, as when God created morning and evening, and together they made *yom echad* ("one day") (cf. Genesis 1:5). Or when Adam and Eve, through marriage, became *basar echad* ("one flesh") (Genesis 2:24).

This whole debate hinges on interpreting the *Shema* as a creed; that is, "the LORD is one" is a statement about what kind of being God is. But, interestingly, one of the most widely-read Jewish Bible translations now renders Deuteronomy 6:4 as "The LORD is our God, the LORD *alone*" rather than "The LORD our God, the LORD is *one*."[10] It does so because in recent decades, scholars have come to believe that the original, ancient sense of *echad* in this verse was more likely to be "alone" than "one." In Zechariah 14:9, for instance, *echad* has this sense: "The LORD will be king over all the earth; on that day the LORD will be *echad* and his name *echad*" (pers. trans.). This is a vision of the messianic age, when all of humanity will cease to worship idols and revere *only* God and call on his name *alone*.

Jewish scholar Jeffrey Tigay asserts that even though the Scriptures clearly preach monotheism, the *Shema* itself is not a statement of belief. It's an oath of loyalty. He calls the first line of the *Shema* "a description of the proper relationship between YHVH and Israel: He alone is Israel's God. This is not a declaration of monotheism, meaning that there is only one God.... Though other peoples worship various beings and things they consider divine, Israel is to recognize YHVH alone."[11]

Why is this important? Because it changes the sense of what the *Shema* communicates. Rather than merely being a command to a particular belief about God, it is actually a call for a person's absolute allegiance to God. God *alone* is the one we should worship; him only shall we serve. As often as the *Shema* is called a creed or a prayer, it is better understood as an oath of allegiance, a twice-daily recommitment to the covenant with the God of Israel.

As Western Christians we are used to reciting creeds and statements of belief in order to define our faith. We expect to find one here too. So we easily could misunderstand that Jesus was saying that it is extremely critical that we believe in God's "oneness." But when properly understood, this line shows that the greatest commandment is actually a call to commit ourselves to the one true God.

Reading the line this way solves another mystery about what Jesus was saying. If he was asked what the greatest commandment was, why does he begin by quoting a line about God being "one"? Because if you read this line as about committing oneself to God as one's Lord, it flows directly into the next line in the *Shema*, explaining *why* we should love God with every fiber of our being. If the Lord *alone* is our God, and we worship no other gods, we can love him with all of our heart and soul and strength. The two sentences together become one commandment, the greatest in fact — to love the Lord your God.[12]

Once again, in the light of their Hebrew context, we find that Jesus' words call us beyond what is going on in our brains. We are not just to "hear" but to take heed, to respond, to obey. And we are not just called to believe in the oneness of God, but to place him at the center of our lives.

To do that, we are to love God with all of our heart and soul and strength and mind. Each of these words, in their Hebrew context, can expand our understanding of our calling and the very essence of the Scriptures, as Jesus understood it. We'll consider that next.

Wisdom for the Walk

1. Read the three passages of the *Shema* on pages 195–96 at the end of this book. Why do you think these passages were chosen for repetition every morning and evening? What questions do they raise in your mind?

2. Read 2 Chronicles 6:19–27, which is Solomon's prayer at the dedication of the first temple. How does knowing the wider Hebraic meaning of "hear," *shema*, enrich your understanding?

3. In what ways may you have heard (intellectually understood something) but not obeyed (acted on your knowledge)? Why does this happen? What can you do about it?

4. The *Shema* is often interpreted as a statement of monotheism, that God is one. But it can also be translated as "the LORD alone is our God." How does this translation change or deepen your understanding of God and how to relate to him?

5. Paul also quotes the *Shema* in 1 Corinthians 8:4. How does he use it in his teaching?

CHAPTER 3

Loving God
with Everything You've Got

Be as strong as the leopard, swift as the eagle,
fleet as the gazelle and brave as the lion
to do the will of your Father in heaven.

—Judah ben Tema[1]

In the bitterly cold predawn, icy winds sliced through Viktor Frankl's threadbare uniform. Yet another eternally long day was beginning for him and his fellow inmates as they wearily marched through the gates of Auschwitz to the day's work site. Trudging through puddles and slush down a stony, gutted road, the group clustered together to keep warm.

From behind an upturned collar, a man next to him whispered, "If our wives could see us now! I do hope that they are better off in their camps and don't know what is happening to us." Thoughts of his own wife suddenly flooded into Frankl's mind. In his mind's eye, he could see her with uncanny clarity—her warm smile, her frank but encouraging nod, the way her eyes squinted when she laughed. A powerful wave of love for her overwhelmed him, carrying him away from his bleak, hopeless reality. In *Man's Search for Meaning*, Frankl writes:

> I understood how a man who has nothing left in this world still may know bliss, be it only for a brief moment, in the contemplation of his beloved.... For the first time in my life I was able to understand the meaning of the words, "The angels are lost in perpetual contemplation of an infinite glory."[2]

In his darkest hour, love for his wife filled him with such joy that he grasped why the angels could spend all of eternity in worshipful love of God. For a few moments, Frankl glimpsed the essence of the greatest commandment, "Love the LORD your God with all your heart and with all your soul and with all your strength" (Deuteronomy 6:5).

As Christians who have understood Christ's sacrifice for us, we have no problem understanding why loving God with all our hearts is our appropriate response. But what does this second line of the *Shema* really mean, in terms of your heart, your soul, and your strength? What should it look like in our lives?

How Do You Command Love?

This first word Jesus quoted is *ve'ahavta* (veh-a-hav-TAH) — literally, "and you shall love." It is understood to be a command, even though it sounds as if it is a statement about the future. In some sense, you could read it as describing the future. When we finally stand before Christ and see what he accomplished on our behalf, we really *will* love the Lord our God with all of our hearts. Just like the angels, we'll find nothing difficult about worshiping God for eternity.[3] This is what heaven really is — dwelling forever in the presence of our beloved Savior.

But the plainer sense of *ve'ahavta* is not about the future, but a command for today. In the Middle Ages, the famous Jewish philosopher Maimonides wrote:

> What is the love of God that is appropriate? It is to love God with an exceedingly strong love until one's soul is tied to the love of God. One should be ... like a person who is "lovesick," whose thoughts cannot turn from his love for a particular woman. He is preoccupied with her at all times, whether he is sitting or standing, whether he is eating or drinking. Even more intense should be the love of God be in the hearts of those who love him, possessing them always as we are commanded "with all your heart and with all your soul" (Deuteronomy 6:5).[4]

Maimonides was basing this sermon on a line that comes a little later in the *Shema*, that the hearers are to think about God's words when they're sitting at home or walking along the road, when they lie down and when they awake (Deuteronomy 6:7).

Rabbi Jeffrey Spitzer connects the idea of God being *echad*, the only one, with being in love. He writes:

> When one falls in love, this is what it is like. The object of one's love is all there is; the love and the relationship create a complete unity of experience. A person in love wants to shout out "Do you hear! I am in love! This is the one!" That's not too far from "Hear, O Israel, the LORD is our God, the LORD is one!" When one falls in love, one wants to learn everything about that person ("and you shall speak of them"), the conversations last all day and even through the night ("when you lie down and when you rise up").[5]

As wonderful as this passion for God might be, love is more than the tingling high a person gets from swaying to an hour of praise songs. Pastor Brian McLaren points out that some "spiritual infatuation addicts" wander from church to church, looking for just the right combination of a tear-evoking message and heart-swelling music to float away in a spiritual euphoria. Certainly God's presence is real, and it can be quite palpable. But for some, the worshipful ecstasy of "The Feeling" becomes all that matters. Responding to the message or joining the church community is simply not on their agenda.

"Sometimes I wonder if too many of us assume that 'The Feeling' is the whole point of worship—worse, that it's the whole point of Christianity," McLaren comments. He imagines God as asking, "If you never felt 'The Feeling' again, would you keep worshiping me anyway—for me, and not just for the feeling?"[6]

Knowing more about the wideness of the Hebrew word for love, *ahavah* (a-hah-VAH), can shed light on what the command to love God is really about. Besides the common understanding of love as affection toward another, *ahavah* goes beyond emotions. It is like *shema* in that it can also describe actions associated with love, not just an inward mental state. *Ahavah* can also mean "to act lovingly toward" or "to be loyal to." You see this in ancient treaties, when an enemy king who signed a covenant would pledge to "love" the king with whom he was making peace. This meant that the enemy king would act loyally, not that he would have warm thoughts about what a great guy the other king was every time he came to mind.

This nuance of *ahavah* solves another puzzle. How could God order people to "love" him in the sense of having a certain emotional response toward him? Actually, he didn't. When the Israelites were commanded to love God as part of their covenant, we can read it as not so much about passionate feelings as much as an utter commitment to loyalty toward God, the one they obeyed.

As Pastor Chuck Warnock puts it:

> Love meant action. Love meant living a certain way, a way that distinguished God's people from all other people. Loving God meant worshipping the One, True God — not hedging your bet by making idols to the sun god, and the moon god, and the god of the harvest, and worshipping those, too. No, loving God meant throwing your lot in with the One God, the God of Abraham, Isaac, and Jacob.[7]

It's not that emotions weren't important. But emotions came afterward, when God's people experienced his generous care, his mercy for their sinfulness, and his answers to prayer. King David's passionate love for God made him burst into undignified dancing, tossing aside his robes and regal etiquette in worshipful joy (2 Samuel 6:14–16).

This full-bodied definition of the word "love" also teaches us that loving others must include action, not just mental feelings. We cannot fully obey God's command to love our neighbors by just thinking nice things about them. To love them encompasses getting up off our chair and showing them God's love by helping them in any way that we can.

I often tell my sweet little black tuxedo cat Daniel how much I love him, which seems to be a special kindness in

> *Be a disciple of Aaron: love peace and pursue it, love your neighbors, and attract them to Torah.*
> —Mishnah, *Avot* 1:12

light of his chronic health issues and odd appearance. A year ago a food allergy made him itch, so he licked off all his fur from his chest to his tail. His front looked fine, but his back half was naked and wrinkly, like a sphinx cat. We finally solved the itch but even now his fur is only partially restored, so he still is half bald.

It struck me one day that all the warm inner thoughts I had toward Daniel weren't really love if they didn't cause me to organize my life around giving him his meds every morning and evening, clean up after his unending litter-box mess, and dole out money each month to the vet. Love is *both* inward and outward, both the warm fuzzies and the actions that result from them.

When we understand the active side of love, *ahavah* can shed light on Jesus' words. When he commanded us to love our enemies, he may have been thinking more about our actions toward them than our inner affections. If you read his words this way, the phrase that you should "love your enemies" becomes synonymous with the next phrase, "do good to those who hate you" (Luke 6:27). You *live out* love toward your enemies by treating them fairly, praying for them, not taking revenge, and being kind no matter how unkind they are to you. When someone acts cruelly toward you, you don't need to deceive yourself into thinking that he or she is really a wonderful person. But if you do your best to act with love, your feelings are bound to change over time.

With All Your Heart

In English, we speak of the "heart" to refer to our emotions, sometimes even contrasting our "hearts" with our "heads," our rational thinking. But in Hebrew, the heart (*lev* or *levav*) doesn't just describe your emotions; it also refers to your mind and thoughts as well. It is the center of all your inner life. With a primitive grasp of physiology, it's not hard to see how the Israelites came to this conclusion. Many ancient cultures assumed that the heart is the seat of intelligence because it is the only moving organ in the body, and strong emotions cause the heartbeat to race. And when the heart stops beating, a person is dead.

Knowing that the word "heart" often meant "mind" or "thoughts" can clarify some Bible passages. For instance: "These commandments that I give you today are to be on your hearts" (Deuteronomy

6:6) really means "These commandments are to be a part of all your *thoughts*." And Proverbs 16:23, "The heart of the wise instructs his mouth and adds persuasiveness to his lips" (NASB) really means, "The wise person thinks through his words, so that he can speak persuasively." Whenever you read "heart" in the Old Testament, consider it in terms of the intellect as well as the emotions, because in Hebrew it can also refer to your mind.

This means that we are also to use all of our *thoughts* as well as our emotions to love the Lord. As Paul says, "we take captive every thought to make it obedient to Christ" (2 Corinthians 10:5). If there is one thing we can learn from Jewish culture over the ages, it is an utter passion for learning one's religious faith. A rabbi of Jesus' day would have been expected to draw insight from his memory of the entire written Torah and the rest of the Scriptures and to possess an encyclopedic memory of oral commentary. Jesus held his own with the best, earning their respect as a result of years of learning in his childhood and adult life.

> *Just as the goad directs the heifer along its furrow to bring forth life to the world, so the words of the Torah direct those who study them from the paths of death to the paths of life.*
> —Talmud, *Hagigah* 3a[7]

Even today, Orthodox rabbis memorize vast amounts of commentary texts. One scholar gave his twenty-volume Talmud to a student because he didn't need it anymore. Like others, he'd repeat its tractates by the hour to keep them fresh in his mind. Because he was a professor at Hebrew University, strangers recognized him on the streets of Jerusalem for his prolific knowledge and would buttonhole him to get his opinion on a difficult text.[8]

When I first heard about this kind of memorization, I didn't think it was humanly possible. But then I started noticing all the pop culture we know by memory. Test yourself by turning on an oldies radio station. See if you can't rattle off verse after verse of hundreds of songs you haven't heard in years. If you're of my generation, it's "Monday, Monday, can't trust that day ..." and "Yesterday, all my troubles seemed so far away...." I bet if you just heard the words, "Here's the story of a lovely lady ..." you could sing the rest of the

Brady Bunch theme song. How about *Gilligan's Island?* Our brains are filled with sitcoms and top forty hits, whereas people of Jesus' time filled their minds with psalms and Scripture and prayers, which were often chanted or sung.

You might think that an education that revolved around memorizing the Bible is excessive, but in most societies from ancient times up to the present, people have been far more literate in their sacred texts than we are today. Indeed, our modern Western culture is one of the most secular in the history of the world.[9]

With All Your Life

We tend to read right past the phrase about loving God with "all your soul." In our culture, saying you love something with your "heart and soul" means that you love it with your spirit and emotions, and very passionately. But what we read as "soul" (*nephesh* — NEH-fesh) also has a different sense in Hebrew than just one's spirit or inner being. *Nephesh* means *life* as well, as long as you have breath. So the Jewish interpretation of this line is that you are to love the Lord with *all of your life*, meaning with every moment throughout your life. Loving God with all of your life is the exact opposite of our culture's expectation that you'll wedge a few moments for God in between work, hobbies, sports, TV, and the latest movie.

Loving God with all your *nephesh*, your life, also means that you're even willing to sacrifice your life for him. If Jews are able, they will quote the *Shema* at their death to make a final commitment to their God. Many a Jewish martyr has exclaimed the *Shema* with his last breath as a testimony to that fact.

A powerful story is told about Rabbi Akiva, who lived in the first century AD and who was tortured to death publicly by the Romans for teaching the Torah. It was the time of saying the morning *Shema*. During the torture, his students heard him reciting the *Shema* instead of crying out in pain. His students called out to him, "Teacher, even now?"

The dying rabbi explained, "All my life I have wondered about the phrase that says 'Love the Lord your God with all of your soul,' wondering if I would ever have the privilege of doing this. Now that the chance has come to me, shall I not grasp it with joy?" He repeated the words of the *Shema*, "Hear O Israel, the LORD is our God, the LORD alone," until his soul left him.[10]

This is what Jesus was calling us to do and what he did himself: he loved the Lord (and us) with all of his life, until he breathed his last.

Hesed: Long-Acting Love

Hebrew has a word for lifelong love that is richer and deeper than English has ever conceived of: *hesed* (HEH-sed). (While not in the *Shema*, I cannot imagine not sharing it here.) Based in a covenantal relationship, *hesed* is a steadfast, rock-solid faithfulness that endures to eternity: "Though the mountains be shaken and the hills be removed, yet my unfailing love [*hesed*] for you will not be shaken" (Isaiah 54:10).

Hesed is a love so enduring that it persists beyond any sin or betrayal to mend brokenness and graciously extend forgiveness: "No one is cast off by the Lord forever. Though he brings grief, he will show compassion, so great is his unfailing love [*hesed*]" (Lamentations 3:31–32).

Hesed is to love as God loves. When God's presence passed by Moses on Mount Sinai and revealed his very essence, God proclaimed his great *hesed* (Exodus 34:6). Biblical scholar John Oswalt describes it this way:

> The word *ḥesed* ... [is] the descriptor par excellence of God in the Old Testament. The word speaks of a completely undeserved kindness and generosity done by a person who is in a position of power. This was the Israelites' experience of God. He revealed himself to them when they were not looking for him, and he kept his covenant with them long after their persistent breaking of it had destroyed any reason for his continued keeping of it.... Unlike humans, this deity was not fickle, undependable, self-serving, and grasping. Instead he was faithful, true, upright, and generous — always.[11]

Like other Hebrew words, *hesed* is not just a feeling but an action. It intervenes on behalf of loved ones and comes to their rescue. After Abraham's servant miraculously found a wife for Isaac by bumping into her at a well, he praised God "who has not abandoned his kindness [*hesed*] and faithfulness to my master" (Genesis 24:27). Because *hesed* is often active, it is translated as "mercy" or "loving-kindness," but neither of these words fully conveys that *hesed* acts out of unswerving loyalty even to the most undeserving.

Hesed is a bone-weary father who drives through the night to bail his drug-addicted son out of jail. *Hesed* is a mom who spends day after thankless day spoon-feeding and wiping up after a disabled child. *Hesed* is an unsung pastor's wife whose long-suffering, tearful prayers keep her exhausted husband from falling apart at the seams. *Hesed* is love that can be counted on, decade after decade. It's not about the thrill of romance, but the security of faithfulness.

My parents celebrated their sixty-third wedding anniversary before my father died two years ago. I was born last of seven, after they had been married twenty-some years. The love I saw between them was not newlywed passion but a calm commitment to travel through life's highs and lows together. They were hardly unusual in their generation, but the gift they gave their children is getting rarer every day —a sense that our lives were stably anchored in a loving family. By weathering life's storms together, year after year, they embodied God's *hesed*.

I wonder if *hesed* is becoming harder for people to grasp nowadays. To us, love is dating and romance—a candle-lit restaurant and a sunset walk along the beach. We focus on love in the short term. Our movies tell us that a housewife who dumps her balding, boring husband for a shadowy stranger with a passionate kiss has discovered true love. Is this because lifelong loyalty is becoming so rare? As more and more of us grow up in broken families, are we losing our ability to imagine love that never ends?

More and more, Christians even talk about our relationship with God as a romance. We reminisce about the day we accepted Christ, fondly remembering the night we first met. Does that mean that we're only dating and not married? On my crabby, grumpy days, God's *hesed* is what I hang on to. For better or worse, he's stuck with me — no matter what.

With All Your Very?

Imagine that next Valentine's Day you open your mailbox to discover a fancy, romantic card. And inside, your beloved has written only one line:

I love you with all of my very.

With all your *very*? What kind of sentiment is that? Why would a person buy a card with such an odd typo? But this strange phrase is actually the last line of the commandment to love God. Love the Lord with all of your heart, and all of your soul, and all of your *very*. Hebrew speakers find the phrase as strange as we do. You can almost hear the crowd of puzzled Israelites murmuring when they first heard Moses' words: "With all my very?... Very *what*?"

The word, *me'od* (meh-ODE), "very," is a common adverb that is used the same way as we use "very," to intensify adjectives. Outside of the *Shema*, it's almost never used as a noun.[12] You'll likely find it on the first page of your handy Berlitz phrase book. A common first line (to a man) is "*Mah shlomkha?*" ("How are you?"), and the usual response is, "*Tov me'od*" (TOVE meh-ODE, "*very* well"). And in Genesis 1:31, when God looks back on all his handiwork, he proclaims his creation not just *tov*, "good" — but *tov me'od*, "*very* good."

Hebrew scholar Randall Buth reads the *Shema*'s phrase "with all of your very" as saying, "with all of your *oomph!*" The word itself pushes you to love God heartily, earnestly, zealously — or as we read it, with all of your *might*.

Once English speakers hear *me'od* defined as "strength" or "might," we see the issue as solved and move right on. But remember that the wording, actually, is "all of your *very*." Every time Hebrew speakers uttered the strange phrase, it provoked them to meditate on what this odd construction was really saying.

You can find several discussions in the first-century writings about what your "very" really means. As you'd expect, one way of interpreting it was as "all of your much-ness" in the sense of "strength." But interestingly, another interpretation was that it means all of your *mind*—your thoughts, consciousness, and intelligence. (This meaning is also inherent in "all your heart," but preachers also associated it with "all your very.") Sometimes the word's vagueness prompted expositors to explain *me'od* with two meanings, side by side, and expand the *Shema* from three parts to four.

More than one scholar believes that this is the reason why Jesus' version of the *Shema* in some gospel texts has four aspects rather than three, as in Deuteronomy.[13] In Mark 12:30 it has four components: heart, soul, mind, and strength. In Matthew 22:37 it has only three: heart, soul, and mind. But in Matthew, "mind" takes the place of "strength."[14] (Luke 10:27 has four components, like Mark's version, but a lawyer quotes it rather than Jesus.)

So what did Jesus actually say? Simple, if he was talking about Scripture. He didn't speak the Greek words that we see in the Gospels. He quoted the Hebrew text of Deuteronomy. But when the gospel writers interpreted his words for their audiences, they explained the strange word *me'od* the way they understood it, as "mind" and/or "strength." Since the word *me'od* is ambiguous, sometimes they even gave it two explanations, as other teachers did, so that the greatest commandment became fourfold instead of three.

Believe it or not, they had yet another explanation of *me'od* that can also teach us today. Your *me'od* is also about your *mammon*, your money. This is because "all your very" can be understood to mean "all your increase." Everything God has given you over your lifetime has "increased" you. Your wealth and possessions, your family and children—all are gracious gifts from him. Loving God with everything you have is a high calling indeed.

How do you love God with your money? Obviously, one way is by sharing with those in need, and both Jesus and Jewish tradition expected that we would do so—more about that later. But you could also look at loving God with your money in terms of financial integrity. Moneywise, discipleship has a "cost," even in the smallest decision you make. When you show a sales clerk that she undercharged you on an item, you'll get a little less change back. As you tally up your tax return, if you decide to not exaggerate a deduction, a few dollars will come off your refund. If your business forgoes a questionable opportunity, your bottom line will decline. And if you dent another car as you're parking and leave a note rather than driving away, it might cost you *a lot*. Rather than gritting your teeth at each of these little "expenses," you could see them as ways of saying "I love you" to a righteous God.

A Modern *Shema*

Rereading the text that Jesus considered the very essence of God's Word, we can capture it in this modern way:

"Listen up, Israel — The LORD is your God, he, and he alone!! You should love him with every thought that you think, live every hour of every day for him, be willing to sacrifice your life for him. Love him with every penny in your wallet and everything that you've got!"

Or if you want to say it in Hebrew,[15]

> *Shema Israel, Adonai elohenu, Adonai echad!*
> *Ve'ahavta et Adonai elohekha*
> *b'khol levavkha,*
> *uv khol nafshekha,*
> *uv khol me'odekha!*

Wisdom for the Walk

1. In what ways is your love for God romantic and passionate? What are the advantages and disadvantages of thinking of love as a feeling? How important are feelings in your walk with God?

2. How can you love God through your mind? What can you learn from the Jewish tradition of memorization and study of Scripture?

3. Think through your activities last week. Does God compete with an infinite number of other distractions, like sports, hobbies, investments, movies, Facebook, and TV? If so, how can you reorient your life to keep your focus on God?

4. How can you demonstrate God's *hesed*, his merciful and loyal love, in your marriage, your family, your friendships, and your church? How might you demonstrate loyalty and commitment in a culture that prizes mobility and self-fulfillment?

5. How do you show your love for God with your money?

CHAPTER 4

Meeting Myself
Next Door

In everyone there is something of his fellow man....
Hence, "love your neighbor"—
for he is really you yourself.
— Rabbi Moses Cordovero[1]

Have you heard the story of Al, who hit rock bottom in life at age twenty-two? In a letter to his sister he rued the day that he was born, declaring that he was nothing but a burden on his family. As a youngster, Al had been labeled retarded and taken out of school more than once. Even the family maid referred to him as "the dopey one." After dropping out for a while, Al had managed to finish high school, but he couldn't get into tech school, much less college. Now he needed work badly, but he couldn't get a job to save his life. Finally, a friend's father, Fred Haller, cut Al a break. He gave him a probationary job at the office where he worked, taking a chance that Al wasn't as hopeless and clueless as everyone thought him to be.

But then radio commentator Paul Harvey, who tells this story, goes on to explain, "Al was not inexorably destined to guide lesser minds through ... intricacies of space and time. In fact, at twenty-two, he stood at the brink of utter uselessness, until Fred Haller gave him a chance at the Swiss Federal Patent Office. Inspired by that first success, he learned to live up to his potential. From that beginning came the incomparable genius, *Albert Einstein*."[2]

For years, Paul Harvey held audiences spellbound by telling the "rest of the story"—the hitherto unknown details behind notable people and events. Often he retold a person's early history without the optimism of later fame, so that listeners could see their heroes from a fresh perspective. When his audience discovered the surprising beginnings of a well-known figure, their achievements glowed in a whole new light.

Jesus' words often have a "rest of the story" too, when you discover their Jewish context and their origins in the Scriptures Jesus knew. We've already seen how the greatest commandment, to "love the LORD your God," overflows with new meaning in its original Hebraic context. According to Jesus, another command is just like it: "Love your neighbor as yourself" (Matthew 22:39). Indeed it is—this line also unfolds to reveal deeper layers of wisdom, once you know the "rest of the story."

Thinking in Terms of "We"

The overwhelming importance of the command to "love your neighbor" echoes throughout the New Testament. Paul declared that the whole of the Law is fulfilled by obeying this one command (Galatians 5:14). Peter also exhorted his followers to "above all, love each other deeply" (1 Peter 4:8). And in John's letters, he wrote that "this is the message you heard from the beginning: We should love one another" (1 John 3:11). James called the command to love your neighbor the "royal law found in Scripture" (James 2:8).

Jesus' first Jewish followers put this command at the top of their marching orders, devoting themselves to fellowship, communal prayer, and breaking bread together (Acts 2:42–47). The emphasis on community was one of the outstanding characteristics of the Jerusalem church, responsible for its magnetic witness and strength during persecution.

Surprisingly, not only did they gather together, they also remained active in the larger community, joining the rest of the Jewish people in daily worship at the Temple. They didn't denounce the world around them and cloister tightly with like-minded friends. As a result, they enjoyed the favor of outsiders and daily welcomed new believers.

Even though the early Jerusalem church emphasized community, within only a few centuries Gentiles brought into the church an emphasis on individual piety and private devotion.[3] By AD 400, many Christians believed that the hermit's utter solitude was the path to God. Modern Christians, especially American Protestants, still maintain a strong sense of "Jesus and me" individualism, emphasizing one's "personal relationship with Christ" as the essence of faith.

By contrast, Judaism throughout the centuries has declared that "life is with people." Religion, in their thinking, is inherently communal. Whereas Christians seek out solitude for drawing close to God, many Jewish prayers can only be recited in the presence of a *minyan* (min-YAHN), a group that contains at least ten adult Jewish men. In his article "You Can't Be Holy Alone," Ismar Schorsch explains the premise behind this practice: when people gather to worship God, his presence among them sanctifies the place.[4]

Recently the difference became quite palpable to me. In my own Christian "quiet time" I decided to read from the *Amidah*, the Jewish daily prayer liturgy, knowing that it's typically recited communally.[5] I was reciting lines like this:

> Heal us and we shall be healed, help us and we shall be helped, for you are our joy. Grant full healing for all our wounds, for you, O God and King, are a true and merciful physician. Blessed are you, O LORD, who heals the sick of His people Israel.

All by myself I was praying these ancient lines that were exclusively framed in terms of "we" and "us" and "our people" (as is the Lord's Prayer, of course). A few days later I attended a large Christian worship service. There, the focus of every song was on God and *me*: "I love you, Lord, and I lift my voice" … "Just as I am, without one plea" … "Here I come to worship, here I come to bow down." Hundreds of us were worshiping side by side, a sea of voices resounding together, and every one of us was pretending to be all alone.

Love as You'd Want to Be Loved

I mentioned before how surprised I was when I first saw that both of the "love" commands come out of the Torah, the "Law of Moses." While "love the LORD your God" comes from Deuteronomy 6:5, "love your neighbor" actually comes from Leviticus 19:18:

> Do not seek revenge or bear a grudge against anyone among your people, but *love your neighbor as yourself.* I am the LORD.[6]

Because both Deuteronomy and Leviticus verses share the word *ve'ahavta* ("and you shall love"), Jesus tied the two "love" commands together by using a fascinating rabbinic rule called *gezerah sheva*, "a comparison of equals." Because the two verses share a common word that is only found a couple other places in the Scriptures, one could assume that one line was expanding on the other, as an explanation of how to love. So loving God requires, and is indeed expressed best, through love of our neighbors.[7]

How do you actually "love your neighbor as yourself"? Scholar James Kugel believes that an early sermon about this verse may have given rise to the Golden Rule. He writes:

> Loving one's neighbor every bit as much as one loves oneself … seems like a tall order indeed, virtually an inhuman one. So perhaps the commandment was intended in some other sense, something like, you shall love your neighbor as you yourself *would be loved,* that is, treat your neighbor with love in the same way that you yourself would want to be treated.

He goes on to point out that around 10 BC, Hillel declared, "Whatever is hateful to you, do not do to your fellow; this is the whole Torah and the rest is commentary." This is similar to Jesus' "in everything, do to others what you would have them do to you, for this sums up the Law and the Prophets" (Matthew 7:12).[8]

In *Sitting at the Feet of Rabbi Jesus,* we noted that Hillel's formulation of the Golden Rule focuses on what *not* to do rather than pointing toward the ultimate goal of love. His words may sound as if they set the bar too low, but you have to admit that even Hillel's minimum is beyond most of us. Can any of us go a day without doing something to another that we wouldn't want done to ourselves? As we aim for Jesus' ultimate goals, we can often learn from rabbinic thinkers how to do so.

In *Love Your Neighbor as Yourself,* Rabbi Joseph Telushkin points out that Hillel's negative phrasing does achieve a practical purpose.

He tells about a school teacher who asked his sixth graders to compose two "Golden Rule" lists, one of the actions they would want others to do to them, and the other of actions they would not want done. Their "Do" lists were brief and somewhat vague, containing things like "love," "respect," and "help." But the "Don't" lists were much longer, with practical prohibitions like "Don't hit," "steal," "laugh at," "snub," or "cheat." The negative version was clearer to the students because it was concrete and specific. As a result, it was more likely to change their behavior.[9]

> *Love is not affectionate feeling, but a steady wish for the loved person's ultimate good as far as it can be obtained.*
> —C. S. Lewis

Who Is My Neighbor?

Even though a rabbinic discussion was already going on about "love your neighbor" in the early first century, Jesus did, in fact, say something new. To see how he did this, we need to look at the words of "love your neighbor" more closely and how his parable about the good Samaritan brought his interpretation of the love command to a whole new level.

As we've seen before with Hebrew, the words behind "love your neighbor as yourself" can be read in more than one way. The Hebrew text reads:

> *ve'ahavta* (veh-ah-hav-TAH — and you shall love)
> *l'reahkha* (le-rey-ah-KHAH — [to] your neighbor)
> *kamokha* (ka-MO-khah — as/like yourself)

We always roll our eyes at the lawyer who asks, "Who is my neighbor?" in Luke 10:29, hearing his question as a sly attempt to undermine the text's obvious meaning. But actually his query was reasonable. The word *reah* (REY-ah), which we translate as "neighbor," typically means "companion," "fellow," "kinsman," or "friend." It doesn't usually apply to just any person on earth. The lawyer likely assumed that in this verse *reah* went beyond one's closest friends, but various opinions existed.

For instance, "love your kinsmen" was how some read this verse. One early text preaches, "Among yourselves, be loving of your brothers as a man loves himself, with each man seeking for his brother what is good for him, and acting together on the earth, and loving each other as themselves."[10] The focus was on loyalty to one's own companions, not on loving all humanity. As insular as this interpretation is, could we even start by doing that? Showing love to the people around us is actually a lot harder than feeling a lofty, vague affection for the whole world. As Charlie Brown's friend Linus used to say, "I love mankind! It's people I can't stand."

Yet another interpretation of "love your neighbor" has puzzled scholars for centuries. In Matthew 5:43, Jesus says, "You have heard that it was said, 'Love your neighbors *and hate your enemy*'" (italics added). Often Christians have accused the Pharisees of teaching this, but it occurs nowhere in rabbinic writings. When the Dead Sea Scrolls were discovered in the 1940s, the answer came to light. The authors of these documents, the Essenes, gave "love your neighbor" this spin. Every day they pledged themselves to "love all the sons of light, each according to his lot in God's design, and hate all the sons of darkness, each according to his guilt in God's vengeance." They were ticking down the days until the Messiah would arrive to start the war on evil and slay all the wicked on earth.[11]

Your Neighbor Is Just Like You

Many others had commented on what "love your neighbor" meant in Jesus' time. But Jesus had yet another way of reading this verse. The key to understanding how he interpreted "love your neighbor" is actually in the last word of the verse—*kamokha*, which literally means "like yourself." It also has more than one possible rendering. Traditionally, we read it "as you love yourself," so that we should love others as much we love ourselves, which is certainly a great goal. But *kamokha* can also be read in another way. Instead of comparing the two kinds of love, it can compare *yourself* with your *neighbor*: "Love your neighbor *who is similar to yourself.*"

Supporting this interpretation, just a few lines later in Leviticus

19:34, the phrase has exactly this sense. It reads, "The foreigner residing among you must be treated as your native-born. *Love them as yourself*, for you were foreigners in Egypt." More plainly this means, "You shall show love to foreigners, because *they are like yourselves* — because you were once foreigners in Egypt." You should have empathy for them when you realize how similar their situation is to your own experience.

> *Better a sinful person who knows that he has sinned, than a righteous person who knows that he is righteous.*
> — Rabbi Yaakov Horowitz

The idea of comparing your neighbor to yourself might not seem earth-shattering, but consider how this reveals the true wisdom of Leviticus 19:18: "Do not seek revenge or bear a grudge against anyone among your people, but love your neighbor [*who is like*] *yourself*. I am the LORD." When you're angry with your neighbor, don't forget — you're just the same way.

I've seen this in my own life. A friend of mine used to cook up exciting plans, and after I'd gotten excited and reorganized my life around them, he'd change his mind and cancel. Not just once, but time and time again. After being irritated about this for years, I found myself doing the same thing to others. I'd promise something and then back out, much to their dismay. Then I realized that I genuinely *wanted* to do the things I promised, just as he did. We were both a bundle of good intentions! But good intentions aren't the same as follow-through. It was only when I saw myself in him that I got over my anger.

When you realize that you're guilty of the same sins that others are, you realize that you shouldn't bear grudges against them, but you should forgive and love them instead. All people, including ourselves, are flawed and sinful, but we need to love them because we ourselves commit the same sins. We're alike in our weaknesses and frailties. We are to love those who do not seem worthy because *we ourselves are unworthy* and need God's mercy.

In Jesus' day, some actually did read "love your neighbor" in this sense. One early sage taught: "Forgive your neighbor the wrong he has done, and then your sins will be pardoned when you pray. Does anyone harbor anger against another, and expect healing from the

Lord? If one has no mercy toward *another like himself,* can he then seek pardon for his own sins?"[12]

Understanding "love your neighbor" this way reveals the logic behind Jesus' line in the Lord's Prayer, "Forgive us our debts, as we also have forgiven our debtors" (Matthew 6:12). Another way you could pray it would be, "Please love us even though we are sinners, as we love other sinners who are just like ourselves."

When you think about it, forgiving sins is one of the strongest tests of love. It's easy to love someone who has treated you rightly, but loving someone who has hurt you is far more difficult. God must love us greatly if he keeps forgiving the sins we commit against him.

Why a Samaritan?

To answer the lawyer's question, "Who is my *reah*," Jesus responded by telling the story of the good Samaritan, one of the most familiar parables to Christians today. A man is attacked by thugs while traveling from Jerusalem to Jericho, and he is lying next to the road near death, stripped, wounded, and bleeding. Both a priest and a Levite see him by the wayside but pass by without stopping to help. But a despised Samaritan comes to the man's aid, bandaging his wounds and treating them with oil and wine. Then he gently lifts the man onto his own donkey and transports him to an inn, generously paying for his expenses (Luke 10:30–35).

No one can miss the parable's beautiful picture of human compassion. Yet most of us don't get the punch line quite right. The question Jesus was asked was, "Who is my neighbor?" and on first blush it sounds as if the answer is "the man dying by the road." But look again. In Jesus' response he turned the question on its head, saying, "Which of these three do you think *was a neighbor* to the man who fell into the hands of robbers?" Jesus' question rules out the crime victim as the neighbor. To answer Jesus, the neighbor was the Samaritan!

But the great irony was that a Samaritan was the last person on the planet who should qualify as a neighbor. The Samaritans were hardly known for hospitality to Jews, and in fact they often attacked pilgrims who were traveling to Jerusalem for the Temple feasts.[13] Even as Jesus told this parable, his disciples were likely recalling their own fresh memories of Samaritan obnoxiousness. Just a chapter earlier, a Samaritan town had rudely rejected Jesus' entourage. The disciples fumed to Jesus, "Lord, do you want us to call fire down from heaven to destroy them?" They were itching to use their new powers to blow the Samaritans to smithereens (Luke 9:51 – 55).

Making the Samaritan the "neighbor" undoubtedly needled Jesus' still grumbling disciples and pressed the rest of his audience to realize that their "neighbors" might include even their most despised enemies. But perhaps Jesus also had in mind one other thing, an obscure event out of the dustiest pages of Israel's history books.

Deep in the book of Chronicles, buried within its interminable accounts of Temple tributes, tribal heads, and the exploits of idolatrous kings, we find a remarkable story in 2 Chronicles 28:1 – 15. This event took place after the tribes of Israel and Judah had separated; both of the tiny kingdoms were living a tenuous existence, consumed by battle after battle against surrounding nations in a fight for sheer survival.

At a low point in their history, the tribes whom God had brought through the Red Sea together, who had wandered the desert and entered the Promised Land together, fell at each others' throats. Israel attacked and soundly defeated Judah, putting 120,000 of their own brothers, the Judeans, to the sword. The soldiers were on the verge of leading another 200,000 back to Samaria as slaves.

But then Oded, a prophet of the Lord, stopped them in their tracks. The only reason God had allowed Israel to defeat Judah, stormed the wizened prophet, was to punish the Judeans for dabbling in idolatry. But Israel was far more guilty of idol worship! If Israel enslaved its Judean brothers, it would compound their guilt. God's fury against them would reach up to the heavens.

The Israelites were cut to the quick by the prophet's rebuke. You'll hardly believe what the leaders of the soldiers did next:

> Then the men who were designated by name arose, took the captives, and they clothed all their naked ones from the spoil; and they gave them clothes and sandals, fed them and gave them

drink, anointed them with oil, led all their feeble ones on donkeys, and brought them to Jericho, the city of palm trees, to their brothers; then they returned to Samaria. (2 Chronicles 28:15 NASB)

We rarely read of such compassion between nations at war, where one side binds the wounds of its enemies and gently restores them to freedom. This unimaginable act of kindness was a remarkable moment of grace between the tribes of Israel and Judah. By anointing the prisoners with oil and putting them on donkeys, it even hints that they were treating them as royalty—coronations of kings were performed this way (1 Kings 1:38–39).

You can see hints of this story in Jesus' parable in several ways. First, Jesus focuses the action in Jericho, one of the few times he mentions a specific place in a parable. The victim in his story was stripped naked, as some of the Judeans had been, and the Samaritan anointed the man, put him on his donkey, and carried him to Jericho, just as was done to the Judean prisoners. As Jesus unfolded his parable, the teacher who questioned him would have undoubtedly recognized these details and realized that the Samaritan was living out a scene of great compassion that had taken place long ago.[14]

Having these details in mind sheds even more light on Jesus' brilliant answer to the lawyer's question: "Who is my neighbor?" The Samaritan, his enemy. And not only this, but his enemy who was showing mercy to others, as his ancestors had done long ago. The take-home message was clear: the lawyer should go and do likewise. Act like the Samaritan, and even love the Samaritans, who at that time were some of his most despised enemies.

Indeed, the point when the ancient "good Samaritans" repented and decided to love their enemies was exactly when they became aware of the truth of Leviticus 19:18—that their enemies were their own brothers and that they were sinners just like them! They showed love to their neighbors because they realized they were alike, both in their humanity and their sinfulness.

And now you know ... the rest of the story.

Wisdom for the Walk

1. As you have grown up in faith, are you more at home worshiping God alone or with others? What difference does it make to sing or pray as "we" or as "I"? Why do we need to live out our faith within a community?

2. A wise friend once said to me, "What you're like as a neighbor is what you're like as a person." What kind of neighbor are you, literally, to those who live next door to you?

3. Consider someone who has made you angry recently, or someone you've disliked for a long time. In what ways is this person like yourself?

4. Make your own list of how "not" to love others—things you are prone to doing to others that hurt when you've been on the receiving end.

PART II

LIVING OUT *the* WORDS *of* RABBI JESUS

Sometimes you have to admit that Jesus' words are a puzzle. Why does he warn against having a "bad eye"? Why pray about "hallowing God's name"? When you know the Jewish idioms he used and the ideas that he built on, you can discover fresh, practical insights for living as his disciples today. Themes Jesus preached on, like judging others and guarding one's tongue, have resonated in Jewish thought down through the centuries, and they yield surprising wisdom for walking in the footsteps of our Rabbi Jesus.

CHAPTER 5

Gaining
a Good Eye

Whoever has a good eye, a humble spirit
and a modest soul is a disciple of Abraham our father ...
who enjoys this world and inherits the world to come.
—Mishnah, *Avot* 5:19[1]

Remember Amelia Bedelia? Whether you remember her books from childhood or read them to your kids, you'll recall the misadventures of the housemaid who follows every instruction to the letter. When her employer asks her to "dress the chicken," she sews a tiny pair of overalls and fits them onto the bird. When she's told to "put out the lights," she unscrews all the bulbs from their fixtures and hangs them on the backyard clothesline. The author, Peggy Parish, based her character on a maid in Cameroon who made comical errors by following the instructions of her English employers in a woodenly literal way.

Even kindergarteners laugh at the mistakes that Amelia Bedelia makes by not grasping how language works. But some of us make the same error as we read our Bibles. That's because all languages have idioms, figures of speech that don't make complete sense outside of their native context. You simply cannot decipher phrases like "beat around the bush," "kick the bucket," or "get someone's goat" by breaking them down word by word. Your best guesses might lead you wildly astray. To "catch a person's drift," you need to know the culture.

Understanding a few Jewish idioms can unlock Jesus' strange saying about what kind of "eye" we should have:

The eye is the lamp of the body. If your eyes are healthy, your whole body will be full of light. But if your eyes are unhealthy, your whole body will be full of darkness. If then the light within you is darkness, how great is that darkness! (Matthew 6:22–23)

Over the years, these mysterious lines have invited all kinds of speculation. One New Age teacher, Elizabeth Clare Prophet, interprets them as meaning that right in the middle of your forehead is a third, invisible "inner" eye that is the key to spiritual enlightenment. Another believes Jesus was calling us to perceive our oneness with God's divinity.[2] Countering these ideas, one pastor teaches that Jesus was simply speaking about healthy vision, encouraging his listeners to appreciate their ability to see.[3]

How can we really know what Jesus meant? The answer lies in the fact that Jesus was not a New Age guru or a twentieth-century pastor but a Jewish rabbi. We can crack this cryptic saying about the "eye" by hearing it within its Hebraic context and grasping the figures of speech Jesus was employing.[4] The Hebrew language uses "eye" in many idioms that describe a person's attitude toward others.

Jesus was most likely comparing the idea of having a "good eye" with having a "bad eye," two idioms that have been a part of the Hebrew language from biblical times until today.[5] Having a "good eye" (*ayin tovah*) is to look out for the needs of others and be generous in giving to the poor. But to have a "bad eye" (*ayin ra'ah*) is to be greedy and self-centered, blind to the needs of those around you.[6]

You can find Jesus using the "bad eye" idiom to describe stinginess elsewhere, such as in his parable about a farmer who hires workers all day long and then pays all of them the same at day's end. When the early workers grumble, the farmer responds, "Don't I have the right to do what I want with my own money? Or is your *eye bad* because I am generous?" (Matthew 20:15, pers. trans.).

Both expressions also appear in Proverbs: "The stingy are eager to get rich and are unaware that poverty awaits them" (Proverbs 28:22). In this line, "the stingy" is literally a "*bad eye*." Or this: "The generous will themselves be blessed, for they share their food with the poor" (22:9). Here, "the generous" is literally a "*good eye*." Even today, Hebrew speakers use these idioms. In Israel, a fundraiser for a local charity might knock on your door and say, "*ten b'ayin yaffa* [give with a beautiful eye]," another version of the "good eye."

The idea of having a "good eye" or "bad eye" comes from how Hebrew expands on the concept of "seeing," using it to describe one's attitude and response toward others. To "see" can even mean to respond to a need. Once again a Hebrew verb ties a mental activity to its expected physical outcome.

When Abraham was on the verge of sacrificing Isaac, God provided a ram in his place. So Abraham named the mountain "The Lord Will Provide," which is literally, "The Lord Will *See*" (Genesis 22:14).[7] What Abraham meant was that when God sees our need, he will certainly respond—God has a very "good eye."

Jesus' teachings about having a "good eye" or "bad eye" also show how perfectly he fit into first-century Jewish reality. Only a few decades after him, Rabbi Joshua declared that "a bad eye, an evil inclination, and the hatred of humanity drive a person from this world." He too preached that selfishness and greed destroy our lives.[8]

> *Miserliness shuts a man off from his fellow men and from humanity itself: If you look through a glass window, you see all the world, but if you cover one side with silver, it becomes a mirror and you see only yourself.*
> — M. Zborowski

Another Jewish teacher, Yohanan ben Zakkai (AD 30–90), queried his disciples, "What is the very best path to take in life?" The first answered, "Having an *ayin tovah* [a good eye]." Another said, "Being a good friend." A third, "Being a good neighbor." Yet another, "Being wise about the future." The last replied, "Having a good heart." This final response, Zakkai declared, was the wisest, because it included the rest. If you have a good heart, you will have all the other things, including a "good eye."

If you don't understand these figures of speech about the "eye," Jesus' intended message is subject to all kinds of misinterpretation. But when you read Jesus' words in light of their idiomatic meaning, they make perfect sense. If you're generous, your whole life will show it. And if you are selfish, it will infect your very soul.

Once you realize that Jesus was preaching about sharing one's money with others, this section of Matthew 6 clicks into place like a jigsaw puzzle. Just prior to verses 22–23, Jesus told his followers to "store up your treasures in heaven" (cf. 6:19–21), which is actually another Jewish idiom about giving to the poor.[9] And immediately after this line, Jesus declared that we can't be a slave to two masters —God and money. This entire passage (Matthew 6:19–24) is about sharing our resources with others.

Before I learned that your "eye" is really about your attitude toward money, these three lines appeared unrelated and Jesus' words about having a "body full of light" seemed perplexing and odd. But now his broader message becomes apparent. He was exhorting his followers to cultivate an open-handed attitude toward others and not let money rule over them. Caring for those around us isn't merely a nice habit to cultivate; Jesus says that it is central to our character as a whole.

Believe it or not, yet another idiom lurks nearby. In Matthew 6:1, Jesus tells his followers not to do their "acts of righteousness" in order to impress others. You might think he's talking about any kind of righteous deed. But in Jewish parlance, "righteousness," *tzedakah* (zeh-dah-KAH), is commonly used to mean "charity." Jesus' very next words show that this is actually what he means: "[But] when you give to the needy, do not announce it with trumpets" (6:2). *Tzedakah* has been a common Jewish idiom for giving to the poor for two thousand years. This expression suggests that helping others is not over-and-above; it is simply doing the right thing, doing what God expects of us as his people. Jesus expected it too. He didn't say "*if* you give to the needy," but "*when*." He very much expected his followers to be charitable, as Jews over the ages have been.

The Importance of the "Eye"

Why is a person's "eye" toward others so critical to Jesus? Because our relationship with money reveals our relationship with God. To have a "bad eye" is to cling to the little that you have, resenting those with more and refusing to help those with less. Your attitude shows how convinced you are that God is stingy, that he is either unwilling or unable to care for you. And it also reveals how disconnected you are from the struggles of others. No wonder Jesus says that life becomes dark indeed when you've cut yourself off from both God and those around you.

On the other hand, if you're radically convinced of God's caring presence in your life, you're also confident that God will provide for your needs — not just materially, but emotionally and spiritually as well. You may not be wealthy by the world's standards, but you have a rock-solid understanding that what you have is *enough*, that ultimately your own situation is secure. The fruit is a generous attitude, a "good eye" toward others. How can your life not brighten when you think this way?

Having a "good eye" or a "bad eye" also points toward a more fundamental issue — what is your primary motivation in life? Is your driving concern your own comfort, or do you look beyond yourself? Ever more our Christian culture reinforces our self-centeredness, as sermon titles increasingly aim to entice us through the church's doors by appealing to our *felt needs*: "God's Secrets to a Successful Marriage" ... "Jesus' Plan for Organizing Your Life" ... "Biblical Foods for Beauty and Weight Loss." Our desires may be legitimate and the sermons good messages. But after a steady diet of self-therapy, we simply won't tolerate a sermon that points out sin or pushes us to care about others. All we want to hear about is, "What's in it for me?"

Amazingly, we even find preachers who appeal directly to our "bad eye." Recently, Benny Hinn prophesied that a great "wealth-transfer" from the wicked to the righteous will occur just prior to the rapture, which is imminent. He then declared that if listeners send in their seed-gift today, God will bestow on them a "prosperity-anointing."[10]

Jesus' message was exactly the opposite of Benny Hinn's. He promised his followers that if they had a "good eye," their lives would be illumined from within. But is this just pie in the sky? What if Jesus' disciples actually did follow his marching orders to give to the poor? Would his words about being "full of light" come true?

We find this very thing in Acts — that Jesus' first Jewish disciples actually did carry out his instructions to a tee. They knew just what he meant about what kind of "eye" they should have. The Jerusalem believers overflowed with generosity, caring extravagantly for each other's needs:

> All the believers were together and had everything in common. They sold property and possessions to give to anyone who had need. Every day they continued to meet together in the temple courts. They broke bread in their homes and ate together with glad and sincere hearts, praising God and enjoying the favor of all the people. And the Lord added to their number daily those who were being saved. (Acts 2:44–47)

The first believers didn't abandon all earthly comforts and live in poverty. They shared from their excess, so that everyone would have enough.[11] They didn't need to cling to possessions for status or security, because they were convinced, beyond a shadow of a doubt, that their wonderful, loving God would always provide. Their Rabbi Jesus had preached that they should have a "good eye," and they lived out his words with passion. And their lives shone brilliantly because of it.

Passing the Plate

Even if Jesus' words about the "eye" aren't clear, his emphasis on giving comes through elsewhere. But in *Passing the Plate: Why American Christians Don't Give Away More Money*, Christian Smith and Michael Emerson point out that his message doesn't seem to be sinking in nowadays. In their 1996 poll of charitable habits, 35 percent of U.S. Christians reported that they gave no money to charity. Even among regular churchgoers, one fourth gave *nothing* to any religious or secular cause at all—not even a token five dollars a year. On average, Christian giving per family amounted to about $200 per year.[12]

Why do so many Christians have such a "bad eye"? One major factor is consumerism, which convinces us that our worth as a person is linked to how nice a car we have. We're bombarded by advertising that reminds us of all the products that we *don't* have, comforts that are just out of reach. If you don't yet have a perpetually dissatisfied "bad eye," you're not listening to enough ads. Back in 1930, one advertising trade journal declared that making people unhappy is actually the goal: "Advertising helps to keep the masses dissatisfied with their mode of life, discontented with the ugly things around them. Satisfied customers are not as profitable as discontented ones."[13]

In our world it's not hard to become like *Veggie Tales'* Larry the Cucumber, when he zoomed past Bob the Tomato in his new Soobi Action Jeep. When Bob remarked, "You must be really happy to get a cool toy like that," Larry replied, "Well, almost ... there's just one more thing I need to be *really* happy—the Soobi Action Camper."

"So once you get the camper, then you'll be happy?" probed Bob.

"Oh, I don't know. There's always the Dirt Bike ... and the Jet-ski ... and the Soobi Action Hanglider...." Larry sighed.

"Larry, how much stuff do you need to be happy?" exclaimed Bob.

"I don't know. How much more stuff is there?"[14]

Of course, many of us wish we could be more generous, but there's not much left at the end of the month. Smith and Emerson point out that often the problem isn't our income, it's our major purchases. They write:

> For many families with money, a mere two buying decisions —the purchase of home and cars—are enough to lock household budgets into tight budgetary situations for decades. The mortgages and automobile loan payments alone, which are often maxed to the upper limit of affordability, are enough to make people feel that they can barely pay their bills.... It is not that they do not actually have the annual incomes to give generously. It is rather that they ... commit most of their money to be spent in ways that leave little left over to give away.[15]

Many of us pray intently over a potential spouse or career, knowing how critical our decision is to serving God. What we might not consider is that our next car or house purchase is just as important.

Just imagine if Jesus were a real-estate agent, taking you around to see the options for your growing family. "This next place is lovely. It's got five bathrooms, a Jacuzzi, and a pool in the backyard. The price is $400,000—pretty high, but the schools are great here ... Oooohh, but check out this place next door. It needs some work, but it's only $250,000. You know, if you buy this house, what you'll save in loan payments could support an entire orphanage in Kenya.[16] Hey, haven't you been praying lately for a way to really make an impact? I know a great little place just outside of Mombasa that I could call. Your money could save the lives and souls of hundreds of children — really *sweet* kids, I have to say ... Let me find their number, just give me a minute here ..."

Jewish Wisdom for Giving

Despite their emphasis on giving, Judaism takes a pragmatic approach. Orthodox Jews are expected to give at least 10 percent away to charity. But there's an upper limit to giving too. Unless one is enormously wealthy, people are discouraged from giving more than 20 percent. Why? Because giving everything away causes *you* to become impoverished, and then you can't help anyone else. One sage commented, "It's better to give one shekel a thousand different times than a thousand shekels at once, because each time you give, you become a kinder person."[17]

And be gentle in judging those in need, one rabbi pointed out. "When a poor man asks you for aid, do not use his faults as an excuse for not helping him. For then God will look at your offenses, and he is sure to find many."[18] If we can't be compassionate to others who've made unwise choices, why should we expect God to help us when we make mistakes ourselves?

It's hard to overstate the Jewish emphasis on giving — not just to the poor, but to every kind of religious and civic need. In observant communities, at every turn in life there is a reminder to give. Collections are taken at every holiday celebration, wedding, or funeral. One of the highest compliments a person can be given is to be called a *ba'al tzedakah* — a "master of charity," a person who always has an open hand to share with those in need and an open door to extend hospitality.[19]

Who is rich?
He who is happy
with what he has.
— Mishnah, *Avot* 4:1

In past centuries, the woman of the house often took charge of the giving. You can see this in the time of Jesus, when his patrons were wealthy women like Joanna and Susanna (Luke 8:3). Children are always involved, in order to teach them generosity from their earliest years. They are the ones who drop the coins into the family's *tzedakah* box to be given later to a worthy cause. Children also hand over the money when fundraisers knock on the door.

As many Christians switch over to giving to the church electronically, we might want to consider this. How will we teach our children about giving if they don't see us put our check into the plate each week?

In the past few years it's certainly gotten tougher to make ends meet. But there's another way to show a "good eye" toward others, by doing *gemilut hasadim* (gem-i-LOOT hah-sa-DEEM) — "acts of lovingkindess" (*hesed*). As important as charity is, this is understood to be even better. Handing a ten dollar bill to a hungry homeless man is charity. But inviting him to have lunch with you at McDonalds is an "act of lovingkindness." It's something you do with your own hands to help others.

Three classic types of *gemilut hasadim* are visiting the sick, comforting mourners, and burying the dead. Some Jews make a point to use part of their "giving dollars" to do *gemilut hasadim*. One lady I met in Jerusalem loved to read, so she invested in a library of books and then regularly found ways of loaning or even giving them to others.

Considering as much money as we spend on entertainment, wouldn't an alternative be to make a "hobby" out of a particular form of *gemilut hasadim*? My friend Bruce makes a habit of stopping to help or offer a cell phone when he encounters people stranded with car trouble. Yet another friend, Hillari, who teaches classes on professional skills, enjoys helping friends hunt for jobs and prepare for interviews. My friend Kathleen finds ways to buoy up coworkers' morale, acting as "mom" to her whole office. How about making a "hobby" of inviting single or elderly people home for dinner after church?

We like movies and amusement parks because we can escape for a little while, as fleeting and artificial as the enjoyment may be. But my friends who do *gemilut hasadim* experience pleasure that is authentic and long-lasting, as God reveals his *hesed* to others through them.

Being Frugal with a Good Eye

This year my car turned twenty years old. And my favorite clothing boutique is Ditto's, a second-hand store in town. My sister-in-law has concluded that I'm "pathologically frugal." With the lean economy in recent years, many others have discovered thriftiness too.

A few years ago, when I was part of another tour of Israel, I got a different perspective on frugality. My fellow travelers and I had mentally prepared ourselves to haggle at the markets, ready to bargain down to the last shekel. But then our guide reminded us that recent years had been terrible for merchants. Political events had kept tourists away, and the streets had been empty for months. Many shops were barely keeping their doors open. For us, a few shekels' difference was a source of pride at how cheaply we could get a souvenir. For them, the money would feed the family for another day.

We realized that sometimes what we call frugality is actually stinginess. Being frugal is when we deny ourselves something in order to save money. But when we deny others what is due them, by underpaying workers or giving miserly tips, or even bargaining excessively, then we are selfishly saving at others' expense.

It is the way of the kind-hearted to run after the poor.
—B. Talmud, Shabbat 104

One friend of mine, a business owner, never uses coupons. He empathizes with storeowners because he knows how tough it is to make a living in business nowadays. It's his way of living with a "good eye." He realizes that we need to look beyond our pocketbooks to consider others' needs as well.

What the Torah Taught

Caring for the poor has been central to Judaism for millennia. Where did they get this idea? From God's unique commands in the Torah. Many of us are glad to skip past the Old Testament's legal codes. Its laws about unclean foods and ritual impurity strike us as strange and distasteful. But these rules likely didn't surprise the Israelites, because sacrifice and food laws were common among Israel's neighbors.

What *would* have shocked Moses' first listeners were God's lengthy list of commands for caring for the less fortunate. Yearly tithes were to be gathered for the poor, and farmers were to leave some of their crops behind for widows and aliens to glean (Leviticus 19:9 – 10). Loans to the needy were to be without interest, and if they couldn't be repaid in seven years, they were to be forgiven (Deuteronomy 15:1 – 3). If hard times forced a farmer to sell his land, it was to be returned in the year of Jubilee, which took place every fifty years (Leviticus 25:28).[20]

The gods of Israel's neighbors concerned themselves with sacrifices and ceremonies. They were not terribly moral, and they were often fickle and cruel. The God of Israel was unique in tying worship of him with compassion for others.[21] When his people began to believe that rituals were all he required, God sent prophets to remind them that justice to the poor was his greatest concern. This was the heart of Jesus' teaching too.

Today, people wonder what difference it makes that Jesus was Jewish. What about his culture should affect us here and now? The rituals and food laws of first-century Israel were similar to those of other nations in many ways. But the distinctive feature of the Torah was its great concern for society's vulnerable. When Jesus came along, he emphasized the same thing. The more we read Jesus' words in their Hebraic setting, the more we discover that if we want to follow Jesus as his first Jewish disciples did, we need to learn to have a very "good eye."

Wisdom for the Walk

1. Before you knew about the "eye" idioms, how did you understand Matthew 6:22–23?

2. In your heart, how solidly assured are you that God is providing for your own financial and emotional needs? How does it influence how you share with others?

3. As you look back over this chapter, does anything from the rabbis add perspective to what you've heard from Jesus?

4. Can you name anyone in your church, neighborhood, or work who is in need? (If you can't, what does that say about how you've chosen to live?) Consider how much you think about how those around you are coping. Do you have it on your mind how you can help out?

5. In what ways does your use of money reflect selfishness—a bad eye? In what ways does it reflect generosity and kindness—a good eye?

6. What is your philosophy and practice of giving and tithing? For example, do you tithe only to your church? Do you like to give in small or large amounts? Do you support numerous causes, or do you choose just a few? With all the causes clamoring for your attention, how do you make decisions about where to give?

CHAPTER 6

The Mystery of the Name

What is the Sanctification of the Name?
Conduct which leads people to love the name of God.

—Talmud, *Yoma* 86b

As a Lutheran missionary in Madagascar, my grandpa Tverberg was used to encountering the strange and unusual. But late one Saturday evening, as he was preparing his sermons for the next day's services, a knock at his door took him far outside his comfort zone.

Earlier that day, a Malagasy man named Fanala who had heard him preach declared, "I am going to become a Christian. I hate to serve the devil." To show his commitment, Fanala handed over a basket full of charms and divination tools to be burned. But that night, a villager arrived at my grandpa's door saying, "Fanala has the devil; you have to come drive him out!"

My grandpa rose from his book-strewn desk and hastily strode toward the village. Nothing in his seminary textbooks had prepared him to cast out demons. Lutherans are good at liturgy, passing the peace, and serving Jell-o salads. Exorcisms just aren't on their list.

Hastily, Grandpa thought back to how the disciples commanded demons to leave, hoping that their prayer was what he should pray too. As he neared Fanala's hut, he caught sight of a crowd seated in a circle, an unearthly chant rising from the group. Fanala was in the middle, pacing to and fro, whistling and frothing at the mouth, waving his arms wildly.

Grandpa put his hand firmly on Fanala's shoulder and commanded, "In the name of Jesus, go out!" Immediately, the man fell backward as if he was dead, and the incredulous villagers exclaimed,

"There went the devil!" In a few minutes, Fanala awoke in his right mind. The next day he was baptized, and he never experienced possession again.[1]

Throughout history, people have prayed, been baptized, and even cast out demons "in the name of Jesus." And Jesus himself taught us to pray to his Father by saying, "Hallowed be your name." But we stumble over these phrases and others that speak about the "name." The Hebrew language still uses these idioms, and Jewish culture has discovered great wisdom about what it means to hallow the name of God.

In the Name of *El Al?*

Years ago, while disembarking from a flight to Israel, I discovered a clue to the mystery of "the name." Achy and rumpled from the ten-hour ride, I was pulling a squashed suitcase from the overhead bin when my rudimentary Hebrew caught the very last line of the end-of-flight announcements: *"B'shem El Al, shalom."* Literally, "In the name of El Al, peace." The flight crew wasn't using the airline's name to cast a spell of blessing on its customers. They were saying, "As official representatives of the *El Al* airline, we bid you farewell."

From biblical times until today, the phrase "in the name of" is a Hebrew idiom that often means "on behalf of" or "for the sake of." We've picked this up in English when a policeman shouts, "Stop in the name of the law!" The officer represents an authority greater than himself, and he is letting the perpetrator know it. In the same way, my grandpa was acting as Christ's official representative. Because Jesus is the true Lord of creation and because he wields authority over the spiritual world, the demon obeyed my grandfather.

Reading the phrase "in the name of" literally, you also might think that it is critical to pronounce the name correctly, to form your lips into the proper sounds. More than one group has felt so strongly about pronouncing Hebrew names correctly that they've made new translations of the Bible with all of the names respelled.[2] But my grandfather's experience proves otherwise. When he was praying, the name of that crossed his lips was actually *Jesosy*, pronounced zhe-SHOO-shee, in the Malagasy dialect of the area.

The power of the name of Jesus is not about uttering a certain word, but in the supreme authority of the One who is named. In Hungarian, they call him *Jézusnak*; in Maori they call him *Ihu*; in Haitian Creole, they call him *Jezi*. Around the world, people have called on Christ as they have known him, and he has gladly answered their prayers.

Yeshua, God's Salvation

Jesus' Hebrew name was *Yeshua*, pronounced "yeh-SHU-ah." Many who study his Jewish context prefer to call him as *Yeshua* in order to be sensitive to his Jewish life and reality. In this book, and more generally, I use "Jesus" because it is the pronunciation most familiar to English speakers.[3] Part of the reason is from what I've experienced as I've seen people get interested in their Jewish roots. Sometimes in their enthusiasm, they take on a whole new vocabulary that creates barriers between themselves and others. My thinking is that if you've discovered insights that bring you closer to God, you're obligated to share them. To do so you need to be a bridge, not an island. So I deliberately use a more widely known vocabulary.

All that said, when you know that Jesus' name originally was *Yeshua*, you become more aware of its wonderful meaning, "God's salvation." The angel told Joseph to call his future son by the name *Yeshua* because he would save his people from their sins (Matthew 1:21). This is because the name *Yeshua* sounds like "he will save." It is actually a contracted form of *Yehoshua* (which we translate as Joshua), which literally means, "The Lord's salvation."[4]

Sometimes Jesus' name became part of his message. One day, as Jesus was traveling down the dusty road outside of Jericho, a flash of royal blue caught his eye from the tree ahead. Peering more closely, he caught sight of Zacchaeus, the fabulously wealthy chief tax collector, who was trying to get a glimpse of the great rabbi as he passed by. Pausing below the aged sycamore, Jesus called him down, boldly declaring that he must eat with him that day. Why? Because when

Zacchaeus repented of his corruption, "salvation" (*yeshua*) had come to his house that day. Jesus was using the meaning of his own name to proclaim that Zacchaeus's sins had been forgiven and he had found salvation (Luke 19:1 – 10).

What's in a Name?

It's hard to overstate how important names were in biblical times. In ancient thought, without a name, an object or being didn't even exist. Egyptian documents describe the time before creation as "when no name of anything had yet been named."[5] After God called each piece of the universe into existence, he completed its creation by naming it: day, night, heaven, earth, sea. By doing so, he was also exerting his sovereignty, because the one who names another has authority. When God gave Adam the task of naming all the animals, he was giving him his first exercise in ruling over creation (Genesis 2:19).

In the ancient Near East, a person's name was intimately linked to his or her identity and reputation. When God reoriented a person's life, he also changed his name. "Abram" became "Abraham" and "Jacob" became "Israel" to show the new direction God had given them. Sometimes a person changed her own name when it seemed not to fit anymore. Naomi, whose name means "pleasant," wanted to rename herself Mara ("bitter") after losing her husband and sons (Ruth 1:20). Her life, at that point, seemed to be nothing but bitter.

Because names were so significant, a common pagan practice was to try to manipulate the spiritual world by using divine names in incantations. The gods of polytheism were understood to be finite and subject to magical forces more powerful than them. If you knew their names, you could petition them to do your bidding.

But throughout the Bible, God refused to respond when divine names were used Harry Potter-style, as magical incantations. In Acts 19, the seven sons of Sceva learned this the hard way. The exorcists attempted to cast out a demon "in the name of Jesus whom Paul preaches." But the demon just laughed at them, retorting, "Jesus I know, and Paul I know about, but who are you?" Then it assaulted them, beating them until they ran away naked and bleeding (Acts

19:13 – 16). Undoubtedly these men were calling on the correct Jesus, even pronouncing his name with a perfect Hebrew inflection. But because they weren't Jesus' disciples, they had no authority to issue commands in his name.

In the Name of a Prophet ...

Several idioms come from the connection between a person's name and his or her identity. The phrase "your name" can sometimes even substitute for "you," especially in poetry. For instance, Psalm 75:1 says, "We praise you, God, we praise you, for your Name is near." What the psalmist really means is that *God* is near, not just that his *name* is near.

Grasping the idiomatic way "name" was used can unlock one of Jesus' stranger sayings: "He who receives a prophet in the name of a prophet shall receive a prophet's reward; and he who receives a righteous man in the name of a righteous man shall receive a righteous man's reward. And whoever in the name of a disciple gives to one of these little ones even a cup of cold water to drink, truly I say to you, he shall not lose his reward" (Matthew 10:41 – 42 NASB).

At first glance, Jesus' words here are mystifying. How can a person receive a prophet "in the name of a prophet"? The NIV (1984 ed.) clarifies this line by explaining the idiom: "Anyone who receives a prophet *because he is a prophet* will receive a prophet's reward." Here, "in the name of" isn't actually about a person's name at all. In this case, it's an idiom that really means "because of someone's identity."

Solving this puzzle also requires knowing that these words reflect Jesus' Jewish habit of "hinting" to his Scriptures to make a point, expecting his audience to know their Bibles well enough to get his message.[6] Jesus was reassuring his disciples as he sent them out that God would take care of them. He did so by recalling two heroic women who took care of God's representatives because they knew they had been sent by God.

The widow of Zarephath was the one who "received a prophet in the name of a prophet." She shared her meager supplies with Elijah during a famine because she knew he was a prophet sent by God

(1 Kings 17:9–16). As a result, God gave her a "prophet's reward" —he sustained her family through the famine, just as he did Elijah.[7] And Rahab, the Canaanite prostitute, was the one who "received a righteous man in the name of a righteous man." She sheltered the spies Joshua sent out because she believed in Israel's God (Joshua 2:1–21). Because she recognized the spies' mission as "righteous," Rahab was declared "righteous" and received the same reward—she was allowed to live in the land along with the Israelites.[8]

Jesus was using these examples from Scripture to show his disciples that God would take care of them as they went out proclaiming the gospel, just as he had done for his representatives in ages past. If anyone gave Jesus' disciples so much as a cup of water because they supported their mission, he'd make sure they'd be rewarded. Not only would God provide for Jesus' disciples; he'd even take care of those who took care of them!

Hallowing the Name

What then, does it mean, to "hallow" or sanctify God's name? Obviously it literally means to make God's name holy. But here, the word *name* really refers to God's reputation. The phrases "hallowed be your name," "your kingdom come," and "your will be done on earth" are related to each other in meaning. All of them express the desire that God's reputation will grow on earth, that people will accept God's reign over their lives and desire to do his will.

You might not think that God's reputation would be important to him, but the idea of his reputation expanding throughout the world is a central theme of the biblical story. At first, God taught only Israel how to live, but he intended that they'd be a "light to the nations." In a world where other nations prostituted themselves to idols and slit their babies' throats on the altars of demons, the Israelites were to worship the true God and show how he wanted them to live.

> *To avoid a sin or to obey a command, not from fear or ambition but purely out of love of God, is to sanctify His name in public.*
>
> —Maimonides

In the coming of Christ, God made his

identity more clear. He revealed his heart for sinners and his sacrificial love. Then he sent out his disciples to "make disciples of all nations" (Matthew 28:19). The overall idea is that God's reputation would expand throughout the earth as people came to know who God is. Salvation now ripples throughout the world as people hear good things about God and accept Christ as their Savior. His ultimate plan is that "the earth will be filled with the knowledge of the LORD as the water covers the sea" (Isaiah 11:9). God's kingdom will fully come when God's "name" is *echad*—that is, when he alone is worshiped by all the nations (Zechariah 14:9).

God's reputation, his "name," is therefore of critical importance for his plan of salvation. In the light of this, we can gain much insight from hearing rabbinic wisdom about what it means to "hallow the name"—*kiddush hashem* (ki-DOOSH ha-SHEM). Its opposite is *hillul hashem* (hi-LOOL ha-SHEM), to "profane the name." These two phrases are rich with significance in Jewish tradition, having been used from the first century until today.

A story was told about Simeon ben Shetach, a Jewish sage who lived about a hundred years before Jesus. His disciples bought their impoverished teacher a donkey from a wealthy Arab trader, to ease their mentor's daily burdens. When they combed through its mane, they found a jewel that had fallen from one of its expensive loads. The disciples rejoiced at their teacher's newfound wealth. But Shetach refused it, ordering his disciples to find the Arab and return the jewel. When the disciples located the trader, he was breathless at regaining his prize, declaring, "Blessed be the God of Simeon ben Shetach!"

Because of the rabbi's great honesty, the foreigner gave praise to God. This is what it means, in rabbinic parlance, to "sanctify God's name," *kiddush hashem*. It means to live in such a way as to bring God glory among those who do not know him. The rabbis described it as one of three things: to live a life of integrity; to do some heroic deed, like risking one's life to save another; or even to be martyred to honor God.[9]

The idea of *kiddush hashem* suggests an insight into an age-old debate among Christians. Some of us emphasize Christian witness as sharing the gospel, using words to evangelize the world. Others feel that the best Christian witness comes through social action, by building houses for the homeless and meeting physical needs. Often we split into two camps, choosing one way or the other. But the idea of *kiddush hashem* is to associate loving deeds with God's reputation. Sharing the gospel without caring for people's needs comes across as hollow. But doing charitable acts without revealing that you're serving Christ doesn't sanctify God's name either. When Jesus sent his disciples out, he told them to heal the sick and proclaim the kingdom, as he did himself (Matthew 10:7–8). Not one or the other, but *both*. We need both words *and* deeds to bring God glory.

Profaning the Name

In contrast, *hillul hashem*, "profaning the name," is an extremely serious sin. The rabbis found this in the way they interpreted the third commandment, "You shall not take the name of the LORD your God in vain, for the LORD will not leave him unpunished who takes His name in vain" (Exodus 20:7 NASB). Christians interpret this commandment as a prohibition against swearing. But of all ten, this is the only commandment that God promises to punish. Aren't other sins far more serious?

In Jewish thought, this commandment is understood to have a much greater meaning. The text literally says, "You shall not lift up the name (reputation) of the LORD for an *empty thing*." One of the ways that the rabbis interpreted this was as doing something evil publicly and associating God with it. It is a sin against God himself, who suffers from having his reputation defamed.

A few examples clarify why this sin is so serious. Consider Nidal Hasan, who opened fire on a crowd of soldiers preparing for deployment at Fort Hood, Texas, killing thirteen. As he did so, he cried out, "*Allahu Akbar*"—Allah is great! But rather than bringing glory to Allah, the world silently wondered, "What kind of wicked god do you serve who commands you to do such terrible things?"

But the same could be said about Terry Jones, the Florida pastor who announced that he would burn the Qur'an on September 11, 2010, and carried through on his threat a few months later. He intended to denounce the falsehood of Islam, but instead, he caused Muslims to despise Christ and see his followers as godless blasphemers. In their minds it proved that Jesus' famous command to love one's enemies had fallen on deaf ears. And Americans of all faiths were horrified that a pastor would recklessly endanger other people's lives and foment war. His actions succeeded in bringing shame on the name of Christ around the world.

Even outside of the public eye, in the lives of average people, we can be guilty of *hillul hashem*. How many stories have we heard of people who were treated unfairly by fellow Christians and have never returned to the church? They've declared, "I don't want anything to do with you or your God." When a churchgoer is dishonest in business, rude to the neighbors, or uses pornography, it is a witness *against* Christ to the world around us. Each of us is easily capable of profaning God's name, a serious sin indeed.

> *Better a letter of the Sacred Torah itself be blotted out than that the Divine Name be profaned.*
> —Talmud, *Yebamot* 79a

The Ultimate *Kiddush Hashem*

Just as evil actions can damage the reputation of God in the world, good actions can bring him great honor. Jonathan Miles is a Christian who founded the ministry of *Shevet Achim* in Jerusalem.[10] His team brings Palestinian and Iraqi children to Israeli hospitals for heart surgery. Their work has a powerful impact on the Muslims and Jews who see them regularly risk their lives, in the name of Christ, to serve others. And Muslim families are stunned by the compassion Jewish doctors and nurses show toward their children.

Once, Jonathan was at a police station in Gaza when a fearsome-looking Palestinian glared at him from across the room. The hulking man approached him and verbally assaulted him for several minutes, demanding to know why he had come to Gaza. (Jonathan later learned that he was a member of a terrorist organization and was even being recruited to be a suicide bomber.) Jonathan explained that he was expecting to meet the family of a child needing heart surgery. It was getting late though, and the people hadn't yet arrived.

His questioner's hostility deflated like a balloon pricked with a pin! Eager to help, the huge man led Jonathan from house to house through the village, knocking on each door to hunt for the family. The two have since become friends, and the man avidly seeks to know more about Jesus. That is the power of one obedient disciple — that by his example he could reach a would-be murderer and cause him to consider following Christ.

The ultimate example of *kiddush hashem*, sanctifying God's name, is Jesus himself. He declared, "I have made Your name known to them, and will make it known, so that the love with which You loved Me may be in them, and I in them" (John 17:26 NASB). As God incarnate, his death on the cross proclaimed to the world that the God of Israel is a merciful, self-sacrificial God. No one who believes that Jesus is God can claim that God is cruel or uncaring. Jesus has proven otherwise through his own actions on our behalf. Because of Christ's great sacrifice, God's reputation has expanded to the ends of the world.

As Jesus' followers, we are commanded to be like him to bring his light to the world. As he said, "Let your light shine before others, that they may see your good deeds and glorify your Father in heaven" (Matthew 5:16). We need to always be aware that the world is watching, so that our actions reflect the holiness and love of the God we serve.

Wisdom for the Walk

1. Read Moses' words to God in Deuteronomy 9:25–29 after Israel worshiped the golden calf. How does Moses appeal to God's "reputation" to plead for forgiveness for his people?

2. What other expressions can you think of in English that use "name" in some of the ways that Hebrew does?

3. Read Ezekiel 36:16–26. How did the people of Israel profane God's reputation? What did God say he would do to restore his reputation among the nations?

4. Look up Deuteronomy 18:5; 1 Kings 5:5; Matthew 18:20; and John 17:11–12. How does understanding idioms about "name" help you interpret these verses?

5. Is there anything that you are doing that might make God look bad to others? How can you change your behavior to reflect God's character?

CHAPTER 7

How to Have
a Kosher Mouth

As long as I remain silent, I control my tongue.
Once I start speaking, my tongue controls me.
— Judah ben Samuel of Regensberg

Being a substitute teacher is never a picnic. With only a few months' experience in the Chicago inner city, Albert Thompson struggled to reign in his unruly fourth-grade class. The classroom had erupted into shouting and fighting, and kids were darting into and out of the room. Blocking the doorway, he scolded the offenders, informing them that he was reporting them to the principal. It seemed to be the logical way to bring order back into his class.

But one spiteful nine-year-old had other plans. Angry at being disciplined, she made up a story that the teacher had molested her, and then bribed ten other children for one dollar apiece to tell the principal the same thing. Unaware of the potential havoc their testimony could wreak, each of the kids repeated the lie about the teacher they so disliked. Thompson was immediately suspended.

A police investigation soon uncovered the children's vengeful plot, and Thompson was cleared of the charges. The girl confessed to having concocted the story out of thin air, and several students identified her as the one who paid them to frame their teacher.

Nevertheless, some parents protested to the school board. They still wanted to press charges rather than acknowledge that their kids had been lying. Thompson was guilty until proven innocent, and even after being proven innocent, because of the children's fabricated testimony. He called the incident "a nightmare. A lot of people were willing to crucify me, rather than hear this story out." He decided to leave teaching behind, saying, "Right now my reputation is soiled. I don't care where I go in the school system, people know about it."[1]

These worldly-wise nine-year-olds had already been taught about the need to report unwanted touching and the devastating impact of sexual abuse. But they hardly realized how their words alone could devastate the life of a teacher. This inflammatory power of the tongue is exactly what James is thinking of when he likens it to a spark that threatens to burn down great forests (James 3:5). Our words contain enormous potential for good or evil. Proverbs declares that "the tongue has the power of life and death" (Proverbs 18:21).

While we know that some of the things we say are wrong, ugly words seem to be a fact of life nowadays. Whole TV programs, even entire cable channels, are dedicated to celebrity gossip. The Internet is saturated with snarky commentary on life today—even Christian blogs sometimes push the edge. Is what we say really of such grave concern?

James seems to think so. He spares no harsh metaphor in portraying the tongue's potential for cruelty:

> Consider what a great forest is set on fire by a small spark. The tongue also is a fire, a world of evil among the parts of the body. It corrupts the whole person, sets the whole course of one's life on fire, and is itself set on fire by hell.
>
> All kinds of animals, birds, reptiles and sea creatures are being tamed and have been tamed by mankind, but no human being can tame the tongue. It is a restless evil, full of deadly poison. (James 3:5b–8)

To James the tongue is a ravenous wolf, a poisonous asp, an agent of hell. His stridency might seem over the top until you recall that a pigtailed little girl can end a teacher's career with one calculated lie.

You might think that James had some special axe to grind about how terrible our tongues are. But wait until you hear Jewish teaching on the subject! Centuries of persecution have forced Jews to live in tightly-knit communities, where poisonous words are especially lethal. Over the ages, rabbis have devoted great energy to expounding on the biblical boundaries for our tongues. Jesus' priority too was on what comes *out of* our lips rather than what goes *into* them. He points out, "What goes into someone's mouth does not defile them, but what comes out of their mouth, that is what defiles them" (Matthew 15:11).

We can preserve a friend's marriage with our wise counsel. Or we can shred the self-worth of a child with criticism or incinerate a friendship with gossip. Wouldn't it be nice to be able to leave a room knowing that no one will say anything unkind about you? Or to not have to worry that a coworker's coolness is because she got wind of your comments about her over lunch last week?

We all fail daily at being consistently Christlike in what comes out of our lips. No one is innocent of harming others through hurtful words. And we've all whiffed the toxic stink of malicious speech when we've been its victims. Some of us are pack-a-day gossips who have puffed away for so long in this smoke-filled room that we don't even notice how its acrid stench clings to our hair and clothes.

Is there any way to improve what comes out of our mouths?

Jewish Wisdom about our Tongues

For thousands of years, Jewish teachers have focused on the promise in Psalm 34:12 – 13: "Whoever of you loves life and desires to see many good days, keep your tongue from evil and your lips from telling lies."[2] Even the apostle Peter quotes this famous verse when he tells his congregation how they should live (see 1 Peter 3:10).

If you're looking for happiness and longevity, the psalmist offers a wonderful promise. But it's contingent on keeping your tongue from evil. But, what exactly is an "evil tongue"? In Hebrew, *lashon hara* (lah-SHON ha-RAH) is the name that Judaism gives to all types of gossip, slander, and malicious speech.

Not only is reigning in your tongue the key to happy relationships, it will also purify your soul. Jesus says, "A good man brings good things out of the good stored up in his heart, and an evil man brings evil things out of the evil stored up in his heart. For the mouth speaks what the heart is full of" (Luke 6:45). In other words, if you have an evil tongue, you have an evil heart.

In the past century especially, Orthodox Judaism has focused its attention on teaching the ethics of speech.[3] Neighborhood groups meet, Jewish high schools sponsor clubs, and thousands attend conferences to learn about *shmirat halashon (shmeer-aht ha-la-SHONE)* —"guarding the tongue."[4] You can even call a 1–800 hotline to ask a rabbi, "Is it all right to say this?" Over time, Judaism has amassed great wisdom about how our tongues should and shouldn't be used.[5]

Some sins of speech are obvious to everyone, such as, "You shall not give false testimony against your neighbor" (Exodus 20:16). But probing more deeply, the rabbis found more categories of speech that the Bible warns against, some of them you may never have realized are wrong.

Motzei Shem Ra — "Slander"

Jesus himself employs some rabbinic idioms for types of evil speech. For instance, to make up lies about others in order to defame them is called "to put out a bad name" (*motzei shem ra — moat-ZEY shem rah*). Jesus uses this phrase to brace his disciples for their difficult mission: "Blessed are you when men hate you, when they exclude you and insult you and 'put out your name as evil' (*motzei shem ra*) because of the Son of Man" (Luke 6:22, pers. trans.). We can expect to be slandered if we are clear in our commitment to Christ.

> *It takes your enemy and your friend, working together, to hurt you to the heart: the one to slander you, and the other to get the news to you.*
> — Mark Twain

Slander was considered to be one of the most evil sins of speech. But you don't need to be old to wield this cruel weapon. The elementary school girl had already discovered how to employ it against her teacher. Parents need to begin training their children into what not to say from almost the day they begin speaking. A child's main classroom is usually what they overhear from their parents' conversation.

Rabbinic commentaries often link *motzei shem ra* and *metzora* ("leper").[6] They connect the two because they sound similar and because God punished Miriam with leprosy for seven days when she slandered her brother Moses (Numbers 12:1–15). The punishment fits the crime, say the rabbis, because leprosy and libel share many common traits. At first the symptoms are hardly noticeable, but over time the disease becomes chronic—a person who smears one person will usually smear others. Moreover, the disease is highly contagious, as the listeners repeat the falsehood. And like leprosy, malicious talk separates wife from husband, brother from brother, and friend from friend.

Lashon Hara—An Evil Tongue

We all can see the wrongness of slander—telling lies about others. But believe it or not, we can also do great damage to others without lying. *Lashon hara* doesn't just include telling lies about others. In fact, this phrase is more commonly used to describe the practice of telling negative *truths* about others that are unnecessary and damaging.

Lashon hara is recounting to your coworkers about how the boss messed up his presentation. It's pointing out to your wife how poorly the worship leader sings. It's complaining to your sister that your husband forgot your birthday *yet again*. Any sentence that starts with "She's a great person, but it's annoying when she …" is always going to end in *lashon hara*. This habit tears down friendships, demeans others, and undermines trust. There are, of course, a few times when a person needs to relay damaging information, but outside of that, this kind of negativity is frowned upon in Jewish law.[7]

We often justify our words with, "Well … I didn't say anything untrue!" But the Golden Rule states that you shouldn't do to others what you wouldn't want done to you. If you'd be hurt and embarrassed by having your own flaws revealed, you shouldn't share those of others.

Why do we gossip about others? One major reason for *lashon hara* is our desire to elevate ourselves by tearing others down. Paul has a solution to this problem: "Do nothing out of selfish ambition or vain conceit. Rather, in humility value others above yourselves, not looking to your own interests but each of you to the interests of the others" (Philippians 2:3–4). If we genuinely care as much about others as ourselves, we will try to protect their reputations as much as we do our own.

A story is told of a habitual gossip who finally decided to repent of his sin. He knocked on the door of the village rabbi and asked, "Is there something I can do to make amends?"

The rabbi stroked his beard and replied, "Go home and come back with a pillow."

Relieved, the man soon completed the odd errand. Would such a simple gift be all that was needed to atone for this sin?

When he returned, the rabbi continued. "Now, slice it open."

It was a windy day, and the breeze picked up the feathers, wafting them over the housetops and into the fields.

"Now, go gather all of the feathers again and put them back in the pillow."

"But that's impossible!" exclaimed the man.

"In the same way, it's impossible to repair all the damage that your words have done."[8]

Remember how Jesus compared lust to adultery, and anger to murder? He was inflating the gravity of these sins to emphasize the seriousness of their consequences. The rabbis did exactly the same thing with sins of the tongue. Often *lashon hara* is compared to murder: "A slanderer stands in Damascus, but kills in Rome."[9] Defamatory statements are like Patriot missiles, computer-guided bombs programmed to annihilate their targets at long distances. The victim doesn't even realize who the cowardly perpetrator is.

Interestingly, later rabbis went further, pointing out that *lashon hara* isn't just murder; it's the murder of three people. Obviously, the object of the gossip is one victim. But the listener is also a victim, because his or her relationship with the one being gossiped about is negatively affected. Also, the listener is

> *Have you heard something? Let it die with you. Be brave, it will not make you burst.*
> —Sirach 19:10

tempted to share the rumor with others. The third victim of *lashon hara* is the speaker! Over time, as people realize that a gossip can't be trusted, they distance themselves to avoid being betrayed. It's like slow suicide.[10]

Why did rabbinic commentaries (as well as James) go to such lengths to declare the potential for the wickedness of our tongues? Because nothing except our own vigilance is stopping us from uttering words that will wound loved ones and shatter our dearest relationships. Once a word exits our lips, we can't get it back.

Furthermore, now that a few strokes of a keyboard will broadcast our thoughts across the planet in the blink of an eye, it is even more critical to consider wisely each word we use. Not only do our words go much farther, they last much longer. If you insult someone on your own blog, you might decide later to edit or delete your post. But if someone else quotes it and then others find it, you're powerless to remove it from everywhere it might go.

"The Dust of *Lashon Hara*"

Believe it or not, you can commit a sin of speech without even saying a word. When someone says, "Well, you wouldn't want to hear what I think of so-and-so," all you need to do is roll your eyes and smirk knowingly. An eyebrow raised in disdain or a lip curled in disgust unmistakably communicates your ill opinion of someone else. In rabbinic parlance, they call this *avak lashon hara* (ah-VAHK lah-SHON ha-RAH) — "the dust of *lashon hara*."

Imagine one day you open your newspaper to find a letter to the editor by a neighbor you dislike. If you hand it to your wife so that she'll sneer at his ludicrous opinions, that's *avak lashon hara*. It's the same thing if you forward an email that has stupid spelling errors so that others can ridicule the author, or if you pass on an unflattering photograph in order to embarrass someone. You may never have spoken a word, but if the object of your feelings observed what you had done, he or she would get justifiably angry with you.[11]

Surprisingly, the category of *avak lashon hara* also includes seemingly innocuous comments that may cause others to speak *lashon hara*.

Rabbinic teachers were excellent psychologists, pointing out that if you say something nice about a person to someone who dislikes them, often your listener will follow with disparaging remarks. If you mention Rush Limbaugh to an impassioned liberal, or Barak Obama to a right-wing conservative, you can be almost sure that the next thing your conversation partner will say will be *lashon hara*. In Jewish thought, we're responsible for the actions of our community, not just ourselves. We should guard not just our own words, but even the words that we cause others to speak!

> *Words kill, words give life; they're either poison or fruit — you choose.*
> —Proverbs 18:21, The Message

Halbanat Panim — "Whitening the Face"

Yet another kind of speech that you may never have thought of as wrong is called "whitening the face," *halbanat panim* (hahl-bah-NAHT pah-NEEM), humiliating someone in public. Its name comes from the fact that the embarrassed person's face blanches out of shock, as the blood drains away. The rabbis also considered it a kind of murder, likening the victim's face to that of a corpse. Here, it's the person's reputation that has been assassinated. "The pain of humiliation is more bitter than death. Therefore, one should rather fling himself into a fiery furnace than humiliate someone in public," declares the Talmud.[12] While Christians know intuitively that humiliating others is wrong, it is good to remind ourselves of the severity of its effects, especially on our spouses and children.

Jews are particularly sensitive to the sin of humiliation, having been ridiculed for their piety over the centuries. They have a long list of ethical rules to prevent shaming of others. They say that a husband must not insult or correct his wife in front of others, and vice versa. And teachers shouldn't ask a student a question in class if they don't think the student can answer. Even in death, Orthodox Jews are buried in a plain wooden box in a simple white garment, so that the poor would not be humiliated by their own inability to afford an elaborate burial.

Sometimes humiliating someone publicly actually *is* murder.

Alexis Pilkington was a lovely, talented seventeen-year-old, a well-liked athlete who had already landed a soccer scholarship to college. In the wee hours of Sunday, March 21, 2010, she made one last comment on her Facebook page: "So done with everything." Then she committed suicide. What had driven her to take her life? She had been suffering from depression, but her friends are convinced that what pushed her over the brink were the vicious, lewd comments posted about her online by anonymous classmates. Their cruelty didn't even end after her death. Scrawled one vile hand, "she was obviously a stupid depressed b**** who deserved to kill herself. she got what she wanted. be happy for her death. rejoice in it."[13]

Geneivat Da'at — "Stealing Knowledge"

There's yet another way you can sin through your lips without ever uttering a single untrue word. "Stealing knowledge," *geneivat da'at* (gen-ey-VAHT dah-AHT), is to fool someone into having a mistaken assumption, belief, or impression, even if no lying is involved. If a shopper is convinced that he's buying a top quality item and the clerk never mentions that it's defective, that would be "stealing his knowledge." Or, if a store increases its prices temporarily so that it can advertise huge markdowns, that is *geneivat da'at*.

We all know what it's like to be taken in by this type of deception. When we realize we have been duped, it feels like someone has stolen something from us. And interestingly, the rabbinic thinking is that we *have* been robbed. The sages noticed that the phrase includes the word *ganav*, "to steal." They concluded that the commandment "Do not steal" also prohibits "stealing another's knowledge," or deceiving others. Indeed, the rabbis defined seven types of thieves, and the worst is the one who "steals the mind."[14]

But we're often guilty of this too. *Geneivat da'at* is to spend half an hour grilling a computer store salesman about laptops, pretending like you might buy something when you're really planning to buy one online. It's to invite someone to a party when you know the person can't attend, or to offer something to a friend, knowing that the other person won't accept. You may never utter an actual falsehood, but all these things "steal" others' goodwill, understanding, or deliberately create a false impression of yourself.

Rabbi Joseph Telushkin relays this story:

> Some years ago, a woman I know attended a dinner hosted by a wealthy cousin at an exclusive restaurant. When the waiter brought the bill, her cousin blanched; the meal clearly had turned out to be far more expensive than he had anticipated. Noticing his unhappy reaction, the woman offered to split the meal's cost. The man smiled and happily accepted the offer. Yet, in reality, the woman, who had much more limited means than her cousin, was furious. Never having expected him to accept her offer, she felt betrayed when he did.[15]

But then Rabbi Telushkin points out that the woman didn't have anyone to blame but herself, because she had committed *geneivat da'at*. She had tried to create an impression of generosity when she didn't actually *intend* to be generous.

When we remember that we're serving the God of truth, we realize that he doesn't approve of such forms of verbal manipulation. How many times a day do our words not match our intentions? We may not give a second thought about all the little ways we're deceptive, but we should if we want to be God's people of integrity.

Pilates for the Tongue

Have you ever tried Pilates, the exercise program that focuses on strengthening your abdominal muscles? You'll certainly remember having a sore midriff after your first session of what seems to be a thousand and one variations on the sit-up. If you can control your abs, your "core," they say, you'll stand straighter, breathe deeper, and enjoy a better quality of life.

James tells us that the key to getting fit spiritually is to focus our workouts up a little higher, on our tongue: "Anyone who is never at fault in what they say is perfect, able to keep their whole body in check" (James 3:2). Rabbinic teachers agree, quipping, "Who is strong? He who overcomes his evil inclination."[16]

Some years ago a friend of mine decided she was going to focus on watching her tongue. No longer would she complain about her boss to her coworkers or repeat the secrets others had confided in her. Often she found herself straining to hold in some juicy little tidbit that just *had* to be said—but shouldn't. She bit her tongue until she practically drew blood. Slowly she found other ways to deal with frustrating people than to regale her friends with her snarky tales of woe.

The struggle was worth it, she told me one day. It felt as if she had gone on a tone-up and workout plan for the soul. She ceased worrying about who might have overheard her snide comments. No longer did she keep a nervous watch of who poked their head into her cubicle or hovered over her email inbox. A calm had descended because there was nothing to hide. Her blood pressure seemed to decrease by ten points.

Before, each morning, she used to look in the mirror at a sorry sight—a backbiting jerk who was always ready to smear someone with a catty comment. But now she gazed at a woman who could be trusted, who wouldn't betray a friend. Sure, she wasn't perfect, but she was a lot better. Others might have a trimmer figure, but her soul had become shapely and beautiful.

Wisdom for the Walk

1. Read Matthew 18:15–17. How do Jesus' words about going to someone who has sinned against you fit in with Jewish ideas about ethical speech?

2. On the Internet, which of the categories of sinful speech do you think are most common? Which are most dangerous?

3. Consider your own memories of hurtful words spoken either by yourself or others. What lessons can your past teach you about how not to use your tongue?

4. Can you think of a recent example you've experienced of *geneivat da'at*—"stealing another's knowledge"?

5. What other things can you think of Jesus saying about how we use our tongues? See, for instance, Matthew 5:37; Luke 6:28; 17:3.

CHAPTER 8

Taking My Thumb Off the Scale

One who judges his neighbor favorably
will be judged favorably by God.
—Talmud, *Shabbat* 127a

My keys clattered onto the countertop, a relieved sigh escaping from my lips as I slipped off my Sunday coat. The morning had been filled with small irritations: the coffee I splattered on my new sweater, the nosy prayer chain coordinator who grilled me on every detail of my recent illness, the lady behind me who refused to shake hands during the service. And I was still quivering with anger over the guy who nearly crashed into me on the way home from church —who knew speed-demons drove minivans?

But what had really ruffled my feathers that morning was another stiff conversation among the small group I recently joined. Today's lesson was on Jesus' words, "Do not judge." The discussion had produced nothing but platitudes and strained silence. A middle-aged mom proposed that once we take the log out of our own eyes, we can and should judge. But then a hip twenty-something with funky glasses challenged the group to truly love people by ignoring what we call "sin." After a painfully long pause, an elderly man awkwardly countered by voicing his indignation about seeing the words "Do not judge" on a billboard put up by a local gay-rights group. No one seemed to know quite what to make of Jesus' words.

Few sayings of Jesus have caused more frustration than his words about judging. From everything else Jesus taught, we know Jesus wasn't telling us just to turn a blind eye to sin. So we struggle to find a way to sort out sin without actually calling it that, so that we won't sin by judging. Or we just file this line in the "impossible" category, like "love your enemy" — it sounds great and preaches well, but it's well nigh impossible to actually live out.

But this teaching of Jesus grows much more applicable when we hear how it fits into the wider conversation going on among Jewish thinkers. From centuries before Jesus was born "judging" has been a topic of discussion, filtering down through the millennia to inform Jewish practice right up to today. Jesus was, in fact, building on some wise thinking and bringing it to a new level.

"Judging" in Jewish Thought

In about 120 BC, Yehoshua ben Perachia, one of the earliest rabbinic sages, shared the following wisdom: "Judge each person with the scales weighted in their favor."[1] The saying evokes the imagery of the ancient marketplace, where a merchant measures out grain by pouring it into one pan of a hanging scale until it swings level with the weighted side. A friendly shopkeeper will heap a little extra on, letting the pans tilt past the balance point. The idea is that you should "weigh" the deeds of others on the side of generosity. Simply put, give others the benefit of the doubt.[2]

Jesus employed a similar metaphor about judging: "A good measure, pressed down, shaken together and running over, will be poured into your lap. For with the measure you use, it will be measured to you" (Luke 6:38). Jesus too says that we should let our scales of justice fall past the balance point, bestowing on others a little more than they deserve.

But how do we actually live out this big-hearted lifestyle? A rabbinic parable illustrates:

> A man worked on a farm for three years. On the eve of the Day of Atonement, he went to his employer and asked for his wages to take home to his wife and children. The farm owner said to him, "I have no money to give you."
>
> The farm hand protested, "Well, give me some of the crops I've helped grow."

The farmer replied, "I have none!"

The worker cried, "Well then, give me some of the sheep that I've helped to raise!" The farmer shrugged and said that he had nothing he could give him. So the farm hand gathered up his belongings and went home with a sorrowful heart.

After the holidays, the employer came to the farmhand's house with all of his wages, along with three carts full of extra gifts. They had dinner together, and as they ate, the farm owner asked, "When I told you I had no money, what did you suspect?"

"I thought you had seen a bargain and used all your cash to buy it," the worker replied.

"And what did you think when I said that I had no crops?"

"I thought perhaps they were all leased to others."

"And what did you think when I said I had no animals?"

"I thought that you may have dedicated them to the Temple."

The farmer answered him, "It was just this way. My son wouldn't study the Scriptures, and the day you came to me, I had rashly dedicated all my possessions to God. But, just a couple days ago, I was absolved of my vow so that now I can pay you. And as for you, just as you have judged me favorably, may the Lord judge you favorably!"[3]

In this parable, the hired hand always gives his employer the benefit of the doubt by imagining the best possible motivation for actions that otherwise seemed suspect. This is what the rabbinic saying means about judging your neighbor "with the scales weighted in his favor." Doesn't the last line of this story remind you of Jesus' words, "With the measure you use, it will be measured to you"?

While this is a nice thought, it hardly seems to be an earth-shattering insight on Jesus' words. But what happens when you try to live it out? I thought back to my morning at church, considering how I might "judge favorably" in each situation.

... Maybe the prayer chain coordinator was genuinely concerned about my illness rather than just trying to be nosy.

... Maybe the woman who wouldn't shake my hand was new at

church, or uncomfortable meeting people. Maybe she had a cold and didn't want to spread it.

... Maybe the driver of that minivan was in a hurry because he was late for something. Maybe his kids were driving him crazy. Maybe he had to go to the bathroom!

By simply reconsidering my unkind assumptions about other people's offenses, I could feel my anger drain away and my ruffled feathers settle back down. My attitude took a 180-degree turn once I reviewed the morning's irritations in a new light.

In almost every situation, a person can either look for a good or a bad motive behind other people's behavior. The way you choose to interpret others' motives has a profound effect on the way you react to them. Personally, I've found that when I make a habit of trying to "judge favorably," it transforms me into a kinder, more patient person. My attitude grows more loving when I assume the best instead of the worst about the people around me.

I'm still working on putting this into practice, but imagine the possibilities if I consistently looked at other people in the best possible light. I'd start saying things like, "Maybe the boss was short-tempered today because of problems at home." If I had an argument with a friend, I'd assume she was defending what she considered a sensible opinion rather than that she was attacking me. When I heard someone insulting my faith, I might say, "That person must have had a bad experience with the church in order to make him feel that way."

Truly, this small practice can change your entire outlook on life.

Judging Favorably in Jewish Culture

Jewish culture has emphasized the need to "judge favorably" for thousands of years. The rabbis declared that "judging others in favorable terms" is actually as important as visiting the sick, praying, or teaching the Scriptures to your children!

In *Love Your Neighbor*, Rabbi Zelig Pliskin describes a group in Jerusalem that meets regularly to train themselves to "judge favorably." Members discuss perceived hurts and brainstorm together to find excuses for behavior that seems unkind. When someone doesn't receive an invitation to a wedding, they'd say, "Perhaps the person is under the impression they have already sent an invitation," or "Perhaps the couple can't afford to invite many people." If someone was walking with a heavy load and his next door neighbor drove right past, the group would hypothesize, "Perhaps he was only going a short distance," "Perhaps he has already committed himself to pick up some other people," or "Perhaps he had a problem that weighed on his mind so heavily that he couldn't think of anything else."[4]

When I first heard about this idea of inventing excuses for people, it seemed a little silly. Why should I make up lies when I know that someone has done something wrong? Over time, I started to realize that my first ungracious assessment was often no more plausible than the other scenarios. My "scales" of judgment were seriously askew, weighted heavily toward guilt rather than innocence. Only by consciously forcing them back the other way could I see how off-balance they were in the first place.

Universally, we're all butchers with our thumbs on the scale, and often we're completely wrong in how we size others up. In *The Grace Awakening*, Charles Swindoll confesses his own experience of judging unfairly. At a week-long Bible conference, he met a couple the first night who seemed enthusiastic about hearing him speak. But as the days went on, he noticed that the man nodded off at every sermon he gave, without fail. Growing more and more annoyed, Swindoll concluded that the man was a "carnal Christian," someone who talked one way but lived another. On the final evening, a chat with the man's wife revealed that he couldn't be more wrong. Swindoll writes:

> She stayed after the crowd and her husband had left. She asked if she could speak with me for a few minutes. I figured she wanted to talk about how unhappy she was living with a man who didn't have the same interest in spiritual things as she. How wrong I was. She said their being there was his idea. It had been his "final wish." I didn't understand. She informed me he had terminal cancer and had only weeks to live. At his request they attended the conference where I was speaking even though the

medication he was taking for pain made him sleepy — something that greatly embarrassed him. "He loves the Lord," she said, "and you are his favorite Bible teacher. He wanted to be here to meet you and to hear you, no matter what." I was sincerely stunned. She thanked me for the week and left. I stood there, all alone, as deeply rebuked as I have ever been. I had judged my brother, and I was as wrong as I could possibly have been.[5]

As nice as it would be to always "judge favorably," it would be hopelessly foolish (and unbiblical) to think that no one sins willfully and intentionally. Often a person's intentions and actions are obviously evil. Rabbi Telushkin comments:

> Judging fairly does not mean judging naively. If someone does many bad, even wicked things, we are not obligated to devise far-fetched explanations to excuse her behavior. Indeed, viewing such people favorably can have a negative impact on our own character. "One who gets into the habit of ignoring the acts of wicked people [or trying to explain them away] will begin to condone their practices.... We must oppose them and take a stand against them."[6]

Even when people are clearly in the wrong, it's a lot easier to forgive once you've started thinking things like, "Maybe she didn't realize how hurtful her actions would be." Judging favorably even helps when you are confronting sin. Imagine that your best buddy is having an affair with a colleague. You might say, "John, I know Sue is attractive and you two have been working long hours together. And I know that you and Helen have had your difficulties, and you've needed someone to talk to. But no matter why you've gotten involved, please don't do this to yourself and Helen!" By giving your coworker the benefit of the doubt even when he is clearly in the wrong, you can more easily share your concern.

Other Ways of Judging Negatively

Once you see judging (or actually, judging negatively) as believing the worst about others, you discover that this attitude takes many shapes and forms. Being critical of others and being a chronic complainer both come from searching for the negative everywhere you can find it. Even being thin-skinned and having feelings that are easily hurt means that you interpret other people's words to you in the worst possible light.

Our culture is saturated with negative judgments. Democrats accuse Republicans of ugly, self-interested motives for every action they take, and Republicans return the favor. Comedians delight in holding up the faults of the famous for ridicule. Editorials overflow with cynicism about the government's evil motives and its inept handling of international affairs. Christians often reflect this pervasive cultural habit of condemnation, hardly realizing how wrong it really is. We don't even see how it poisons our relationships with those whom we love.

While a few children grow up scarred from physical abuse, many more grow up scarred from relentless criticism from parents who judge them unfavorably. Indeed, the worst "judges" are often those who have never received mercy themselves and never learned to extend it to others. We should even refrain from condemning the most judgmental among us, because we don't know how much criticism they have endured.

> *Remember that you are not so good, and the world is not so evil.*
> — Rabbi Zev Wolf of Strikov

Gossip relies heavily on judgment. No one passes on the news about Linda and Bob being alone in the office at midnight if they don't think some hanky-panky went on. People who love to gossip usually have a habit of hunting for wrongdoing in a person's life in order to share it with others. Like flies that always land on an open sore, said the rabbis, they ignore people's good traits and only focus on their faults.[7]

Giving people the benefit of the doubt might seem unimportant in the grand scheme of things. But your propensity toward judging positively or negatively plays a large role in whether your marriage will last. Psychologist John Gottman points out that couples tend toward one of two states: "positive sentiment override" or "negative sentiment override." He explains:

Positive sentiment override [is] where positive emotion overrides irritability. It's like a buffer. Their spouse will do something bad, and they'll say, "Oh, he's just in a crummy mood." Or they can be in negative sentiment override, so that a relatively neutral thing that a partner says gets perceived as negative.... If their spouse does something positive, it's a selfish person doing a positive thing. It's really hard to change those states, and those states determine whether when one party tries to repair things, the other party sees that as repair or as hostile manipulation.[8]

As newlyweds, a couple's rose-colored glasses overlook every slight, but over time, hurts and disappointments can build until both partners view each other in the worst possible light. Once a couple has gotten trapped in a downward spiral of negative, critical judgment, Gottman comments, escaping it is as difficult as backpedaling while whitewater rafting.

After interviewing thousands of couples and tracking which marriages lasted and which failed, Gottman has identified what he calls the "Four Horsemen" that clip-clop onto the scene when a relationship is in serious trouble: defensiveness, stonewalling, criticism, and contempt. Of these, one overshadows all the others—an attitude of *contempt*. This toxic emotion reveals itself through insults, name calling, mocking, or ridicule. When one or both partners habitually speak to the other with disdain or disgust, even if they just sneer or roll their eyes when the other is talking, the marriage is often moving toward divorce.[9]

Criticism, as Gottman defines it, is to point out your partner's sins: "You're self-centered, you drink too much, and you're mean to the kids." But contempt is far worse, because it doesn't just expose the sin, it damns the sinner: "You're a failure as a father!" "Worthless loser! You'll never amount to anything!" Contempt is the end product of condemnation, which comes from a history of judging unfavorably and without mercy. It is a way of saying, "I have judged you, and I have reached my verdict, and there is *nothing* good in you."

Jesus' Words on Judging

As wise as the Jewish commentary is on judging, what light can it shed on Jesus' words? Jesus' audience may have already known about "judging favorably," about assuming the best about others' intentions. Undoubtedly Jesus would have agreed with the rabbis' emphasis on generosity in dealing with others. But his ideas on judging have a slightly different slant.

One thing you might wonder is what "judge" meant in the original languages. In the Greek of the Gospels, the verb is *krino*, which can potentially mean "discern," "decide a court case," "pass judgment," or "condemn," depending on the context. The Hebrew words for "judge," *dan* and *shafat*, have the same ambiguity. In other words, in both Greek and Hebrew, the words for "judge" are ambiguous and can mean either "discern" or "condemn," just as in English. Jesus was talking about judging in the sense of condemnation rather than discernment.

Jesus does not teach us to ignore wrongdoing. Paul explicitly declared that the church must judge sinful practice among its members: "What business is it of mine to judge those outside the church? Are you not to judge those inside? God will judge those outside" (1 Corinthians 5:12–13). And if the wrong is committed against us personally, Jesus tells us to show the person the sin in hopes that he or she will repent and be forgiven (Matthew 18:15–17). Leviticus 19:17 also says, "Do not hate a fellow Israelite in your heart. Rebuke your neighbor frankly so you will not share in their guilt."

Let's look at a passionate warning that Jesus gives in Matthew 5:22: "I tell you that anyone who is angry with a brother or sister will be subject to judgment. Again, anyone who says to a brother or sister, 'Raca' ['empty' or 'worthless'], is answerable to the court. But anyone who says, 'You fool!' will be in danger of the fire of hell." Jesus' words here may be a head-scratcher, but grasping two things about his Jewish preaching style will shed light on his words.

For one, he's using *parallelism*, which is characteristic of Hebrew.[10] When making a speech, people repeated their ideas or rephrased their words twice or more for emphasis. Jesus' words, statements, and even stories often came in twos or threes, like the twin parables of the lost sheep and the lost coin in Luke 15:4–10. The idea was to drive home a point by proving it in multiple ways. When you see parallelism, you should look for commonalities rather than differences. In Matthew 5:22, "Raca" and "fool" are rough equivalents for speaking angrily, and "court" and "the fire of hell" are metaphors for judgment. Three times Jesus says almost the same thing—anger and insults lead to judgment.[11]

It also helps to know that Jesus was teaching in a culture accustomed to overstatement. Jesus' contemporaries often exaggerated their words in order to drive home a point: "*Lashon hara* is as terrible as the murder of three persons," they expounded. "Humiliation is worse than death, so you should fling yourself into a furnace rather than embarrass someone." When Jesus preached about plucking out an eye that causes you to sin, or being drowned by a millstone rather than leading a child astray, his audience would have heard his words in this light (cf. Matthew 18:1–10).

> A man prone to suspect evil is mostly looking in his neighbor for what he sees in himself.
> —Baal Shem Tov

How does this help us read Jesus' words in Matthew 5:22? Jesus was issuing a strong warning on passing judgment on others. His first line is about anger. Being angry, I've discovered, usually indicates judgment. If a person won't shake my hand, I don't get angry unless I assume that they're being haughty—that they think I'm beneath them. If someone forgets to pick me up, I don't get angry unless I assume they're thoughtlessly ignoring my needs. Whenever I get angry, I look for the selfish or wrong-headed motive that I assume lies behind the person's actions.

The two other lines of Matthew 5:22 are about insults, which by definition are negative judgments. If I meet a woman who is assertive and I like her, I'll say she's "bold and self-confident." But if I dislike her, I'll call her "arrogant and loud-mouthed." My best friend might be "disorganized," but my enemy is a "slob." A store clerk who can't answer a question might simply be uninformed, but in my judgmental head, I'll call him "stupid" and "clueless."

Insults like "*raca*" or "fool" show contempt. They render the final verdict on the *person*, not just the sin. A person who is ignorant can learn, but for a "fool" there is no hope. Jesus is saying that when you show contempt, you dare God to judge you because of your own judgmental attitude toward others. The same mind-set that will end a marriage will get you on God's bad side too.

How can you discern sin without condemning the sinner? One wise idea comes from Hillel, who lived a few decades before Jesus' time. He said, "Judge not your fellow man until you yourself come into his place."[12] While you might be able to discern another's sin, you don't have full knowledge of the person's life experiences. You can't know the inner struggles or the difficult experiences that others have lived through. Imagine that the lady next door yells at your kids and swears at your dog. She's obviously rude, beyond a shadow of a doubt. But do you know if she grew up in an abusive home? Could she be struggling with depression?

While you can discern sin in practice, only God knows the whole motive of the heart. We can (and should) discern outward wrong-doing, but we aren't qualified to slam down the gavel and declare God's condemnation on the person as a whole. To judge another is to presume to have both the knowledge and authority of God himself. Paul writes, "Judge nothing before the appointed time; wait until the Lord comes. He will bring to light what is hidden in darkness and will expose the motives of the heart" (1 Corinthians 4:5). Or as James puts it, "There is only one Lawgiver and Judge, the one who is able to save and destroy. But you—who are you who judge your neighbor?" (James 4:12).

Just Like Yourself

As wise of an idea as "judging favorably" is, Jesus' teachings on judging start with a different assumption. When you judge favorably, you assume that a person is basically good. Jesus' assessment of humanity was less optimistic. His words about judging are based on knowing that your neighbor is a sinner, but so are you. If you declare God's condemnation of others, you invite him to condemn you too.[13] Once again we hear the great commandment as Jesus preached it: "You shall love your neighbor as one who is *like yourself*"—both precious to God but guilty of sin. Rather than saying, "Judge favorably by assuming the best about others," perhaps Jesus would say, "Judge mercifully, since you know you're a sinner too."

I can't judge others because I don't know their hearts. Indeed, the only one I really *can* know is my own sinful heart. So if I want God to have mercy on me, I need to extend mercy. Jesus brought home this potent message by putting it into a sevenfold parallelism:

> Be merciful, just as your Father is merciful.
> Do not judge, and you will not be judged.
> Do not condemn, and you will not be condemned.
> Forgive, and you will be forgiven.
> Give, and it will be given to you.
> A good measure, pressed down, shaken together and running over,
> will be poured into your lap.
> For with the measure you use, it will be measured to you.
> (Luke 6:36–38)

Wisdom for the Walk

1. Think of a recent time when you have gotten really angry with someone. What was the outward circumstance? What wrong-headed inner motivation are you assuming about them that makes you think they deserve your anger?

   Think up two possible things that could excuse their conduct (at least in part). Is either reasonable? What would Jesus say about what you should do?

2. Think about a current issue about which you have strong opinions, one that makes you angry with anyone who defends the opposite side. Why are you angry? What selfish or wrong-headed motivation are you assuming your opponent is guilty of?

   Consider two ways that your opponent could have reached his or her perspective (even if they are completely wrong) that would allow them to sincerely believe what they say.

   Are either of these a possibility? Can you actually know your opponents' motivation? What would Jesus tell you to do about your feelings toward those people?

3. Is there anyone for whom you have feelings of contempt?

CHAPTER 9

Praying
with *Chutzpah*

The issue of prayer is not prayer.
The issue of prayer is God.
— Abraham Heschel[1]

A surefire way to immerse yourself in the culture of Israel is to take a public bus in Jerusalem. Because of the bumper-to-bumper traffic, everybody, rich and poor, rides the "Egged" buses around town. Ethiopian Jews wrapped in swaths of white fabric sit next to wizened Russian babushkas. A college-age girl in army fatigues chats on a cell phone. Little boys in black suits clamber up the huge steps, side curls and tassels bouncing in the breeze. Their long-skirted, head-scarved mother follows closely behind.

One afternoon when I was riding downtown, I got an even stronger taste of the culture. A grey-haired, matronly retiree climbed aboard and plunked herself into an empty seat halfway back. She hadn't, however, paid any fare — she had just shuffled past the driver, feigning ignorance. Craning to make eye contact in his mirror, the driver called back to her over the crowd. "*Eifo geveret?*" (Where to, ma'am?)

At first she stared out the window, pretending not to notice.

"*Eiyyyfo, geveret?*" The whole bus looked on.

Finally, she barked back a gruff response, completely impenitent. A flurry of indecipherable Hebrew filled the air, the gist of which was obvious: either buy a ticket or get off. But the woman was immovable — glued to her seat, adamant. The driver threw up his hands at her, the universal (and widely used) Israeli gesture of annoyance and disgust.

And the bus didn't move either. Right in the middle of Nevi'im Street, a major artery with only a single drivable lane, the driver shifted into park, snapped open a newspaper, and sat back to read the headlines. Blocks and blocks of traffic snaked to a standstill behind us. After what seemed forever, the woman slowly rose and exited the side doors.

Half of Jerusalem came to a stop for this lady. That's what you call *chutzpah*—utter nerve, sheer audacity that borders on obnoxiousness. Both the woman and the bus driver knew how to push the boundaries of propriety for their purposes!

If you grew up as a small-town Midwesterner like me, you'd find this behavior nearly unimaginable. I come from the land of "Minnesota Nice," where we'd rather die than violate our code of mild-mannered courteousness. For me, the bus ride was a cultural journey to the ends of the earth. We're not in Minnesota anymore, Toto.

But an attitude of *chutzpah* (HOOTS-pah) has been part of Middle Eastern culture since ancient times. If you were one of Jesus' first-century disciples, you'd be familiar with this kind of behavior.

Consider, for instance, the Syrophoenician woman who wouldn't take no for an answer after pleading with Jesus to heal her daughter (Matthew 15:21–28; Mark 7:25–30). Jesus and his weary disciples had taken cover in a house in Tyre, hoping to evade the crowds, but her continual pounding at the door threatened to expose their hideout.

Exasperated, the disciples could tolerate her no longer, imploring Jesus, "Send her away, for she keeps crying out after us!" But the distraught young mother pushed right past them, bowing before Jesus himself. Surprisingly, he rebuffed her too, like the Israeli bus driver: "It is not right to take the children's bread and toss it to the dogs." His mission, at that point, was only to the Jews. But the desperate woman boldly contradicted the greatly esteemed rabbi. "Yes it is, Lord.... Even the dogs eat the crumbs that fall from the master's table."

Unlike the lady on the bus, this woman's tenacious, brazen nerve won out. Jesus healed her daughter and congratulated her for her *chutzpah*.

Jesus Liked a Little *Chutzpah*

Believe it or not, Jesus actually liked this kind of boldness. When he was preaching about prayer, he even told a parable where the heroine is just like the Syrophoenician lady:

> In a certain town there was a judge who neither feared God nor cared what people thought. And there was a widow in that town who kept coming to him with the plea, "Grant me justice against my adversary."
>
> For some time he refused. But finally he said to himself, "Even though I don't fear God or care what people think, yet because this widow keeps bothering me, I will see that she gets justice, so that she won't eventually come and attack me!" (Luke 18:2–5)

To catch Jesus' drift you need to hear the utter irony of his parable. The judge in the parable cares nothing about the needs of the widow, but God is exactly the opposite! He is the passionate defender of widows. God issues the strongest of warnings to anyone who mistreats them: "Any widow or orphan you are not to afflict. Oh, if you afflict, afflict them...! For then they will cry, cry out to me, and I will hearken, hearken to their cry, my anger will flare up, and I will kill you with the sword so that your wives become widows, and your children, orphans!" (Exodus 22:22–24).[2]

In fact, God was well-known as "father to the fatherless, a defender of widows" (Psalm 68:5). But the word for "defender" here is actually *shophet* (sho-FET), or "judge." A *shophet* is one who brings justice, in the sense of defending the helpless and vindicating the wronged. The hard-boiled magistrate of Jesus' parable couldn't be farther from God's reality.

You can hear Jesus smirking as he makes this laughably ironic comparison. If even a callous court official will help out an old lady who keeps pestering him, how much more will God, who passionately cares for widows and orphans! In this story, Jesus was exhorting his followers to be persistent in prayer, prodding us to boldly keep coming to God.

In Luke 11:5–8, Jesus tells yet another parable about having *chutzpah* in prayer. In the wee hours of the night, a man raps gently but insistently on a friend's door. Out-of-town visitors have just arrived, but he doesn't have any food to share. Could he have a few loaves of bread?

It was a small but urgent request, because in the ancient Middle East, it was quite a *faux pas* to not be able to extend hospitality to a guest. Jesus' first listeners likely expected the groggy man to hasten to his kitchen to save his friend from a social disaster. It was such a simple, obvious need—who wouldn't help out? Indeed, they'd half-imagine the man loading down his friend with a pantry's worth of supplies, because it was the neighborly thing to do.

But instead, the man shooed his desperate friend away with the lamest of excuses. "Don't bother me. The door is already locked, and my children and I are in bed. I can't get up and give you anything." Jesus' audience would have been shocked at such a contemptible response. Such gall! In their mind's eye, they imagined the sleepy neighborhood overhearing the late-night conversation through open windows and being equally aghast. How unthinkably rude!

The man at the door would be outraged by such a brush-off from someone he thought was a friend. Of course he would keep pounding on the door, brazenly, shamelessly, until the old grouch got up and helped him—not because he's a nice guy, but just so that he could crawl back into bed. Responding to *chutzpah* requires yet more *chutzpah*, as the bus incident revealed.

Once again, the humor of the parable is in the fact that God is so completely unlike the drowsy, lazy neighbor. To the contrary, "He who watches over Israel will neither slumber nor sleep ... the LORD will watch over your coming and going both now and forevermore" (Psalm 121: 4, 8).

In both parables, Jesus was using a classic method of rabbinic reasoning called *kal va'homer* (kahl vah-ho-MAIR, lit., "light and heavy"). He does this whenever he says "how much more" or contrasts a small thing with a much greater thing in a parable. You don't get the point until you grasp the utter irony of the comparison. If an apathetic neighbor and a lousy judge will respond to a needy person who begs for their help, how much more will a loving God answer our bold and persistent prayers?

Jesus made this same point more directly, through yet another example of *kal va'homer*: "Which of you, if your son asks for bread, will give him a stone? Or if he asks for a fish, will give him a snake? If you, then, though you are evil, know how to give good gifts to your children, how much more will your Father in heaven give good gifts to those who ask him!" (Matthew 7:9–11). Once again we hear the irony in Jesus' words—even a wicked man has enough love in his heart to respond to the pleas of his children. And even the best father in this world is evil in comparison to our supremely good Father in heaven. If this is so, then how can we not be confident that he'll respond in love when we come to him in prayer?

In *Jesus the Jewish Theologian*, Brad Young explains that underlying Jesus' words is an ancient Jewish assumption that an intimate faith in God is tenacious, even to the point of being a little pushy at times, because God is worthy of our trust:

> The Snake was cursed that it will "eat dust all the days of your life." But why is it a curse to have one's food everywhere, at all times? Because the fact that our livelihood is not readily available to us, and we are in constant communication with G-d to request our daily bread—that's life's greatest blessing.
> —Rabbi Bunem of Peshischa

> One prays with bold determination because God is good. He is *not* like the contemptible friend who would not help his neighbor. He is *not* like the corrupt judge who feared neither God nor man and refused to help a needy widow.... Jesus uses irony and humor to illustrate the nature of God.

> ... People mistakenly pray as if God is a friend who does not care or a judge who does not deal justly. By role-playing with the divine nature and by using an exaggerated characterization of what God is not like, Jesus teaches his followers what God is like. In many ways the theme of these colorful illustrations can be summarized by saying "God is your good friend." Because God is good, perseverance in prayer will receive an answer. Faith in God is defined as bold persistence.[3]

It Started with Abraham

The Jewish tradition of boldness toward God stretches all the way back to its founding father, Abraham. In Genesis 18:16–33, Abraham has a conversation with God that might shock you. When God informed him of his plans to destroy Sodom because of its wickedness, Abraham responded with protests and bargaining. You'll hardly believe his nerve. Just listen:

> Will you sweep away the righteous with the wicked?... Far be it from you to do such a thing — to kill the righteous with the wicked, treating the righteous and the wicked alike. Far be it from you! Will not the Judge of all the earth do right? (Genesis 18:23–25)

And then, like a savvy Arab merchant, Abraham haggles with God over the city. What if there are fifty righteous people — would he spare it for fifty? How about forty-five? What about thirty, or even twenty? Would the lives of ten innocent people be enough? Each time God agrees, eventually promising to withhold his hand for even ten people.

We might hear Abraham's words as appallingly irreverent, but Jewish thought sees his actions positively.[4] His boldness is a sign of his tremendous trust in God. Abraham is like a little boy who keeps tugging on his father's coattails, refusing to stop pestering him until he gives in. Even though his father seems stern and unapproachable, the little boy knows that ultimately his dad is soft-hearted, and he can be a little bold in begging for a treat.

Some commentators even suggest that God started the conversation with Abraham as a teachable moment, knowing full well that Abraham would argue with him. They imagine that God's responses to him are laden with gentle bemusement, like a dad tussling with a little boy. In the wrestling Abraham would learn about God, and he'd teach his children how to wrestle with God too. After all, the name *Israel* means "wrestles with God."

In *The Gospel according to Moses: What My Jewish Friends Taught Me about Jesus*, Athol Dickson meditates on Abraham's difficult questions for God and realizes that these interrogations exhibited a stronger faith than his own pious attempts to suppress all doubt. He writes:

> It takes more faith to ask than it takes to fear the asking. It takes faith to be ready for whatever answer comes, and faith to persevere with more questions if that answer is not understood.... Sometimes asking questions is a way to demonstrate humility, because inherent in the question is the assumption that I do not have the answer, God does. Sincere questions give God respect. They acknowledge his power. They honor him.[5]

God's answers to Abraham's impudent questions reveal several things. First, unlike the deities that others worshiped, God *is* righteous. He has standards for human conduct, but he himself does not flout his own laws. He is not a cruel, capricious deity who kills people indiscriminately. God agrees with Abraham's desire to withhold judgment on a whole city to protect a very few, yet Sodom didn't contain even that minimum quota of people.[6]

Throughout the Bible, we find faithful Jews addressing their concerns to God with a surprising bluntness. After Moses' first unsuccessful encounter with Pharaoh, he didn't hesitate to let God know about his disappointment in quite an un-Minnesotan way:

> Why, Lord, why have you brought trouble on this people? Is this why you sent me? Ever since I went to Pharaoh to speak in your name, he has brought trouble on this people, and you have not rescued your people at all. (Exodus 5:22–23)

You hear this same unflinching honesty in David's psalms and in Job's laments especially, but it winds through the whole Scripture.

A comfortable, almost impertinent attitude lingers on in later Judaism too. Remember Tevye's prayerful musings with God in *Fiddler on the Roof*? After his mule injured a foot Tevye sighs:

> Dear God. Was that necessary? Did you have to make him lame just before the Sabbath? That wasn't nice. It's enough you pick on me. Bless me with five daughters, a life of poverty, that's all right. But what have you got against my mule?... Really, sometimes I think, when things are too quiet up there, you say

to yourself, "Let's see. What kind of mischief can I play on my friend, Tevye?"[7]

Many of us Christians are so used to pious, solemn reverence toward God that we blush to hear someone addressing him in such a relaxed, almost teasing way. And yet behind this habit is the assumption that God is our loving Father, whom we can approach without trepidation or timidity.

One Jewish man who was particularly known for his bold prayers lived about a century before Jesus. Honi was a humble man who was known for his great piety and prayerful walk with God. Once, when drought gripped the country, people begged Honi to pray for rain. At first when he prayed, no rain fell. So Honi drew a circle and stood in the middle of it and prayed, "Lord of the world! Your children have turned to me because I have a close relationship with you. I'm not moving from here until you take pity on your children!"

It began to rain, drop by drop.

Unsatisfied, Honi prayed, "This is not what I wanted, but rain for filling up cisterns, pits, and caverns." Then it began to rain violently.

So again he prayed, "This is not what I wanted, but rain of good will, blessing, and graciousness." Then it began to rain in just the right way, nourishing the crops and restoring the land.

The Jewish leaders were horrified by Honi's brashness toward God. One scolded him, "Had it been anyone else but you I would have had him excommunicated. But what can I do to you when you implore God and he grants your requests? You're like a spoiled child begging his indulgent father. Whatever he wants his father gives him."[8]

Honi pushed prayer to its limits. But even those who opposed him recognized that he had come to God in childlike humility, trusting that God was his loving Father. Honi was so certain of God's loving-kindness that he was acting like a spoiled brat, knowing that his doting Father would happily indulge him. And God did!

The Issue of Prayer Is God

How can we tell if our prayers are appropriate? The renowned twentieth-century Jewish theologian Rabbi Abraham Heschel makes a profound observation: "The issue of prayer is not prayer. The issue of prayer is God." How you pray reveals what you believe about God. Since I heard this, I've listened more closely to what I pray and what it says about what I believe about God.

One prayer that I used to pray, which I've since rethought, took place when I've asked God to forgive me for worrying. More than one sermon I've heard interprets Jesus' words "Do not worry" (Matthew 6:25–34) as condemning worry as a sin that we need to repent from. But the gist of Jesus' sermon is to warmly reassure his listeners of God's care, not to identify yet another category of wrongdoing. Of course God wants us to place our trust in him, and as we mature in faith we learn to worry less and less. But when we pray for forgiveness for worrying about our problems, it seems to assume that God is a heartless perfectionist who gets angry even with our weaknesses.

And if we pray tenaciously, with *chutzpah*, what do we put our faith in? Some people think that only when they have enough belief will God perform a miracle. Many hurting hearts have been crushed by being told that their faith was too weak for God to answer their prayers.

A few years ago an insight occurred to me in the middle of a relatively minor crisis in prayer. My little cat Raisin, who is very shy, got loose outside when I was out of town. She had wandered out onto my apartment balcony and jumped down onto the ground, about eight feet below. When I arrived home she had been lost for several days, starving, unable to come back because of her skittishness around people. To my great dismay, friends thought they spotted her hiding under cars in our parking lot, crawling up inside their engine compartments in order to be "safe." Every morning I'd wander around my apartment complex, calling her and begging the Lord to bring her home.

As I was praying I wondered, *Am I supposed to have perfect faith in the idea that I'd get my cat back in order for God to answer my prayer? Is the sheer force of my imagination somehow supposed to force God's hand?*

Then it hit me that the faith that we're supposed to have is not in the *outcome*, but in *God himself*. God wants us to be absolutely convinced of his love for us and of his power and desire to take care of us. So my prayer changed. I said, "Lord, I know that you are good and that you have heard my prayer, and I can trust your answer to my prayer, whether or not you bring Raisin back." My emphasis shifted from my cat to the fact that God was good and that I could always trust him.

> *Lord, when my wife died, my daughter was there to comfort me. Now that my daughter, too, has died, only You remain to me, so You must now comfort me.*
> — Prayer of Menachem Mendel of Rimanov

It was a true surprise when a couple days later a seeming miracle brought Raisin home. After days of fruitless searching, a friend lifted her car hood and found Raisin curled up on top of her engine's air filter — dirty, gaunt, and with a paralyzed paw.

I'm almost embarrassed to share this story when so many desperate prayers seem to go unanswered. But it taught me that God didn't really need me to fervently imagine a certain outcome before he'd respond. Any time God answers prayer, he does so out of sheer grace, not because our prayers "earned" a response. God is good, powerful, and loving, and whatever answer he gave, I could still be assured of this most important fact of all.

We can pray boldly because we know that God is good and loving. But there are limits to how we should speak to God. There is a fine balance between speaking to God out of loving trust and treating him with back-slapping overfamiliarity.

Jesus did also say, "And when you pray, do not keep on babbling like pagans, for they think they will be heard because of their many words" (Matthew 6:7). What is the difference between this and praying persistently out of faith?

I think the answer lies in another comment that Jesus makes about pagans, that their lives focused on "What shall we eat?" "What shall we drink?" and "What shall we wear?" (see Matthew 6:31). Because polytheists believed that their gods were subject to magical forces greater than them, they thought that if humans performed the correct rituals and repeated the right incantations over and over, their gods would be compelled to respond by producing wealth and fertility. The ultimate goal of pagan prayers was to manipulate the gods into serving one's own personal prosperity.

When you think about it, there really is not much difference between ancient pagans and teachers today who claim that you can use prayer to "claim your blessings" or "speak prosperity into your life." Any time you try to coerce God into doing your bidding, so that he'll pad your pocketbook and expand your stock assets, you're treating God the same way that pagans treated their gods, as a tool to serve their own ends.

But at the same time, God lovingly listens to our smallest requests, even for things like lost cats. Any mom or dad knows that children come running to them daily with an endless list of tiny concerns. The key seems to be that you humbly come to him as your heavenly Father, rather than ordering him around as your servant.

Chutzpah on Behalf of Others

The Jewish attitude toward persistent, bold prayer differs in yet another way than "name-it-and-claim-it" kinds of prayer. Most often, this unabashed prayer was not for one's self, but on behalf of others. Honi wasn't demanding the latest model donkey to drive; he was pleading for rain for his desperate nation. Abraham too was interceding with God on behalf of the Sodomites, not even for his own people.

In fact, Abraham's tenacious wrestling with God over Sodom was considered especially heroic because he was pleading for God's mercy for sinners. He had compassion for the suffering of others, even if the wicked city deserved God's punishment. From Abraham's example the Talmud teaches, "Whoever is merciful to his fellow beings is without doubt of the children of our father Abraham; whoever is unmerciful to his fellow beings certainly cannot be of the children of Abraham our father."[9]

Israel's greatest heroes were all distinguished by this self-forgetful pleading for God's mercy toward others. In the desert, when the Israelites had abandoned their covenant and God threatened to destroy them, Moses begged God to refrain from judgment.[10] Moses even turned down God's offer to make his own family into a great nation in Israel's place (Exodus 32:10). King David also pleaded for the people of Israel when God sent a plague as punishment, asking him to strike his own family instead (2 Samuel 24:17).

In contrast, Noah was told of the destruction of all humanity but did nothing to warn others. He just built his own boat and loaded up his family, sailing away from the troubles of the world.[11] Jonah was even worse—he rebelled when God instructed him to warn the Ninevites about God's judgment, and he even got angry when God had mercy on them! Noah and Jonah were never as highly regarded as Abraham, David, and Moses in Jewish thought.[12]

Jewish thinkers note that for some mysterious reason, God wants us to plead on behalf of sinful people. He says in Ezekiel, "I looked for someone among them who would build up the wall and stand before me in the gap on behalf of the land so I would not have to destroy it, but I found no one" (Ezekiel 22:30). God does not want us to stand by passively and watch judgment come on others. He wants us to intercede, both telling them to repent and begging God to be merciful.

Interestingly, Jesus fits into the first category of showing *chutzpah* on behalf of others, like Abraham, David, and Moses. He pleaded for God's mercy on the perpetrators of his crucifixion, because "they do not know what they are doing" (Luke 23:34). In fact, his whole ministry was for the purpose of seeking the lost sheep who had wandered from God's enfolding embrace. And finally, by bearing our sins, Christ's heroic *chutzpah* on the cross became the ultimate triumph in gaining God's mercy for a world full of sinners.

Wisdom for the Walk

1. Consider how you typically address God in prayer. What do your prayers say about your perception of God?

2. Read Matthew 15:22–28. What's the difference between seeing faith as belief and seeing it as *chutzpah*?

3. Take a look at Genesis 18:20–33 and Exodus 33:12–23. Where, in your estimation, is the line between boldness and irreverence in prayer?

4. Have you ever prayed a prayer as frustrated and forthright as Psalm 74?

5. Do you react to the sinful world around you by secluding yourself and ignoring it? Or do you concern yourself with those who don't know Christ?

CHAPTER 10

Thinking
with Both Hands

The task is not yours to complete,
but neither are you free to desist from it.
—Mishnah, *Avot* 2:21

In *Fiddler on the Roof*, do you remember how Tevye ruminates out loud when his daughters plead to marry their true loves instead of waiting for the matchmaker's choice? When Tzeitel begs his permission to marry a threadbare, fledgling tailor, Tevye weighs his decision aloud, bantering back and forth to himself: "What kind of a match would that be with a poor tailor? . . . On the other hand, he is an honest, hard worker . . . But on the other hand, he has absolutely nothing . . . But on the other hand, things could never get worse for him, only better."

Later, when Perchik and Hodel boldly announce their intention to get married, Tevye is dumbfounded by how they are casting aside tradition. But again he mulls it over: "He loves her! Love—it's a new style . . . But, on the other hand, our old ways were once new, weren't they? . . . On the other hand, they decided without parents. Without a matchmaker! . . . But on the other hand, did Adam and Eve have a matchmaker? . . . Oh, yes, they did. And it seems these two have the same matchmaker."

Tevye's amusing habit of weighing two opposing viewpoints is distinctly Jewish, a part of his culture. He takes one side and then argues for and against it. This method of "give and take" (*shakla v'tarya*, as it is traditionally called) has been integral to Jewish thought throughout history. Often two points of view are left unresolved and simply accepted as a paradox.

When I first encountered this kind of thinking, my scientifically trained brain found it a little annoying. It felt vascillating and mushy, a short step away from the postmodern logic of declaring all opinions valid, saying, "You have your truth, and I have mine." But I've since discovered that Tevye's method of reasoning is far more sophisticated than this, and it arises out of the culture in which the Scriptures were written. Grasping how it functions is important for unlocking the way the biblical writers thought.

As a Western-thinking Christian, I've often struggled to find systematic theological treatment of every issue, and I have gotten frustrated by how the Bible sometimes seems to be contradictory. But rather than trying to make the Bible more "logical" by Western standards, I've found that a deeper understanding of it comes from learning to read it with "both hands," as Jesus, Paul, and Jews over the ages have done.

Paradoxes throughout the Bible

Once you think about it, some of the most important truths of the Bible are paradoxical. Jesus is both fully human and fully God. God is loving and in control, yet he allows tragedy and injustice to take place. God is everywhere, but at certain times he's present in a unique way, like when his glory filled the Temple.

Jesus also liked to speak in paradoxes, declaring that "anyone who wants to be first must be the very last" (Mark 9:35) and that "anyone who loves their life will lose it, while anyone who hates their life in this world will keep it for eternal life" (John 12:25).

The Bible also sometimes makes seemingly contradictory statements, its authors fully realizing what they were doing. Exodus states that "no one can see God and live"—yet only a few chapters later, the seventy elders of Israel saw God on Mount Sinai (Exodus 24:9; 33:20). In Deuteronomy 15:4, Moses promises that if the Israelites are obedient, there will be no poor among them. But a few verses later he begins, "If anyone is poor among your fellow Israelites ..." (v. 7). Then, just a couple lines further down he tells them to be generous, because "there will always be poor people in the land" (v. 11).

Marvin Wilson notes that often the biblical text uses "block logic" rather than the "linear logic" that we are more used to. Linear logic uses statements that build on each other in a tightly argued fashion: if a = b, and b = c, then a = c. Block logic groups together ideas that may come from opposite perspectives—such as from a human perspective and then a divine perspective. For instance, Jesus said, "Whoever comes to me I will never drive away," yet no one can come "unless the Father who sent me draws him" (John 6:37, 44).[1]

When Westerners find a paradox in the Bible, we often try to resolve the conflict by rejecting one side for the other. For instance, do humans have free will, or does God foreknow our actions? The question has divided Christians for centuries. Some reject free will entirely, such as those who opposed William Carey, the father of modern missions, when he preached the need for world evangelism in 1786. His hyper-Calvinist colleagues retorted, "When God pleases to convert the heathen, he'll do it without consulting you or me."[2] But others reject the idea that God is in control, imagining that God is wringing his hands in heaven, crossing his fingers and hoping that in the end everything will come out OK. Many churches have split over these issues.

> *Making sense of everything is not an obligation or even a possibility. Acceptance of mystery is an act not of resignation but humility.*
> —David Wolpe

Jewish thought takes another approach. One famous rabbinic answer was simply, "Everything is under God's control, yet man has free will."[3] Amazingly, this rabbi simply embraced the two ideas in tension with each other rather than needing to force a resolution. Why? Because passages in Scripture support *both* points of view. Pharaoh hardened his own heart, and yet God hardened his heart (Exodus 7:3, 13; 8:15). God foresaw that four hundred years in the future, the Canaanites would become so evil that he would evict them from their land (Genesis 15:16). But he also offered the Israelites the choice of whether to take on his covenant or not (Deuteronomy 30:19).

While this two-handed conclusion might frustrate our Western rationality, it does have one important advantage—it yields final authority to the Scripture rather than to human logic. It prefers to stay true to the biblical text rather than ignoring what doesn't quite fit.

As a scientist by training, I see the importance of the emphasis on letting the text have the last word. In the laboratory, the temptation is always to ignore results that don't quite fit your model. But good scientists learn to carefully keep track of data that doesn't support their theory, outliers that point to a potential error in their thinking. For theologians, the raw data that can't be neglected (but often is) is the biblical text. Tevye would have made a great scientist, because he kept questioning the limits of his own assumptions and didn't assume that the best answer was as obvious as the first one that came to mind.

> *The whole worth of a kind deed lies in the love that inspires it.*
> —Talmud, *Sukkah* 49b

Another reason for the difference between Jewish and Western logic is the assumption that God alone can understand all things. Jewish thought is much more comfortable with knowing its limits than is Western, Christian thought. Marvin Wilson writes, "The Hebrew knew he did not have all the answers.... He refused to over-systematize or force harmonization on the enigmas of God's truth or the puzzles of the universe.... The Hebrew mind was willing to accept the truths taught on both sides of the paradox; it recognized that mystery and apparent contradictions are often signs of the divine."[4]

In *The Gospel according to Moses*, Athol Dickson points out that acquiring this ability to embrace paradox has allowed him to more fully embrace Christ as both man and God:

> Given what the Torah has taught me about God, I am no longer surprised that the Paradox of Jesus makes no common sense.... Perhaps there are other reasons not to believe in Jesus, but in light of the many paradoxes in the Bible, the idea that God can never be a man is not one of them. All true explanations of God's nature must openly include paradoxical concepts my mind cannot grasp.
>
> Thus it is with the Paradox of Jesus. If I focus on Jesus as man, I miss Jesus as God. If I focus on Jesus as God, I miss Jesus

as man. Is he God or is he just a man? As with all paradoxes of the Bible, the answer is "yes." And "yes."[5]

Certainly there are textual difficulties that a little more scholarly work will resolve, and we shouldn't just give up and label them "paradoxes." But often, biblical "illogic" arises from the fact that it describes a reality beyond human imagining. It's extradimensional, like the fact that you can fly due east from New York to Madrid, then east again to Beijing, and then east from Beijing back to New York. It's only possible because the earth curves around in another dimension than humans once imagined possible.

Rabbi Heschel illustrates the both-handed approach by even applying it to reason itself:

> The demands of piety are a mystery before which man is reduced to reverence and silence. Reverence, love, prayer, faith, go beyond the acts of shallow reasoning. We must therefore not judge religion exclusively from the viewpoint of reason. Religion is not within but beyond the limits of mere reason.... [However] the employment of reason is indispensable to the understanding and worship of God, and religion withers without it.... Without reason faith becomes blind. Without reason we would not know how to apply the insights of faith to the concrete issues of living. The worship of reason is arrogance and betrays a lack of intelligence. The rejection of reason is cowardice and betrays a lack of faith.[6]

Weighing the Laws

Another way that Jewish thought seeks balance is in its approach to the Law. Christians have traditionally understood all of the commandments to be of equal importance. But since before Jesus' time, the rabbinic approach has been to "weigh" the laws so that in a situation where two laws conflict with each other, the weightier one took precedence. For instance, the command to circumcise on the eighth day took precedence over the Sabbath (John 7:22). They described the laws in terms of being "light" (*kal*) and "heavy" (*hamur*). This came out of an effort to live by God's laws in all situations, rather than arbitrarily ignoring some and doing others.

Certain principles derived from the Bible were used to organize laws relative to each other, and the focus of many rabbinic debates was on how to prioritize them. For instance, one principle is *pikuach nephesh* (pi-KOO-akh NEH-fesh), which is the "preservation of life." The sages recognized the preeminent importance that the Torah placed on human life, far more than in other law codes. And the Torah itself says that the Law was given in order to bring life (Deuteronomy 30:16). Jewish thinkers concluded that all laws (except a few) should be set aside to save a human life.[7]

Because of this, Jewish doctors and nurses go to work on the Sabbath, for they may potentially save a life. And if a person is ill, he or she is supposed to eat on Yom Kippur, a day when eating and drinking are strictly forbidden. Even the possibility of saving a life is enough to put this principle into effect.

Contrast this with the Jehovah's Witness policy of refusing blood transfusions in a medical emergency because of the law against drinking blood in Genesis 9:4. Because of this ruling, women bear a forty-fold greater risk of dying of uterine hemorrhage during childbirth.[8] Rabbinic exegesis would never support this interpretation. The weightier law is to save life!

Here's another example. Imagine you lived in Europe during World War II and are hiding Jews in your home. A Nazi pounds on your door, demanding to know where they are. Should you lie or tell the truth? According to the principle of *pikuach nephesh*, you should lie to save their lives. The Bible even provides a precedent: the midwives lied to Pharaoh rather than killing the Israelite boys as they had been ordered, and God rewarded them (Exodus 1:19–21).[9]

But surprisingly, some Christian theologians have come to the opposite conclusion. Augustine said, "Since, then, eternal life is lost by lying, a lie may never be told for the preservation of the temporal life of another."[10] Later, philosopher Immanuel Kant declared that if a man fleeing for his life hides in your house and the murderer asks where he is, "we are forbidden to lie or mislead him."[11] Both men conclude that a person must answer truthfully no matter what. In their thinking, all rules are absolute. This logic forces one to conclude that the law not to stand idly by when a neighbor's life is endangered (Leviticus 19:16) and the law against lying (Leviticus 19:11) are irreconcilable.

Not Yours to Complete

In *The Book of Jewish Values*, Rabbi Joseph Telushkin poses an interesting ethical question, and his analysis illustrates an interesting two-handed approach towards the Law. He points out Jewish law forbids activities that needlessly endanger one's life. Dangerous, thrill-seeking sports like rappelling off cliffs and skydiving from low planes are prohibited. Your life is a precious gift from God. It has a purpose in his greater plan, and it's not yours to gamble with.

So Telushkin asks, shouldn't smoking be prohibited too? Hundreds of years ago smoking was thought to be healthy for one's lungs, and rabbis of that era ruled that it was perfectly permissible. Many Orthodox rabbis were heavy smokers, and some still are. Telushkin argues, however, that if earlier rabbis would have known what a health risk smoking is, they would have forbidden it. He concludes that even though Jewish law allows it, it is unethical to start smoking or to encourage others to do so. Makes sense to me.

But what I found surprising was Rabbi Telushkin's advice to smokers who are thoroughly addicted and who just can't seem to quit: "Regarding those who already smoke, if it is possible for them to break their addiction, they should; if they cannot, then let them at least smoke less."[12]

Smoke less!

I laughed out loud. If smoking is wrong, should we just do it less? I shared that with several Christian friends, and it made no sense to them. If something is a sin we should immediately stop doing it, we all declared.

It might sound as if Rabbi Telushkin is waffling on this issue when he should just take a stand. But his comment actually illustrates a different philosophical approach to the Law in Judaism than in Christianity, something we can learn from. Much of Protestant

Christianity sees the chief goal of the Law as to reveal our sin, how far we are from God's perfection. We often take an all-or-nothing approach to the Law so that when we realize that we can't keep it perfectly, we'll give up and come to Christ for salvation. So if you're like me, your response to an issue like this is to mutter, "Thank goodness I'm saved by grace apart from works," and keep doing what is wrong. Isn't that how we deal with our gossip and lustful thoughts and occasional lies?

The Jewish attitude is different. Contrary to our traditional Christian assumption, their discussions about the Law do not arise out of an anxious striving to earn one's way to heaven. Jewish thought generally assumes that Jews are *already* saved, because God graciously chose Israel as his people. In their minds, the Law teaches them how to live in a way that pleases a loving God and upholds their covenantal relationship.

Because of this, Judaism often shows a surprising pragmatism toward people's weaknesses. People are encouraged to keep aiming to obey God's laws, even if they do so imperfectly. The idea is that if you can't be entirely obedient, do your best to do what you can and try even harder tomorrow. The mere willingness that you have toward trying to submit to God's will brings him joy. Rabbi Nachman of Braztlav (1772–1810) put it this way: "If you are not going to be better tomorrow than you were today, then what need have you for tomorrow?"[13]

In the late first century AD, Rabbi Tarfon summed this up in a delightfully two-handed way: *The task is not yours to complete, but neither are you free to desist from it.*[14] You may not be able, as a sinner, to perfectly obey God's laws, but you cannot give up trying.

Smoke less today and try to quit tomorrow.

At Jewish high schools you'll find a similar approach to tackling the problem of *lashon hara*. In his *New York Times* article, "Weaning Teenagers Off Gossip, for One Hour at a Time," Dan Levin writes:

> At 11:15 each morning at the Stella K. Abraham High School for Girls on Long Island, the voice of Emi Renov, a 17-year-old junior, buzzes over the intercom, gently reminding her fellow

students to refrain from gossiping for the next 60 minutes. What was that? Was she kidding? Telling teenagers that they should not talk about other students behind their backs is like telling them not to try to get a driver's license. Yet for one hour after Ms. Renov's announcement, her schoolmates make an honest attempt to avoid mocking one another's outfits or whispering the latest shocking rumor.

"We can't expect everyone to just stop gossiping forever, even though we all know the rumors and the fights hurt," Ms. Renov said. The program is one small way, she added, "to change how we treat each other, and it really motivates us to speak with respect."[15]

You might laugh that students are only asked to avoid *lashon hara* for one hour. But they know that doing so deliberately for a short time will make them more careful the rest of the day. They figure that even if they are far from perfect, they can at least *start somewhere*.

As Christians, we can learn from this Jewish emphasis on obedience. Doing what Jesus commanded is not about earning one's salvation, but about discipleship. Salvation is a free gift, but discipleship is a lifelong journey of dedicating ourselves to becoming more like Christ. As Paul wrote, "As for other matters, brothers and sisters, we instructed you how to live in order to please God, as in fact you are living. Now we ask you and urge you in the Lord Jesus to do this more and more" (1 Thessalonians 4:1). And Jesus himself said, "Why do you call me 'Lord, Lord' and do not do what I say?" (Luke 6:46). We could paraphrase Rabbi Nachman to say: "If you are not going to be more Christlike, more obedient, more useful in God's kingdom, what purpose do you have for tomorrow?"

I've grown up in a tradition that has emphasized the overwhelming danger of legalism, trying to gain salvation through adhering to rules. But it has greatly underemphasized the opposite danger, which is just as spiritually lethal. By ignoring obedience to Christ we can become useless, worthless disciples, followers who never bear fruit because we're unwilling to conform to God's will. When outsiders wonder if Christ makes a difference, they look at our lives and the answer they come to is, "Not much, I guess."

If you can't stop gossiping altogether, gossip less today. If you can't stop yourself from yelling at your kids, aim to yell less today. If you can't be perfectly honest, keep yourself from lying today. And try again tomorrow, asking the Lord's help to do even better.

Jesus Weighed the Laws Too

Jesus also was using the principle of *pikuach nephesh* when he was arguing what may be done on the Sabbath in Luke 6:9, when he said, "I ask you, which is lawful on the Sabbath: to do good or to do evil, to save life or to destroy it?" Both activities under debate were an effort to preserve life — the plucking of grain to satisfy hunger and the healing of a man's hand.[16]

The point was not that Jesus was throwing aside the Sabbath as unimportant. More than once the Gospels record that Jesus waited until after sunset to heal people, after the Sabbath had ended (Mark 1:32; Luke 4:40). This was because keeping the Sabbath was important, for it was a "sign" of the covenant between God and Israel (Exodus 31:13), like a wedding ring is to a marriage. If a couple needs money, the wife might sell her favorite necklace, but if she sells her wedding ring, it sounds as if the marriage is in trouble. In the same way, not honoring the Sabbath showed contempt for the covenant as a whole (Numbers 15:32 – 36).

In another instance of healing on the Sabbath, a woman who had been crippled for eighteen years was in the congregation one day. Her condition was chronic, not life-threatening, and the synagogue leader pointed out that she could easily be healed any other day of the week (Luke 13:14). But Jesus healed her anyway.[17]

> *He who studies the Scriptures, but does no works of love, lives without God.*
> — Talmud, *Avodah Zarah* 17b

Here, Jesus uses another rabbinic principle called *tza'ar baalei hayim* (TZA-ar bah-ah-LAY hi-YEEM), "preventing suffering to living things." The sages saw that the Torah contains many laws for the humane treatment of animals. An ox that was threshing grain couldn't be muzzled, so that it could eat as it worked (Deuteronomy 25:4). If people found a bird on its nest, they were allowed to take the young, but only after sending away the mother first, to spare her feelings (Deuteronomy 22:6–7). And Genesis 9:4 forbade all of humanity from the cruel act of eating flesh cut from an animal that is still alive. Because of the Torah's sensitivity toward animals, sacrificial practices were designed to end life with a minimum of pain, and an animal that suffered became unkosher.

One of the most humane laws was that on the Sabbath, even the animals were supposed to be able to rest from their labors (Deuteronomy 5:14). To keep a farmer from taking his ox out to the field to get a little plowing done, it was forbidden to untie an animal from its stall. But, because of *tza'ar baalei hayim*, it was permitted to untie animals to lead them out to water, so that they wouldn't go thirsty. In the Gospels, Jesus uses this ruling to say that if a donkey can be "unbound" on the Sabbath to prevent its suffering for one day, how much more should a woman be "unbound" on the Sabbath from what afflicted her all these years (Luke 13:15–16).

Another time, Jesus appeals to a similar ruling of *tza'ar baalei hayim*—that the Sabbath can be put aside to rescue a sheep that falls into a pit rather than waiting until the next day. Here again he employs the reasoning of "how much more" (*kal va'homer*) to say, "If any of you has a sheep and it falls into a pit on the Sabbath, will you not take hold of it and lift it out? How much more valuable is a person than a sheep! Therefore it is lawful to do good on the Sabbath" (Matthew 12:11–12).[18]

Jesus was declaring that as important as it was to honor the Sabbath, human life is even more important: "The Sabbath was made for man, not man for the Sabbath" (Mark 2:27).[19] Jesus was working within the rules, not simply negating them, to show how God longs to take every opportunity to show compassion for the suffering of his people.

Prioritizing Obedience

How, then, do we prioritize our obedience? The idea of "weighting" the laws of the Torah was likely the rationale for the question, "Of all the commandments, which is the most important?" (Mark

12:28–30). The lawyer was asking, "What is our ultimate priority as we try to obey God?" Jesus' answer, of course, was to quote the commands to love God and to love our neighbor. Everything we do should aim toward that goal. He then illustrates with the parable of the good Samaritan, pointing out the wrong priorities of the two characters who went up to worship at the Temple rather than helping the dying man. Of course, the right thing to do in this case was to attend to the needs of the wounded man, showing him the love of God.

Does this mean we can ignore God's standards altogether? Not at all! Reading Matthew 5, one wonders if Jesus was accused of undermining the law, because there he emphatically said that he came not to undermine the law, but to explain it and live by it faithfully. Then he said that anyone who breaks one of the least of these commandments will be called least in the kingdom of heaven. In other words, we should aim to be obedient in all ways, but we should always aim to love, and that sets our priorities for how we should obey. As Tevye would phrase it, on the one hand, be obedient, but on the other hand, choose to love!

This is a wise word for us in terms of discerning what to do when two commands conflict with each other. If you must choose one over the other, choose the one that shows the most love. If you don't typically do yard work on Sunday (or Saturday), but your elderly mother really needs her lawn mowed and it's the only day you can help, you should do it then. If your family celebrates holidays with a tradition that you don't embrace, seek to do what is loving rather than dividing the family over it. Choose the most loving path. Jesus himself would probably do the same thing in your situation. Indeed, he is using you to do it.

Wisdom for the Walk

1. Read Genesis 32:22–30. What paradoxes do you find within that story? How do you make sense of it?

2. What paradoxes in the Bible do you struggle with most? Are there stories or passages that you are tempted to "throw out"?

3. Look through the earlier chapters of this book for other places where you find this "both-handed" logic. Where is it most (and least) helpful?

4. In *Fiddler on the Roof,* even Tevye concluded, "Sometimes there *is* no other hand." What things are nonnegotiable in Christian faith?

5. When was the last time you were in a situation where you had to determine which of two commands was "weightier"? What did you do?

PART III

STUDYING *the* WORD *with* RABBI JESUS

Jesus taught among a people who knew their Scriptures intimately, who regarded study as a form of worship. They found in its lines endless new insights, yet realized that God still did not reveal every answer. Like others, Jesus drew from the Torah, the Prophets, and the Writings. Through his Jewish eyes, we see the passionate longing in his Father's heart to save humanity from the very beginning. From Scriptures he read, Jesus found our calling as God's image bearers and his mission as our redeemer.

CHAPTER 11

The Treasure
of the Text

He who studies the Torah for the honor of God,
his knowledge becomes to him the elixir of life,
as it is written in Proverbs 3:18:
"A tree of life is she to those that lay hold on her."
—Talmud, *Taanit* 7a

In 1946, a little group of Jewish refugees endured months of desperate hardship as they fled from Russian authorities on foot across Siberia toward Western Europe. When they stumbled into their own village in Poland, it had been reduced to rubble, all its inhabitants murdered. All that was left of the burned-out synagogue was a cellar. Descending its stairs they discovered a few charred, water-soaked rabbinic commentaries that were still partly readable. Lighting a nub of a candle, they immediately sat down to read a couple pages together. As another fugitive ran past, he called out, "Are you forgetting that you're fleeing for your lives? The Soviets are closing the frontiers. The American zone is still far off! Flee!" But one of the group waved him off, saying, "Be still. One must learn!"[1]

It's hard to overstate the Jewish love of religious study over the ages. They've long been known as "the people of the book" for their fervency and fondness for study. Why this fascination? One reason, I imagine, is that in Jewish parlance, *Torah* (without the word "the") is often used as an affectionate reference to all of the Bible and Jewish writings, the way Christians speak of the Bible as "God's Word." What we translate as "law," Jews more correctly understand as "guidance" or "teaching." What to many of us sounds like an onerous burden sounds to them as if they are uncovering the very thoughts of God.

You can see this fascination for studying the Bible in the New Testament too, in the first-century synagogue, where educated laypeople shared the public reading and teaching on the Sabbath. Some especially avid lay scholars, humble tradesmen otherwise, would travel from town to town, speaking in synagogues and being cared for by the townspeople. A few decades after Jesus' time these men were called "rabbis," but the tradition of traveling teachers had been established before his birth. Jesus and Paul both knew that the synagogue's open podium would be where they could reach the people who were eager to learn God's Word.

As Christians, we long to think the thoughts of Christ. But the stories he knew, the songs he sang, and the prophecies that shaped his earthly mission lie in the Old Testament, which we've hardly cracked open. Over the centuries, Jews have saturated their lives with these Scriptures. In their minds, study is essential to loving God and living life as he intends. What can their traditions teach us about loving and learning God's Word?

An Iceberg Floating Below

Often Jesus' words in the Gospels presuppose an intimate familiarity with the biblical text. Sometimes Jesus made bold claims about his mission as Messiah through the Scriptures he quoted. If you don't have the text in the back of your mind, some of his powerful statements can sail right past you.[2]

For instance, when John the Baptist was imprisoned, he had his disciples deliver a pointed question to Jesus: "Are you the one who is to come, or should we expect someone else?" Jesus responded by noting the astonishing events that had taken place before their eyes: "The blind receive sight, the lame walk, those who have leprosy are cleansed, the deaf hear, the dead are raised, and the good news is proclaimed to the poor" (Matthew 11:2–5).

Reading this conversation by itself, you'd assume Jesus was simply reassuring John by pointing out the miracles God was doing through his ministry. But actually a deeper discussion was going on between the two teachers, and an iceberg of meaning floats below. In the back of John's mind was Malachi's powerful prophecy that linked his own mission with Jesus. The prophet wrote:

> "I will send my messenger, who will prepare the way before me. Then suddenly the Lord you are seeking will come to his temple; the messenger of the covenant, whom you desire, will come," says the LORD Almighty.
>
> But who can endure the day of his coming? Who can stand when he appears? For he will be like a refiner's fire or a launderer's soap. (Malachi 3:1–2)

From childhood, John knew his calling was to be the "messenger" who would prepare the way. But Malachi goes on to say that when the one who was coming after him arrives, what a day of wrath it would be! Like a white-hot furnace he would purge the Temple of corruption and bring Israel's oppressors to judgment.

But Herod's henchmen had just brought John's God-appointed ministry to an abrupt halt. John had faithfully prepared the way, but now, instead of seeing God's enemies destroyed, the fiery prophet was languishing in chains as their victim. When would Jesus start acting as the "one who is to come"? Out of frustration, John was using Scripture to prod Jesus about his mission — he needed to start stoking the fires of judgment. John's very life depended on it.

Jesus responded by pointing John's disciples toward other prophecies that speak of the "coming" of God, especially Isaiah 35:[3]

> Strengthen the feeble hands,
>   steady the knees that give way;
> say to those with fearful hearts,
>   "Be strong, do not fear;
> your God will come,
>   he will come with vengeance;
> with divine retribution
>   he will come to save you."
> Then will the eyes of the blind be opened
>   and the ears of the deaf unstopped.
> Then will the lame leap like a deer,
>   and the mute tongue shout for joy. (Isaiah 35:3–6)

Jesus knew John would recall the rest of this passage when he quoted just a few words. Here, God reassures the fearful, showing them that his justice would arrive in the end. But his coming would also be signified by great miracles of healing, and these were now taking place in Jesus' ministry. Jesus was telling John that he indeed was the fulfillment of the Scriptures, but in a different way than John had imagined. Now was the time of God's mercy — judgment would come later. The discussion between John and Jesus doesn't unfold itself until you recall the prophecies that form the background of their thinking.[4]

When I first heard about Jesus' expectation that people were well-versed in the Scriptures, I was shocked. I grew up in a home where shelves of Christian paperbacks covered the walls. But the Bible that Jesus read, our Old Testament, was largely a mystery to me. How well do you know it?

Joining the Bible Study of the Ages

Children (especially boys) began learning the Bible when they were very little, as I mentioned in chapter 2. Paul remarked that Timothy knew the Scriptures from infancy (2 Timothy 3:15). By the time they were teens, many boys knew the text largely by heart. After that point, if they kept studying, they'd learn the oral traditions for interpreting the Torah.

All the community, both men and women, heard the Torah read aloud every week in the synagogue. For over two thousand years, a worldwide Bible study has taken place, everyone meditating on the same portion of the Torah (*parasha* — par-a-SHAH) each week.[5] Jesus grew up studying the Torah each week in the synagogue, and the passionate first Jewish church in Jerusalem did the same. In Acts 15:21 James described this practice when he commented, "The law of Moses has been preached in every city from the earliest times and is read in the synagogues on every Sabbath."

Over the centuries, the ongoing religious conversation has united Jews scattered across the continents, linking them to their spiritual ancestors as well. Every fall after the Jewish New Year, the scrolls are rewound from Deuteronomy back to Genesis at a celebration called *Simchat Torah* — "the Joy of the Torah." The study begins again, yet once more.

A second set of texts from elsewhere in the Old Testament is also read each week called the *haftarah*. In the Gospels we find Jesus taking part in this tradition in Luke 4, when he takes the scroll of Isaiah and reads from it. Most likely, he was sharing the *haftarah* reading after having read the Torah portion of the week.[6]

> *If you truly wish your children to study Torah, study it yourself in their presence. They will follow your example. Otherwise, they will not themselves study Torah but will simply instruct their children to do so.*
>
> — Menahem Mendel of Kotzk

A few years ago, my friends and I decided to join this ancient tradition, grappling over the traditional *parasha* readings each week together. Each Thursday night our group ruminated together over the lives of Abraham, Isaac, and Jacob and debated the laws of slavery and sacrifice. Often we discovered the original context of something Jesus quoted and discussed how it influenced our understanding. But in the meantime we struggled to understand the situations we encountered in the Torah. What were we supposed to learn from the patriarchs, with their multiple wives and concubines? What was the point behind all the sacrifices they made?

We learned a valuable lesson from an unlikely group member, a Ugandan pastor, Titus Baraka, who had just arrived to study at the seminary in my hometown. Titus expected to meet Americans with all sorts of odd ideas, but when we invited him to join our Torah study, he thought he had heard it all. He was an evangelist by training, as steeped in the New Testament as we were. Why would we want to spend a year reading God's Old Testament laws? Titus agreed to join us, at first observing our discussions in polite silence. But over the weeks he became our most valuable commentator, his insights revealing a very different perspective. Often it seemed that he read the text as an insider.

We'd wonder, why did Joseph's older brothers hate him so much? And why was he so concerned about Benjamin, his mother's other son, when he was in Egypt? "Ah," Titus would say, "it's always this way in polygamous families. The second wife is usually favored over the first, and the father spoils her children and wants them to be his heirs." Then Titus would point out that Jacob gave Joseph the multicolored coat to declare that he was his chosen "firstborn," because his mother was Rachel, the wife he loved over Leah. Since Benjamin was Rachel's other son, naturally Joseph worried about whether his brothers might harm him too.

Then Titus would explain the importance of being the firstborn in a family. Not only would the firstborn get the lion's share of an inheritance, but where Titus came from, he would be treated with special honor by his siblings, even as a child. No wonder that Joseph's older brothers seethed at his dreams that they'd someday bow before him.

The Biblical Soap Opera

We also discovered that a longer "soap opera" also winds through Genesis over who will inherit God's covenant of blessing. The twelve sons of Jacob will one day become the fathers of the twelve tribes of Israel. To an ancient reader, this was a real page-turner. Who will become the tribe that God ultimately uses to bless the world?

You'd think that Jacob's firstborn, Reuben, would be a shoe-in. But he dishonored his father by sleeping with his concubine, so he is disqualified (Genesis 35:22; 49:4). Next in line are Levi and Simeon. But they lose out too because of their cruel attack on the town of Shechem to defend the honor of their sister, Dinah (Genesis 34; 49:5–6). Who finally wins the blessing? Will it be Judah, the fourthborn son of Leah? Or will it be Joseph, the son Jacob loved? You'll have to tune into this ancient *Days of Our Lives* and see for yourself.

I point this out because one problem we modern readers have with the Bible is that we read it as we did when we were children. Our storybook Bibles split the text into short morality lessons, so we assume that's how we should read the text as adults. But it's actually not meant to be a collection of simple children's stories. It's a sophisticated, epic saga with a complex, interwoven plot. Memory and family history were central to the fabric of ancient Near Eastern culture. Sometimes the Bible includes accounts that hardly seem like moral examples, like Reuben's seamy affair or the ugly incident in Shechem. But they need to be there to explain the deeper meaning of later events.

Admittedly, we find the biblical text difficult. Often the rabbis struggled to understand it as well. One teacher told this parable:

> The Scriptures are like a letter written by a king to a subject whom he loves. But when it arrives, the words have faded and the writing is unclear. Out of love for the king, knowing he's reading the very words written by the king's hand, the subject is happy to decipher it—in fact, he sees the difficulty of the task as proof of his love, strong enough to be put to the test.[7]

Imagine that! When we grapple with difficult texts or dig into boring background information, it shows our love for Christ, that we're willing to put time and energy into discerning his words.

One thing that might help is to admit that the Bible actually *is* a difficult, ancient text. Growing up on Sunday school cartoons and flannelgraphs, you might get the impression that the Bible is supposed to be like Chopsticks, a childhood melody that's playable with a few minutes of practice. It's actually more like a Rachmaninoff concerto, with crashing chords and minor themes that linger through many movements. It might take years of practice to play well, but with even a lifetime of performances, its rich strains never get old.

What can Christians discover in Jewish tradition that can help us learn our Scriptures? One thing is simply its importance. One teacher of Jesus' day declared, "If you have learned much Torah, do not puff yourself up, for it was for this purpose that you were created."[8] The rabbis pointed out that the rewards for learning God's Word come not just in this world but the next. It was said, "Some things a person enjoys as the dividends in this world while the principal remains for the person to enjoy in the world to come. They are: honoring parents, deeds of loving-kindness, and making peace between one person and another. But the study of Torah is equal to them all."[9]

The Bible does not yield its meanings to lazy people.
— Rev. Arthur W Pink

Every person from the lowest beggar to the richest millionaire is expected to spend time in study every day, and no one is too old. My mother turned eighty-nine a few weeks ago. She has a good mind, but she's in a nursing home and struggles to fill her days. Often when we chat on the phone I ask her if she's done her Bible study that day. It's not that she doesn't have stacks of Christian reading material around her. But I think she welcomes the idea that something is still expected of her, that she's still supposed to participate in the learning, or at least to remind herself of God's Word once again.

Drip, Drip, Drip

One day as Rabbi Akiva was shepherding his flocks, he noticed a tiny stream trickling down a hillside, dripping over a ledge on its way toward the river below. Below was a massive boulder. Surprisingly, the rock bore a deep impression. The drip, drip, drip of water over the centuries had hollowed away the stone. Akiva commented, "If mere water can do this to hard rock, how much more can God's Word carve a way into my heart of flesh?" Akiva realized that if the water had flowed over the rock all at once, the rock would have been unchanged. It was the slow but steady impact of each small droplet, year after year, that completely reformed the stone.

When I first started studying the Bible's Hebraic context, I wanted one commentary that would teach me everything, one class that would explain it all. If I could learn all the "right answers" in one marathon event, all the better. I find now that God likes to reveal truth over many years, as I study alongside others. I realize now that big "splashes" aren't usually God's way of doing things. Instead, through the slow drip of study and prayer, day after day, year after year, he shapes us into what he wants us to be.

The rabbis commented that each line of the biblical text is a "jewel with seventy faces" — that we should "turn it, and turn it, and turn it again." God's Word is limitless in its ability to speak into our lives. Abraham Heschel sums it up this way:

> Irrefutably, indestructibly, never wearied by time, the Bible wanders through the ages, giving itself with ease to all men, as

if it belonged to every soul on earth. It speaks in every language and in every age.... Though its words seem plain and its idiom translucent, unnoticed meanings, undreamed-of intimations break forth constantly. More than two thousand years of reading and research have not succeeded in exploring its full meaning. Today it is as if it had never been touched, never been seen, as if we had not even begun to read it. Its spirit is too much for one generation to bear. Its words reveal more than we can absorb.[10]

Wisdom for the Walk

1. Read Psalm 1:1–3 and 119:1–20, substituting the word *teaching* for *law*. How does changing the phrase "law of the LORD" to "teaching of the LORD" change how you hear these psalms?

2. Do you see study of the Word as worship? What are some concrete ways that you can incorporate Bible study into your daily and weekly schedule?

3. How close do you come to doing what God told Israel to do in Deuteronomy 6:4–9? How has the study of God's Word increased your love for God and Jesus?

4. What for you is the most frustrating or difficult aspect of studying the Bible?

5. Our evangelical culture tends to be fond of dramatic conversions and turnarounds. In what ways do you think God has shaped you in slow "drips" of study, prayer, and worship?

CHAPTER 12

The Secrets
That God Keeps

The beginning of awe is wonder,
and the beginning of wisdom is awe.
—Abraham Heschel[1]

It's hard not to be captivated by your first close look at a Torah scroll. Jewish scribes pen each one by hand, observing traditions that are thousands of years old for grinding pigments for the ink and preparing the parchment from the skin of a kosher animal. Painstakingly hand-inked, the Hebrew letters are as mysterious as they are lovely. From the very first quill mark, these ancient shapes breathe the voice of God.

בְּרֵאשִׁית בָּרָא אֱלֹהִים אֵת הַשָּׁמַיִם וְאֵת הָאָרֶץ׃

Beresheet bara Elohim et hashamayim v'et ha'aretz.

In the beginning, God created the heavens and the earth.

Even this very first line of Genesis inspires awe, as we imagine God commanding the universe into existence. But even more remarkable is what this line does not say. Even a four-year-old can tell you what unanswered question lies within.

Where did God come from?

Modern readers often stumble over the Bible's lack of answers to our theological questions. We expect the Bible to prove God's existence if its goal is to bring us to faith. But the Bible's first words simply assume God's reality without proving it.

You might be surprised that ancient readers would have found Genesis just as frustrating. Not so much because they didn't believe in a spiritual world, but because they were consumed by fascination

154

for speculating about the origins and secret lives of the gods they worshiped. Creation myths functioned as an ancient *National Enquirer*, satisfying every curiosity. What scandalous truths lurked undiscovered within the spiritual world? What hidden secrets lay behind our mundane reality? Enquiring minds wanted to know.

Near Eastern mythology was filled with fantastic sagas of the gods' titillating secrets of their love affairs and bloody battles against each other. Did you know Marduk formed the earth by murdering his mother, the monster Tiamat, and arranging it out of her dismembered body parts? Did you know that Cronos castrated his father Uranus, and Aphrodite arose out of the foaming sea where Uranus's genitals fell into water? Who needs to hear about the latest Elvis sighting or UFO landing when you had gory tales like this around the evening fire?

The account of creation in Genesis stands in stark contrast to the graphic, bloodstained melodramas of the surrounding peoples. It was a radical departure from everything the ancient world had known. In his classic work, *Understanding Genesis: The World of the Bible in the Light of History*, Nahum Sarna writes:

> The Hebrew account is matchless in its solemn and majestic simplicity. It has no notion of the birth of God and no biography of God. It does not even begin with a statement about the existence of God.... To the Bible, God's existence is as self-evident as life itself.[2]

The biblical account is unique among the creation stories of its time. Spare in detail, Genesis speaks with understated elegance and lofty grandeur. It was a stunning contrast to the supermarket tabloid creation stories that circulated among Israel's neighbors. No attempt is made to explain how God came into existence. Out of an unapologetic majesty, the God of Israel felt no need to answer this obvious question.

Once you see Israel's God in light of the elaborate myths of the surrounding world, you get a sense that the Bible describes reality rather than fantasy. The Israelites were awestruck by their experience on Mount Sinai, their memories seared forever by a real-life encounter with an unearthly, incomprehensible Being. The true God whom they experienced was utterly beyond the wildest dreams of the myth-spinning pagan world and unlike anything anyone had conceived of before. This mysterious entity refused to be represented by any physical form, separating himself completely from every deity they ever imagined. The Israelites simply had no need to concoct fanciful tales about God's origins in order to convince people of his reality.

What the Bible Does Not Say

Even in the first verse of Genesis, we see that God doesn't answer every question. Jewish thinkers believe that the Bible reveals this even in its very first letter. In a Torah scroll, the first letter of the first Hebrew word, *beresheet* (bare-eh-SHEET, "in the beginning"), stands out in bold, inked larger and darker than the rest of the text. This is the Hebrew letter *bet* (ב). This letter corresponds to our letter B. It is the second letter of the Hebrew alphabet, just as "B" is the second letter of the English alphabet.

The rabbis asked the question, "Why do the Scriptures begin with the second letter of the alphabet rather than the first?" Their answer: "To show that the Scriptures do not answer every question, and not all knowledge is accessible to man, but some is reserved for God himself."[3]

Even the shape of the letter *bet* shows this. It is closed on the right side, but it is open on the left. Since Hebrew is read right to left, it appeared to the rabbis that the Scriptures start with a letter that is open in the direction of the reading, but closed toward the direction of the beginning of the text. The *bet* is a one-way sign saying that you need to start here, at the first letter, and move forward, asking what God's will is and how should you live it out. Because the letter *bet* is closed on the top, back, and bottom, it is futile to speculate about what is behind (what existed before creation), or above (in heaven), or below (in hell).

The point of the rabbinic saying about *bet* is not to discourage study and inquiry, but to teach that the Bible should not be used as a vehicle for endless esoteric exploration. Here we find yet another paradox. You can study God's Word all your life and never reach the end of it. But you cannot force the Bible to answer your every question, twisting and wringing the text until it satisfies your every curiosity. God simply does not choose to reveal some things.

One rabbi I met put it this way: "Speculating about what God has not revealed is like pressing on your eyelids with your fingers. The light that you think you see comes only from your own imagination."

The Torah That Starts with *Aleph*

One place where Jewish thinkers found the idea that God does not reveal everything was in the book of Daniel. After the prophet witnessed great visions of apocalyptic battles in the heavens, he queried the angel, "My lord, what will the outcome of all this be?" To which the heavenly messenger curtly responded: "Go your way, Daniel, because the words are rolled up and sealed until the time of the end" (Daniel 12:8–9).

Jesus often responded this same way when enquiring minds asked him about what was to come. After his resurrection, his disciples plied him curiously, saying, "Lord, are you at this time going to restore the kingdom to Israel?" His reply was as blunt as it was opaque: "It is not for you to know the times or dates the Father has set by his own authority" (Acts 1:6–7).

Jesus himself did not know the hour of his return. "But about that day or hour no one knows, not even the angels in heaven, nor the Son, but only the Father" (Mark 13:32). Some things God just does not reveal.

Rabbinic writings, however, contain a fascinating prediction. When the Messiah comes, he will be a teacher of Torah, and his Torah will start with *aleph*. He will reveal what has not been revealed. In his compendium of Jewish legends, Howard Schwartz writes:

> In the messianic era, the Messiah will transmit a new Torah to Israel that he received from God. Then God Himself will expound the Torah in heaven, before all the righteous and the other inhabitants of heaven, including the angels....
>
> The Torah of the mundane world is worthless compared to the Messianic Torah of the World to Come. This Torah will be

taught by the Messiah, or, some say, even by God Himself. This is the Torah that God delights in, which is studied by the righteous in the World to Come. It begins with *aleph*, the first letter of the alphabet, while the earthly Torah begins with *bet*, the second letter.[4]

Even in his earthly life, we see how Jesus began to fulfill this prophecy. Jesus taught how the Torah should be applied, refining for his followers how they should live it out. And then, through his death and resurrection he revealed the great mystery hidden within the Scriptures throughout the ages. As Paul writes, "I have become its servant by the commission God gave me to present to you the word of God in its fullness — the mystery that has been kept hidden for ages and generations, but is now disclosed to the Lord's people" (Colossians 1:25 – 26).

> *The Jewish God is no philosopher and his path is tangled with logical contradiction.*
> — Leon Roth

But until Christ comes again, all things are still not fully revealed. Paul also says, "Now we see only a reflection as in a mirror; then we shall see face to face. Now I know in part; then I shall know fully, even as I am fully known" (1 Corinthians 13:12). Some things God has chosen to preserve as a mystery to human beings in this present age. At the end of time, when Christ sits down on the throne, he alone will be worthy to open the scroll that was sealed shut before Daniel's eyes (Revelation 5:1 – 5).

Disciples Who Don't Always Know

In this day and age, God doesn't answer our every doubt or explain everything to our satisfaction. How can we deal with our inability to know the answers?

The book of Job reveals some profound Hebraic wisdom. There too we encounter God's reluctance to fully divulge himself. Grieved and in agony, Job implores God to explain why he allows the innocent to suffer. After thirty-seven chapters of arguments between Job and his friends, God finally sweeps onto the scene. But when God speaks, he never answers Job's heart-wrenching queries. Rather, he flips the tables and interrogates Job. Job humbly retracts his questions, and God never discloses the answer to the question of the ages.

But God actually does reveal something to Job through his frustrating "non-answer," when he challenges Job to explain the intricacies of nature and describe how he planted the foundations of the earth. When Job realizes that an infinite chasm separates human and divine intellect, he is utterly humbled. Einstein could explain relativity to an amoeba more easily than God could answer Job. What Job sought to know was utterly beyond his ability to grasp.

God's answer to Job should make all the more sense in light of what we've discovered about the universe. In Isaiah 55:9, God proclaimed, "As the heavens are higher than the earth, so are my ways higher than your ways and my thoughts than your thoughts." To the ancients, the heavens appeared to be a great canopy, perhaps five or ten miles up. But now we realize that the stars are billions of light-years away. It should be all the more apparent that if God revealed even a portion of his wisdom, its sheer magnitude would overwhelm us. We forget that God designed everything from neutrons to galaxies, and that we are just specks in comparison to his unfathomable magnitude. Whole libraries have been written to describe the workings of just one human cell. There is wisdom in the humility to be able to say "I don't know" sometimes, and to let God alone know all things.

The Mistake of Job's Friends

Sometimes our desire to read God's mind can get us into hot water. Consider, for instance, Job's friends. Bildad, Eliphaz, and Zophar were understandably shocked by Job's accusations against God. In response, they argued and debated and reasoned with Job about why he must be wrong. They constructed an airtight defense of their faith: God is all-powerful and perfectly just, and he knows every person's sins. Therefore Job must deserve his trials. Every conclusion Job's friends made can be found in dozens of Bible passages, and the men are pious, orthodox, and sincere. If you didn't know the rest of the story, you might even take their side.

When God finally spoke his mind, however, he was furious at their words! In spite of their seemingly flawless reasoning and elaborate defense of his justice, God stormed at Eliphaz, "I am angry with you and your two friends, because you have not spoken the truth about me, as my servant Job has" (Job 42:7). God considered Job's angry words to be truthful and his friends' virtuous defense to be untrue. How could that be?

Neither Job nor his friends knew God's real reasons for allowing Job's trials. As finite humans, God's eternal plan was utterly beyond them. But in spite of their ignorance, Job's friends had the gall to presume to speak for God, glibly accusing Job of sin. This story should humble us whenever we want to put words in God's mouth. How can we know for sure what he would say?

> *Just as water leaves a high place and flows to a low one, so too, God's voice speaking through the Torah goes past one whose spirit is proud and remains with one whose spirit is humble.*
>
> — *Song of Songs Midrash Rabbah* 2:8

Job's friends were making the mistake that Western Christians do today when we don't have a Hebraic understanding of the "knowledge of God"—*da'at Elohim*. A Westerner opens the Bible and wants to prove God's existence and construct a theology to explain God's nature. We would call that "knowledge of God." But in Hebrew, to "know" someone was to be familiar with him through experience and relationship, as a wife knows her husband. "Knowledge" assumes devotion and loyalty and includes intimacy, even sexually. William Barrett explains:

> Biblical man too had his *knowledge*, though it is not the intellectual knowledge of the Greek. It is not the kind of knowledge that man can have through reason alone, or perhaps not through reason at all; he has it rather through body and blood, bones and bowels, through trust and anger and confusion and love and fear; through his passionate adhesion in faith to the Being whom he can never intellectually know.[5]

While Job's friends had a theoretical knowledge of God, Job *knew* God in this latter, Hebraic sense of the word. Christian philosopher Peter Kreeft writes:

Job sticks to God, retains intimacy, passion and care, while the three friends are satisfied with correctness of words, "dead orthodoxy." Job's words do not accurately reflect God as Job's friends' do, but Job himself is in true relationship with God, as the three friends are not: a relationship of heart and soul, life-or-death passion.... Job stays married to God and throws dishes at him; the three friends have a polite non-marriage, with separate bedrooms and separate vacations.[6]

Understanding "knowledge of God" in this Hebraic sense helps us see how God could declare that Job had "spoken what is right" even when he hurled charges at God: "The fatherless child is snatched from the breast; the infant of the poor is seized for a debt.... The groans of the dying rise from the city, and the souls of the wounded cry out for help. But God charges no one with wrongdoing" (Job 24:9, 12). When Job protested on behalf of the suffering of the poor, he was actually expressing the same passionate concern for the needy that God himself felt. But his friends' theology had little concept of God's love, so it misrepresented God's heart. Neither Job nor his friends knew God's thoughts, but Job at least understood God's great compassion for the hurting. Perhaps God would rather hear us voice angry doubts that show concern for others' pain than to knit ourselves a comfortable theology that shows no love.

As Christians, we struggle with how many people suffer in the world unjustly. But we know that in Christ, God willingly suffered as an innocent person to gain forgiveness for our sins. We can always put our trust in God's empathy and goodness, even if we don't know all of his thoughts. Since we are small and finite, we honor God more by trying to love as he loves than by trying to know all that he knows.

Enquiring Minds and End Times

In spite of Jesus' words that no one knows the hour of his return, many Christians nowadays leave no page unturned in their quest for the secrets of his second coming. In our uncertain world, we're understandably drawn to peer into Bible prophecies. We want to make sense of current events and watch for signs of Jesus' victorious return. But when I recall some of the conversations I've had, I wonder if our desire for this knowledge makes us better disciples.

Late one evening, in the dim light of a restaurant booth, I was chatting with a couple I had met at a Bible study conference earlier that day. As we munched together on a large mound of nachos, the husband relayed the latest news going around his prophecy-oriented church. "We heard that the destruction of Damascus is imminent," he commented, nonchalantly.

Coming from a mainline background, I wasn't sure how to take this prophetic word. For a moment I wondered if I should start putting on my coat. Shouldn't we be gathering a prayer group to plead for God's mercy? Had anyone started collecting for a disaster fund? My dinner companions didn't blink an eye, however. The potential deaths of almost two million Syrians didn't seem to cause much concern. What was important to them was the thrill of being in the know. Pass the guacamole, could you?

Perhaps my new friends had heard so many prophecies that this one just sounded like a long-range weather report. And since most predictions hadn't come to pass, they weren't overly concerned. But that seems to be a problem too—wasn't false prophecy a stoneable offense in biblical times?

This conversation brought to mind an unnerving parallel. Like everyone in America, the vivid scenes of the World Trade Center bombing are still frozen in my mind's eye even now: ash-covered survivors are fleeing through the streets, buildings crumbling behind them, and bystanders stand transfixed, mouths agape at the destruction. One time as the 9/11 footage was replayed, I suddenly recalled a scene from a scratchy, black-and-white Japanese sci-fi movie that had seemed laughably surreal before: a giant lizard stomping through the streets of Tokyo while panicky city-dwellers scurry away, buildings toppling behind them. The two scenes were nearly identical, but the first was a nightmarish reality that still brings tears to my eyes, while the other was a silly fantasy, intended to thrill and entertain.

Could it be that end-times prophecies had become a kind of biblical sci-fi movie to my friends, where explosions are all fake and the crowds all background actors and paid extras? Did they consider the Damascus prophecy as something that might happen to real people, like the devastating reality of September 11? How could they not be tormented by the very thought?

We forget that while Christ's second coming may be a glorious victory, it will also be a time of terrible judgment. God himself puts off that day out of mercy: "With the Lord a day is like a thousand years, and a thousand years are like a day. The Lord is not slow in keeping his promise, as some understand slowness. Instead he is patient with you, not wanting anyone to perish, but everyone to come to repentance" (2 Peter 3:8–9).

Early Christians longed for Christ's return to end their persecution. Revelation's scenes comforted them, promising them that God was in control. We also long for Christ's return to deliver us from the corruption and suffering of this world—an escape hatch out of the madness. But if we have friends and family who are lost, shouldn't we be pleading with God to delay yet one more day? The prophet Amos dreaded the day, preaching:

> Woe to you who long
>   for the day of the LORD!
> Why do you long for the day of the LORD?
>   That day will be darkness, not light....
> Will not the day of the LORD be darkness, not light—
>   pitch-dark, without a ray of brightness? (Amos 5:18, 20)

Jesus often spoke about his return at the end. But he never did so to thrill an audience or pitch his next blockbuster end-times novel. Rather, his message was that we should repent, for the day is short. Just as in Lot's day, no one can guess when the hour will be at hand:

> People were eating and drinking, buying and selling, planting and building. But the day Lot left Sodom, fire and sulfur rained down from heaven and destroyed them all. It will be just like this on the day the Son of Man is revealed. (Luke 17:28–30)

When we read Jesus' words about end times, does it remind us to number our days? Or does it draw us into endless speculation and debate? Do we become more concerned about the lost, or do we become callous spectators? Do we look around for an escape hatch, or do we make sure we're using every moment of our lives to share Christ's love and expand his reign on earth?

Wisdom for the Walk

1. Read Job 1–4 and 40–42. If you were in the middle of their debate, what might you have said? Where do you see the logic of Job's friends begin to go off track? Does Kreeft's idea that Job "is married to God and throws dishes at him" make any sense?

2. How does a "both-handed" logic fit in with the Eastern attitude that God is beyond human comprehension?

3. How much does your own spiritual life focus on "knowledge of God" in the theoretical sense, as opposed to *da'at elohim*, a Hebraic knowledge of God?

4. What kinds of things does God *not* reveal in the Bible?

CHAPTER 13

Our Longing
Father

An arrow carries the width of a field,
but repentance carries to the very throne of God.
— *Pesikta Buber*, 163b

In his book *The Mind's Eye*, neurologist Oliver Sacks describes the fascinating case of Sue Barry, who late in life learned to see in a whole new way.[1] As a child she developed *strabismus* (crossed eyes), though surgery had corrected her misaligned eyesight. She had no idea there was anything still amiss with her 20/20 vision until she was in college, when an eye exam revealed that she lacked binocular vision. Her brain had never learned to merge the images from both eyes into one three-dimensional scene. It would ignore each eye in turn and rapidly shift between the two perspectives. As a result, the world appeared flattened, like a painting or television screen.

To Sue, this seemed to be a minor inconvenience, because she had learned to estimate depth and distance in other ways. Still, she couldn't appreciate why others would "ooh" and "ahh" when they peered through a View-Master or an old-fashioned stereoscope. To most people, the dual images would merge to become strangely real — objects would become solid and round, and buildings would stand out against the skyline. But to her, the two pictures remained stubbornly separate, refusing to focus into one.

It wasn't until her late forties that she began therapy to correct her gaze. For months she did exercises to train her eyes to focus together, but noticed little change. Then one afternoon as she was climbing into her car, a startling sight greeted her — the steering wheel had "popped out" from the dashboard. Over the next few days she started experiencing the world in a whole new way. Grass spiked upward from the ground, and flowers seemed "inflated," not flat as they used to be. At lunch she'd stare at the grape she had speared onto her fork, how it hovered in the air above her plate. "I had no idea what I had been missing," Sue said. "Ordinary things looked extraordinary. Light fixtures floated and water faucets stuck way out into space."

Outside one wintry day, she found a wet, lazy snowfall enthralling, the flakes slowly swirling to the ground. She writes:

> I could see the space between each flake, and all the flakes together produced a beautiful three-dimensional dance. In the past, the snow would have appeared to fall in a flat sheet in one plane slightly in front of me. I would have felt like I was looking in on the snowfall. But now, I felt myself within the snowfall, among the snowflakes … as I watched I was overcome with a deep sense of joy. A snowfall can be quite beautiful—especially when you see it for the first time.[2]

The more I've learned about Jesus, the more I've realized that our inner eyes need to have this same "binocular vision" for reading our Bibles. The image we have of Christ in the New Testament should overlap and fuse together with that of his Father, the God who revealed himself in the Old Testament. Didn't Jesus proclaim, "I and the Father are one" (John 10:30)?

If you grew up reading the Bible the way I did, though, your inner "eyes" may keep them stubbornly separate. Your mind may refuse to merge your perception of Jesus with that of his heavenly Father, if you see Christ's compassion for sinners as an utter contrast to the harsh judgment of the God of the Old Testament.[3]

This habit of separating and contrasting the sternness of Israel's God with the love of Christ pervades Christian history.[4] The practice harkens all the way back to a Turkish churchman named Marcion, who lived only a century after Christ. His Greco-Roman, gnostic leanings caused him to develop an extreme case of "double vision," which split the God of the Old Testament entirely away from Christ. He saw them as two different entities and viewed Israel's God as an inferior, warlike deity whom Christ had defeated and replaced. Marcion wanted to throw out the Old Testament entirely and purge the New Testament of all its influence.

If you sympathize with Marcion's viewpoint, you might be surprised, as I was at first, that the early church condemned him as a heretic. They knew that he was making a shocking error, because Jesus proclaimed that "anyone who has seen me has seen the Father" (John 14:9), and Paul preached that Christ is the "image of the invisible God" (Colossians 1:15).

But what's so wrong with Marcion's thinking? What did the early church know that we've forgotten? The more I've listened to Jesus' words through the ears of his Jewish disciples, the more I've started to see that the God of Israel looks more and more like Christ, and Jesus looks more and more like his heavenly Father.

The God of Mr. Spock

I admit it—as a kid, I was a rabid Star Trek fan. I discovered the original series when reruns began airing after school when I was about eleven years old. The one thing that continually puzzled me was why Dr. McCoy couldn't see the obvious superiority of Mr. Spock's logical approach to life. Spock's philosophy was brilliant, to my preteen thinking. He had purged all emotions from his psyche in order to live only by cool-headed reason. All anger, sorrow, and fear were barred from his thoughts, allowing him to be perfectly rational at all times. Sure, emotions like empathy, joy, and love had to go too. But how could you be wrong when you could calculate every potential outcome to the fifth decimal place?

Later in life, I discovered that Mr. Spock's creators had unearthed this idea in classic Greek philosophy. My pointy-eared Vulcan hero was pursuing the Stoic ideal of *apatheia*—seeking virtue by rejecting all passions, by becoming indifferent to pain or pleasure. Many Greco-Roman philosophers saw emotions as fleshly and evil, uncontrollable and opposed to reason. Obviously, in their minds, the supreme God could not be so weak as to express emotion. God must be *impassible*—impervious to passions like anger and sorrow, unaffected by the misery of the human condition. Aristotle's God was the "prime mover," but he himself was unmoved—he was pure thought, devoid of all feelings.[5]

Much of Marcion's difficulty with the Old Testament came from the fact that the God he found there refused to conform to this philosophical ideal. To Marcion, it was obvious that Christ had come to rescue us from this volatile, vengeful God. Even the church fathers who opposed Marcion agreed that the true God must be imperturbable and placid. Clement of Alexandria (AD 150–215) preached that Christians should imitate God's perfect serenity in every detail of their lives: by sitting correctly, speaking quietly, refraining from violent, convulsive laughter, and even burping gently.[6]

The idea that emotions are irrational and unnatural arose from Greco-Roman philosophy and has influenced Western theology for thousands of years. We moderners find God's passions in the Old Testament embarrassing. But what if we looked at Israel's God from a Middle Eastern perspective, which embraces his emotional reality?

Hearing the story of the prodigal son in Luke 15:11–32 in its native context can shed light on the difference in our thinking. We all know this classic parable of Jesus. A son asks for his inheritance and then leaves town, squandering his money on wild living. When he finally hits rock bottom, he turns homeward, hoping that maybe he can wheedle a job from his father as a hired hand. Instead, his father runs out to meet him, throws his arms around him, and hosts a huge banquet to welcome him home, to the chagrin of his elder brother.

Who is the father in Jesus' parable? Obviously, he brims over with the love of Christ toward his wayward son. We commonly understand that the father represents God, but the merciful love of the prodigal's father may seem worlds apart from the God we find in our Old Testament. More than one interpreter has concluded that Jesus' description of God was something new, even blasphemous to his listeners, who only knew the harsh reality of Israel's God.[7] But if you hear Jesus' parable in its Jewish context and consider it in light of Jesus' Scriptures, you find very much the opposite.

Ken Bailey has discovered a wealth of insight on the parables from his study of traditional cultures of the Middle East. Throughout his travels, he has asked his Arab subjects one question hundreds of times: "Have you ever known a son to come to his father and demand his inheritance?" The answer is always the same: it would be unthinkable. It would be an unspeakable outrage, a gross insult to one's father and family.

To us, the wayward son's sin sounds like just a little youthful foolishness, that he'd asked for cash to go see the world. But as Henri Nouwen notes:

> The son's "leaving" is ... a heartless rejection of the home in which the son was born and nurtured and a break with the most precious tradition carefully upheld by the larger community of which he was a part.... More than disrespect, it is a betrayal of the treasured values of family and community. The "distant country" is the world in which everything considered holy at home is disregarded.[8]

In a Middle Eastern setting, the son's offense was a grievous rejection of his family that could even force them to liquidate their estate early. The son didn't care if his father died or his family lost their farm. His only interest was in being able to enjoy life on his own terms.

Bailey tells the story of one pastor whose parishioner came to him in great anguish, exclaiming, "My son wants me to die!" The man's son had broached the question of his inheritance. In that culture, the son's inquiry expressed a wish for his father's demise. The elderly man was in good health, but three months later he passed away. His wife lamented, "He died that night!" The offense was so great that in a sense, the man died the very night his son had spoken to him.[9]

Bailey's insights on this parable reveal a basic error in how Western Christians understand sin and God's response. We see sin as the breaking of arbitrary rules, as accruing parking violations and speeding tickets in a heavenly court system. If we put our faith in Christ, his atoning sacrifice will pay the fine. In this scenario, God is a callous, uncaring judge whose concern is that the law be upheld and the penalty paid in full.

The portrayal of sin in Jesus' parable, however, is that of a broken relationship, a personal offense against a loving Father. The son's actions would have been profoundly hurtful to his family as he cashed in their property for his own gain. Sin does not just "break the rules" and annoy a strict policeman; it is a direct, personal rejection of our loving heavenly Father, who cares for us deeply.

Our Passionate Father

What might surprise Christians even more is that Jesus' portrait of the prodigal son's compassionate father comes straight out of his Scriptures. Its origins are in the words of the prophets, particularly Hosea and Jeremiah. Jesus' story takes on new depth and dimension when we read it in light of their words.

Hosea prophesied to the northern kingdom of Israel after its people had fallen into idolatry, abandoning the Lord to worship other gods. Most of Hosea's work portrays the nation as an adulterous wife, but later on the prophet interweaves this image with that of a son (poetically called "Ephraim," the largest Israelite tribe) who rejects the father who doted on him from infancy. Both ideas express God's deep sense of betrayal at a painful, broken relationship. In Hosea 11, God recalls how he dandled his precious child, reminiscing sadly over how he tenderly cared for his infant son:

> When Israel was a child, I loved him,
>   and out of Egypt I called my son.
> But the more they were called,
>   the more they went away from me.
> They sacrificed to the Baals
>   and they burned incense to images.
> It was I who taught Ephraim to walk,
>   taking them by the arms;
> but they did not realize
>   it was I who healed them.
> I led them with cords of human kindness,
>   with ties of love;
> To them I was like one who lifts
>   A little child to the cheek,
>   And I bent down to feed them. (Hosea 11:1–4)

A couple generations later, Jeremiah uses the same mixed imagery to reveal God's feelings toward his people:

> How gladly would I treat you like my children
>   and give you a pleasant land,
>   the most beautiful inheritance of any nation.
> I thought you would call me "Father"
>   and not turn away from following me.
> But like a woman unfaithful to her husband,
>   so you, Israel, have been unfaithful to me. (Jeremiah 3:19–20)

God was as aggrieved and wounded at his children's betrayal as any of the Arabs that Ken Bailey encountered, and he mourned for the lost intimacy with his people. Philip Yancey pictures God's response this way:

> Follow around some first-time parents. Their conversation seems limited to one topic: The Child. They crow that their wrinkled, ruddy baby is the most beautiful child ever born. They spend hundreds of dollars on equipment to videotape the first babbling words and the first lurching steps.... Such strange behavior expresses a new parent's pride and joy in a human relationship like no other.
>
> In choosing Israel, God was seeking such a relationship.... His voice sings with pride as he reminisces about the early days: "Is not Ephraim my dear son, the child in whom I delight?" But the joy fades away as God abruptly shifts from the perspective of a parent to that of a lover, a wounded lover. *What have I done wrong?* he demands in a tone of sadness, and horror, and rage.[10]

You might expect God to respond to his people's betrayal with a blast of divine wrath. And in a Middle Eastern context, that's what a father of a rebellious son, by all rights, should do. Considering the great shame that the son had brought on his family, the aged patriarch should have preserved his dignity by ignoring the young man's pleas and driving him off with curses. He should have declared his son disowned, dead in the eyes of his family. But instead, the thought of destroying Israel grieves God. His compassion overwhelms his desire for justice and restrains his hand:

How can I give you up, Ephraim?
    How can I hand you over, Israel?…
My heart is changed within me;
    all my compassion is aroused.
I will not carry out my fierce anger,
    nor will I devastate Ephraim. (Hosea 11:8–9)

Jeremiah describes God's feelings this way:

Oh! Ephraim is my dear, dear son,
my child in whom I take pleasure!
Every time I mention his name,
my heart bursts with longing for him!
Everything in me cries out for him.
Softly and tenderly I wait for him. (Jeremiah 31:20 *The Message*)

Have you ever wondered what went through the mind of the prodigal's father as he spent interminable hours scanning the distant haze, straining to see his son's silhouette on the horizon? Jeremiah was expressing his inner thoughts here in Jeremiah 31, as he described God's yearning for his wayward children to return home.

Jesus finds in Jeremiah's words a profound love that wins out over anger and bursts into joy when a beloved child finally comes home. Here we see the compassionate Father that Jesus knew from his Scriptures, who longs for restoration no matter how grievous his children's rebellion. Here we find that Christ's love for sinners originates within his loving Father.

Was Jesus using Jeremiah and Hosea as the background of his parable of the prodigal son? From how other early rabbis preached from these texts, it seems not unlikely. About a century after Jesus, Rabbi Meir told this parable based on Jeremiah 3:12, 25, and 31:9:

There once was a prince who fell into evil ways. His father, the king, sent a tutor to him who appealed to him saying, "Repent, my son." But the son sent him back with the message, "How can I have the effrontery to return? I am ashamed to come before you." Thereupon his father sent back word, "My son, is a son ever ashamed to return to his father? And is it not to your father that you will be returning?"[11]

Rabbi Meir used Jeremiah's prophecies to show that God is always willing to receive a repentant sinner, no matter how unforgiveable the sin might seem. He too saw a God whose fatherly love welcomes erring children.[12]

God Is Not Indifferent

The wounded anger of a deserted father is a far cry from the aloof judgment that many of us mistakenly see in the God of the Old Testament. Rather than God being distant and unfeeling, a more biblical understanding is that God's anger at sin exists *in tension* with his overwhelming love. The same passionate concern for humanity that causes God's anger is also the source of his tenacious, everlasting love that bursts out in joy when his children finally come home.

All of the prophets, in fact, express God's anguish when his children abandon him, and how he restrains his wrath at sin out of his *hesed*, his mercy and loving-kindness. This is the Old Testament God's answer to our angry question, "How can you be so indifferent to the evil in the world?" Our accusations are actually against the impassible God whom we've conjured up out of our own imagination. The real God is just the opposite, because indifference to evil is *in itself* evil. In *The Prophets*, Abraham Heschel writes:

> There is an evil which most of us condone and are even guilty of: indifference to evil. We remain neutral, impartial, and not easily moved by the wrongs done unto other people.... All prophecy is one great exclamation; God is not indifferent to evil! He is always concerned, He is personally affected by what man does to man.... This is one of the meanings of the anger of God: the end of indifference!
>
> Man's sense of injustice is a poor analogy to God's sense of injustice. The exploitation of the poor is to us a misdemeanor, to God it is a disaster. Our reaction is disapproval; God's reaction is something no language can convey. Is it a sign of cruelty that God's anger is aroused when the rights of the poor are violated, when widows and orphans are oppressed?[13]

If God is not wounded by his people's suffering or angered at their cruelty toward each other, he would be a God who cannot love, theologian Jürgen Moltmann concludes. In *The Crucified God* he writes:

> A God who cannot suffer is poorer than any human. For a God who is incapable of suffering is a being who cannot be involved. Suffering and injustice do not affect him. And because he is so completely insensitive, he cannot be affected or shaken by anything. He cannot weep, for he has no tears. But the one who cannot suffer cannot love either. So he is also a loveless being.[14]

God's passionate reality made perfect sense in a society where tears of mourning and songs of joy were a normal part of life. This was where Job could "throw dishes at God" out of frustration, and King David could dance for joy through the streets of Jerusalem. The Greek rejection of emotions arose out of an intellectual pride that was willing to sacrifice one's full humanity for the sake of being in constant control.

God also described his passionate nature when he called himself *El Kanna (El kah-NAH)*, a "jealous" or "zealous" God (Exodus 34:14). We wince at God's self-description, but here *kanna* has the best sense of the word. It expresses an impassioned protectiveness and commitment that expects utter loyalty in return. God is *not* indifferent or disinterested; rather, he's an Arab father who is crushed by his son's apparent lack of love. God is a mother bear who roars a warning if you get too close to her cubs. God is a jilted boyfriend who's beside himself when he spots his true love on another guy's arm. Israel's God is not less emotional than we are; he is even *more*.

Just as we do, Jewish thinkers struggled with the tension between God's justice and his mercy. One of the ways they contemplated it was by putting it into a parable. Once again, they took a typically "two-handed" approach:

> This may be compared to a king who had a craftsman make for him an extremely delicate, precious goblet. The king said, "If I pour hot liquid into it, it will burst, if I pour ice cold liquid into it,

it will crack!" What did the king do? He mixed the hot and the cold together and poured it into it, and it did not crack.

Even so did the Holy One, blessed be He, say: "If I create the world on the basis of the attribute of mercy alone, it will be overwhelmed with sin; but if I create it on the basis of the attribute of justice alone, how could the world endure? I will therefore create it with both the attributes of mercy and justice, and may it endure!"[15]

This story doesn't use detailed theological terminology to explain how God's justice can coexist with his compassion. It merely points out that both mercy and justice are needed in order for God to reign over creation while allowing it to survive. Once again, the rabbis tried to describe God's actions without expecting that they could fully systematize God's every thought.

Besides being a wise approach to looking at the nature of God, the parable of the prodigal son also illustrates Judaism's pragmatic approach toward life. It points out that a blend of mercy and justice is often what we need in our relationships. Parents struggle with the balance of enforcing rules along with showing grace to their children — not being too strict, yet not letting their kids run wild. When our spouses do something that hurts us, should we overlook it and let it slide, or should we bring our hurt and anger to their attention?

> We are brazen and You are gracious and merciful;
> We are stubborn and You are patient;
> We are imbued with iniquity and You are imbued with mercy;
> We are of fleeting duration, as a shadow, and You are He whose years are endless.
> — Yom Kippur Liturgy

Christians often think that there's only one right way to act in these situations — either never to let sin go unpunished, or always to forgive. But the reality is that we need to have discernment and balance. Even God walks the difficult line between mercy and judgment! We can turn to him for guidance because he knows our struggles beyond what we could ever imagine.

God's Costly Covenant

Rather than embracing the tension between God's mercy and his justice, Westerners want to resolve the paradox. In order to ease the strain, something must break, and what often does is our concept of God. God splits into personalities: "Wrathful Father" (or maybe "Callous Judge") and "Compassionate Son." But what about Jesus being "one" with his Father? If you see dual images of God where Jesus says there's only one, it should tell you that your inner "eyes" aren't focusing correctly.

Even in the beginning of Genesis, a different picture of God emerges. If you're looking for God's unflinching judgment, the place you'd most expect to find it is at the time of Noah. You'd expect to find God nearly exploding with fury at the wicked deeds of humanity, when humankind had filled the world with violence, when "every inclination of the thoughts of the human heart was only evil all the time" (Genesis 6:5).

But instead of wrath, the Bible says that God "was grieved" (Genesis 6:6 NASB), that his "heart was deeply troubled" (NIV). A murderous gangrene had infected his precious children, causing them to destroy themselves and each other. God's anguish was so great that he even "regretted that he had made human beings" (6:6).

In Hebrew there's a connection between God's pain and that of fallen humanity. Because of Eve's sin, her sorrow (*etzev*, ET-tsev) in bearing children will multiply, and Adam will labor in sorrow (*etzev*) to make the earth produce food (Genesis 3:16–19). This is the same word that describes God's sorrow when his heart is "grieved" in Genesis 6:6. Like Eve, God's precious children would now fill his heart with pain; and like Adam, his beautiful earth would now be cursed by human bloodshed. Adam and Eve's sorrows were a small taste of the pain God himself felt at his broken world.

Our world today is still filled with violence; we are no different than the generation that made God regret he had created us. When you consider the mass graves of the genocides of this past century, you realize that humans really are capable of evil beyond the limits of the imagination. Yet, after the flood God promised, "Never again will I curse the ground because of humans, even though every inclination of the human heart is evil from childhood. And never again will I destroy all living creatures, as I have done" (Genesis 8:21).

Why was God's response to evil different than before?

Here, in the Scripture's first pages, I wonder if we don't see God's answer to the classic question, "If God is good and all powerful, why doesn't he destroy evil?" In the flood epic, God revealed what his righteous response to human evil would be—universal judgment. We imagine that God could wave a magic wand and make sin disappear, but this simply isn't an option, any more than God can make triangles with four sides. It's a logical impossibility, Spock might say. God bears with corrupt humanity because the alternative is the death of every sinner on earth. The fact that a good God does not destroy evil is *not* because he's impotent; it's because he's merciful.[16]

> *God does not judge the deeds of man impassively, in a spirit of cool detachment. His judgment is imbued with a feeling of intimate concern. He is the father of all men, not only a judge; He is a lover engaged to his people, not only a king.*
> — Abraham Heschel

We discover God's mercy in his very next words, when he makes a covenant in Genesis 9. Throughout the rest of the Bible, when God made a covenant, it was of monumental importance in his plan of salvation. The covenants with Abraham, with Israel on Mount Sinai, and with King David to send the Messiah were all key events in salvation history. In this very first covenant he made with humankind, he committed himself to find another answer to sin rather than just to destroy sinners. It is the most basic, yet most amazing covenant of all—to promise to redeem humanity from evil rather than to judge it for its sin. In embryonic form, this covenant points toward the coming of Christ.

For God, this decision had an enormous price. Walter Brueggemann explains:

> God resolves that he will stay with, endure, and sustain his world, notwithstanding the sorry state of humankind.... It is now clear that such a commitment on God's part is costly. The

God-world relation is not simply that of strong God and needy world. Now it is a tortured relation between a grieved God and a resistant world.... This is a key insight of the gospel against every notion that God stands outside of the hurt as a judge.[17]

Terrence Fretheim also notes:

> Given God's decision to bear with the creation in all of its wickedness, this means for God a continuing grieving of the heart. Thus the promise to Noah and all flesh in Gen. 9:8–17 *necessitates* divine suffering. By deciding to endure a wicked world, while continuing to open up the heart to that world, means that God has decided to take personal suffering upon God's own self.[18]

God opts to suffer alongside his people because he loves them in spite of their sinfulness. From the moment he made that decision, we see the passionate love that ultimately led to the cross, to bring his prodigal children back to him. And we see his overwhelming joy when a single sinner repents and turns homeward.

The more you see God's heart, the more you see the character of Christ from the very first pages of Genesis. Our dual images of God in the Old and New Testaments start to merge together when we see that the suffering of Christ began in his Father's heart at the dawn of creation, when we see God our Father bearing the cross for our sins. It's only when we focus the two images into one that we gain spiritual "depth perception" and begin to grasp how wide and long and high and deep is the love of God.

Wisdom for the Walk

1. Do you have difficulty seeing Christ as one with his Father? Have you ever resonated with Marcion's feelings that it would be fine to throw out the Old Testament?

2. In your mind's eye, is God far away and indifferent to this world?

3. Read Jeremiah 2–3 and 31. Where do you see the prodigal son story there? How about in Hosea 11?

4. What difference does it make to your conception of God if you see him as being grieved by sin rather than indifferent or enraged?

5. Have you ever struggled with the tension between love and anger?

6. For parents: If one of your children embarrassed and disowned your family and then came home, how would you respond? Do you know anyone who has gone through a situation like this?

God's Image
Stamped in Dust

Whoever destroys one soul is regarded by the Torah
as if he had destroyed a whole world,
and whoever saves one soul,
is regarded as if he had saved a whole world.
—Mishnah, *Sanhedrin* 4:5

One day when Jesus was teaching in Jerusalem, his usual crowd mysteriously filled with Jesus' priestly opponents. Had they finally had a change of heart? Jesus paused, glancing their way as he ended a lesson. From the back, one of their hands quietly rose, signaling a question for the esteemed rabbi. "What about Caesar—should they pay taxes to him or not?"

Everyone knew how loaded this question was. Should the Jewish people support a corrupt regime that oppressed them and opposed their faith in the one true God? A sneer formed across their priestly faces. They knew Jesus would be trapped, whatever he said.

"Pay the taxes"—and he'll be skewered by the zealots.

"Don't pay them"—and the Romans will have his head.

Jesus replied, "Show me a denarius." As the priest's hand fumbled through the folds of his robe to withdraw a coin, guffaws arose from the crowd. As the shiny disk glinted in the sun, the realization dawned on him that he had just revealed his own hypocrisy. Denarii were strictly forbidden from the Temple, because they bore Caesar's blasphemous claim to be divine. Some purists, like the Essenes, refused to touch or even look at this particular coin. But the cleric had no qualms about carrying these pagan money pieces in his pocket. The man's face reddened as he saw how easily the Galilean rabbi exposed his insincerity.

Now it was Jesus' disciples turn to smirk. With a look of feigned innocence, Jesus inquired, "Whose image, whose likeness is on this coin?" Caesar's, of course. It was precisely that image that made the coin forbidden in the Temple. No graven images were permitted, especially not the likeness of an emperor who insisted that he be worshiped as deity. Caesar's taxes were not just about financial support, but about religious veneration. You were honoring the "god" Caesar by paying tribute to him.[1]

Then came the bombshell of Jesus' answer—"Give to Caesar what is Caesar's, and to God what is God's." The way Christians have traditionally interpreted his words is hardly earth-shattering: we should pay our taxes and give to the church.

But Jesus was saying something more. What has God stamped with *his* image? Human beings! Therefore, we should offer our lives back to God. Humans are the handiwork of God. We owe our very existence to him. The fact that we bear his image shows his ownership over us. Caesar was *not* God, so let him have his measly coins back. But humans owe our very lives to God. He's stamped his seal on us to show that it is he alone that we must serve.[2]

Jesus' brilliance is evidenced not only by his evasion of the trick question designed to trap him, but by the zinger of a sermon that he wove into his response. We can surmise that Jesus was making this point because other early rabbis compared God to a king stamping out coins. It was said, "For a king mints many coins with a single seal, and they are all alike. But the King of kings ... minted all human beings with that seal of his with which he made the first person, yet not one of them is like anyone else."[3] It shows the infinite glory of God that we are all stamped with his image, and yet we are unique.

A king engraved his image on his coins to show that he "owned" them—they were under his authority and part of his reign. Wherever his coins circulated, the king was claiming that territory as part of his kingdom. By making this parallel, Jesus was pointing out that because God had stamped his image on us, God's reign was far beyond anything Caesar could imagine—it is over all of humanity. Humans are God's coins, meant to be spent on his world, proclaiming God's kingdom wherever we circulate.

In the Image of God

When Jesus picked up on the "image" of Caesar on his coins, he was using a key motif within biblical and Jewish thought—that we are made "in the image of God." For thousands of years, Jews have ruminated over the implications of Genesis 1:27:

> So God created mankind in his own image, in the image of
> God he created him; male and female he created them.

What does it mean that human beings are made "in God's image"? How can the profound ideas within this phrase shed light on our calling as humans and our mission as Jesus' disciples?

Paul says that we should put off our old corrupt self and live as our new self that is "*created to be like God* in true righteousness and holiness" (Ephesians 4:24, italics added). We are to be "imitators of God," displaying his *hesed*—his compassion and faithfulness to others. It seems fitting, then, that the way Christ chose to train his disciples was that of the ancient rabbis. As his disciples walked with him day after day, they learned his approach to the Scriptures. But even more importantly, they saw how he lived out his own teaching. They would imitate their rabbi's example to learn to "walk in his way," and then go out and disciple others to live that way too.[4]

The nature of that holiness which the true Christian seeks to possess is no other than the restoration of the image of God to his soul.
— William Wilberforce

Paul illustrates this teaching method when he urged the Corinthians to imitate his example, and then sent his disciple Timothy to be with them, saying, "He will remind you of my way of life in Christ Jesus, which agrees with what I teach everywhere in every church" (1 Corinthians 4:17). Paul's goal was not just to give them a new set of beliefs but to change their way of living, so that they would become imitators of Christ too.

Physician Paul Brand relays an experience from when he was training doctors in India that taught him how effective this teaching method is. One morning on rounds, he watched as a young intern interviewed a new patient in the wards. Brand's student kneeled by the woman's bed and examined her for signs of pain as he gently inquired about her private past, his calm demeanor reassuring her all the while.

Suddenly, something caught Brand's eye about the young man's expression. It reminded him distinctly of a mentor of his back in England, Professor Pilcher. The resemblance was uncanny, as if the student had taken acting lessons. Later Brand asked the young man if he had ever studied with the esteemed Dr. Pilcher. At first he and his fellow students stared at him, confused, but then they grinned. "We don't know any Professor Pilcher," one said. "But Dr. Brand, that was your expression he was wearing." Thinking back on his own training with Dr. Pilcher, Brand writes:

> I had thought I was learning from him techniques of surgery and diagnostic procedures. But he had also imprinted his instincts, his expression, his very smile so that they too would be passed down from generation to generation in an unbroken human chain. It was a kindly smile, perfect for cutting through the fog of embarrassment to encourage a patient's honesty. What textbook or computer program could have charted out the facial expression needed at that exact moment within the curtain?
>
> Now I, Pilcher's student, had become a link in the chain, a carrier of his wisdom to students some nine thousand miles away. The Indian doctor, young and brown-skinned, speaking in Tamil, shared few obvious resemblances with either Pilcher or me. Yet somehow he had conveyed the likeness of my old chief so accurately that it had transported me back to university days with a start.[5]

Dr. Brand had been imprinted by his mentor's demeanor and was unconsciously passing it on. In just the same way, as we imitate Christ as his disciples, we carry his image to those around us and cause them to become like him too.

The Exceedingly Ugly Man

Within Jewish thought, being made in the "image of God" carries other important implications. An amusing story was told about a famous second-century teacher, Rabbi Eleazar. One day, as his donkey ambled down the river path on its leisurely trip home from a study session, the rabbi's thoughts lingered back to the profound truths he had unearthed with his fellow *haverim* ("study partners"). He was still basking in the glow of victory, reveling in how he had pulled together three obscure passages to win a heated debate. Only his donkey heard his soft chuckles of self-congratulation.

Or so he thought. As he came around the bend, he almost collided with a bedraggled peasant, an exceedingly ugly man. The homely man's tattered rags seemed almost too elegant for his malformed face, with bulbous eyes and nose to match.

Recognizing the highly esteemed sage, the poor farmer bowed low with the traditional greeting, "Peace be upon you, rabbi!"

But Eleazar's disgust burst out before he could stop himself. "*Raca!* How ugly you are! Is everyone in your village as ugly as you?"

"I don't know," the peasant replied. "But go and tell the craftsman who made me, 'How ugly is the vessel that you have made.'"

Remorse overwhelmed the rabbi. From his donkey he fell to the ground and prostrated himself before the man. "I submit myself to you, forgive me!"

In this classic tale, called "The Rabbi and the Exceedingly Ugly Man," a great scholar is humbled by a simple man's reply to his insult.[6] The rabbi had forgotten that God himself was the misshapen man's creator. God was the potter and the man's features were God's handiwork. To call the man ugly was to suggest that God lacked artistic talent. The peasant had made a profound point — that humans are God's creative work, that we are designed by him. Every human being should be treated as a special creation of God, because all are precious to him.

What might not be as obvious to modern readers is that an even greater comeback was hidden within the peasant's reply. Human beings are not just clay blobs thrown randomly on God's pottery wheel to look like whatever they will. They are fashioned "in God's image." Each person is the Master's own self-portrait in physical form. In light of this, Rabbi Eleazar had not only insulted God by saying that he was a poor artist, but that God was an ugly one too![7]

The New Testament writers said similar things. James tells us, "With the tongue we praise our Lord and Father, and with it we curse human beings, who have been made in God's likeness"—*his very image* (James 3:9). How impossibly ironic it is to proclaim God's greatness in one breath, and then to turn around and insult one of his own precious creations, his self-portraits.

God's Royal Representatives

Typically, Westerners approach the idea of being made in the "image of God" by asking what unique attributes we have in common with God, like reason, intelligence, moral conscience, and the like. In Abraham's time, however, being the "image of God" actually had a different connotation. A god's "image" was its physical representation on earth, like an idol, or the sun or moon. Even more important, kings were said to be the "images" of their gods. A king represented his gods to his subjects, with the belief that the gods reigned over their people through the king's commands.

God's pronouncement in Genesis 1:27 actually has this royal sense. The very next line commands humans to "rule over the fish in the sea and the birds in the sky and over every living creature that moves on the ground." Humans have been appointed to reign over God's creation, to be God's representatives on earth.

Many of us cringe at the idea of humans "reigning" over creation. It sounds like a license to exploit the earth to please our every whim. Since we don't have many kings and queens in our midst, it sounds like we're supposed to emulate Imelda Marcos, plundering her country to expand her shoe collection. But if we represent a loving God, our calling is to show his kindness toward the rest of creation. As biblical scholar Bernard Anderson puts it, "Human beings are to exercise sovereignty within God's sovereignty, so that all earthly creatures may be related to God through them and thus join the creation's symphony of praise to the Creator."[8]

C. S. Lewis weaves this idea into his Chronicles of Narnia. When Peter, Susan, Edmund, and Lucy step through the wardrobe, they discover an ancient prophecy that they are the "Sons of Adam" and "Daughters of Eve" who are destined to become the benevolent, rightful rulers of the land of Narnia. In one conversation, Lewis points out the utter democracy of this calling: "You come of the Lord Adam and the Lady Eve—and that is both honour enough to erect the head of the poorest beggar, and shame enough to bow the shoulders of the greatest emperor in earth."[9]

> *A procession of angels pass before a human being wherever he or she goes, proclaiming, "Make way for the image of God."*
> — Joshua ben Levi

The idea that humans are God's representatives might not strike you as terribly earth-shattering. But in ancient times, the idea that humanity is precious in God's sight expressed a revolutionary, unheard-of truth. Men and women (both!) were God's royal image bearers, and their lives had meaning and dignity in the eyes of God. If you lived in ancient times, this was a radical new idea. Mythologies in the ancient Near East portrayed humans as the slaves of cruel, capricious, callous gods, created so that the gods could enjoy leisure. A pessimism haunted ancient writings that life was worthless and futile. Homer lamented, "This is the lot the gods have spun for miserable men, that they should live in pain; yet themselves are sorrowless."[10]

In much of the ancient world, life was cheap. Historians estimate that if you lived in a tribal society, your chances of dying a violent death at the hands of someone else were about one in six, because war, slavery, and barbaric cruelty were shockingly commonplace.[11] Even murder was seen as a score that could be settled by paying off the offended clan. In one Hittite court case, a man attacked another as he was fording a river, seizing his ox by the tail and letting the owner drown. The murderer's penalty was to move to the victim's village to make up for the lost labor. To the Hittites, the actual loss of life meant nothing.[12]

In biblical thought, however, murder was an offense against

God himself, because humans bear God's image. Because life was of supreme worth, a murderer couldn't buy off his victim's family, but suffered the death penalty (Genesis 9:6; Numbers 35:31).[13] Property crimes like theft, however, were never punishable by death, unlike everywhere else. Israel's laws were unique in reflecting God's great concern for humanity, down to the weakest members of society. When Jewish thinkers grasped how this unique theme shaped their laws, one result was the rabbinic principle of *pikuach nephesh* ("preservation of life") — that in applying the laws of the Torah, human life must always take priority. To us the sacredness of human life is a given. We don't realize how novel this idea was in its time.

Knowing Our Worth

The words of Genesis 1 express a profound paradox: though we are as insignificant as dust, we reflect the glory of God himself. Adam's name reflected the fact that God had formed him from the *adamah* (ah-dah-MAH, "ground" in Hebrew). His task was to work the *adamah*, and when he died he would return to the *adamah*. Adam was the consummate "earthling." And yet God blew his very own breath into Adam, setting humankind apart in a unique way.

One eighteenth-century rabbi put it this way: "A person should always carry two slips of paper, one in each pocket. On one it should be written 'The world was created for my sake,' and on the other it should say 'I am but dust and ashes.'"[14] On days when we feel discouraged and worthless, we should read the first one. On days when we're consumed with pride and our own self-importance, we should read the other.

In *The Weight of Glory*, C. S. Lewis points out how knowing the eternal significance of every person we meet should change how we treat others:

> It is a serious thing to live in a society of possible gods and goddesses, to remember that the dullest and most uninteresting person you can talk to may one day be a creature which, if you saw it now, you would be strongly tempted to worship, or else a

horror and a corruption such as you now meet, if at all, only in a nightmare.... There are no ordinary people. You have never talked to a mere mortal. Nations, cultures, arts, civilizations— these are mortal, and their life is to ours as the life of a gnat. But it is immortals whom we joke with, work with, marry, snub, and exploit—immortal horrors or everlasting splendors.[15]

Often we struggle with knowing our worth, and we try to prove it through competition, pride, and tearing others down. Conversely, we might think that humility is about seeing ourselves as useless, untalented, and insignificant. God's idea of humility, however, is to realize that each one of us is precious in his sight, and yet *everyone else is too*. Perhaps we should write ourselves a third slip of paper: "All of humanity is precious to God, not just me."

Indeed, Heschel writes that seeing that each human being bears God's image leads to the love of one's neighbors, and even of one's enemies:

> We must never be oblivious of the equality of the divine dignity of all men. The image of God is in the criminal as well as in the saint.... The basic dignity of man is not made up of his achievements, virtues, or special talents. It is inherent in his very being. The commandment "Love your neighbor as yourself" (Leviticus 19:18) calls upon us to love not only the virtuous and the wise but also the vicious and the stupid man.... The image-love is a love of what God loves, an act of sympathy, of participation in God's love. It is unconditional and regardless of man's merits or distinctions.[16]

A Palace in Flames

Dust ... it's the most worthless substance imaginable. Yet God squeezed together some soil, blew his breath into it, and formed a noble being appointed to reign over the rest of creation. We're the ultimate silk purse from a sow's ear—royalty brought forth from a clump of dirt. When Adam and Eve sinned, their "feet of clay" showed through, and this became their ultimate penalty. They will disintegrate back into the worthlessness from which they came: "For dust you are and to dust you will return" (Genesis 3:19).

This melancholy theme winds through the Scriptures — that because of sin, all of human striving and glory will crumble into ashes. The wicked are like chaff that the wind blows away. This is the tragedy of the human condition. God created us as his regal image bearers, but instead we perish and decay into dust:

> He brings princes to naught
>> and reduces the rulers of this world to nothing.
> No sooner are they planted,
>> no sooner are they sown,
>> no sooner do they take root in the ground,
> than he blows on them and they wither,
>> and a whirlwind sweeps them away like chaff.
>>> (Isaiah 40:23–24)

Over and over, Paul describes Christ's great redemptive mission in these terms. In Philippians 2, he quotes an early hymn, where Christ, the "very nature [image] of God," the true king over all of creation, deigns to take the image of the "man of dust," even humbling himself to suffer mankind's loathsome fate of death. Because Christ descended to the depths of human devastation, God "exalted him to the highest place and gave him the name that is above every name" (Philippians 2:6–9). Paul promises that because of Christ's victory over death, we will be resurrected in bodies that bear his image: "Just as we have borne the image of the earthly man, so shall we bear the image of the heavenly man" (1 Corinthians 15:49).

Seeing Christ's mission this way sheds light on our own calling. After the Holocaust, Heschel likened the world to a "palace in flames," writing, "The world is in flames, consumed by evil.... This essential predicament of man has assumed a peculiar urgency in our time, living as we do in a civilization where factories were established in order to exterminate millions of men, women, and children; where soap was made of human flesh."[17]

Just imagine: a nation's beloved royal family, its constitutional documents, its finest art treasures — all turning to ashes. Preciousness turning to worthlessness in a blink of an eye. Created in God's image, humans are lovingly fashioned to be his royal representatives. Because they have inestimable worth in God's eyes, their destruction is tragic indeed. Yet, shockingly, humans are the *source* of the devastation on earth.

On the morning of September 11, 2001, thousands of panicked office workers fled the doomed World Trade Center. As they scrambled down the staircases, a remarkable sight greeted them. Wave after wave of firefighters were passing them, not running away from the burning tower but straight *into* it, most all of them to certain death. They were ascending the staircases into the inferno in a heroic effort to save those who were perishing. Bystanders paused and applauded the breathtaking sacrifice they were witnessing.

Christ is the captain of the rescue squad of this earthly palace of flames. He himself heads the charge into the burning devastation and sacrifices himself to redeem perishing humanity. In Revelation, all of creation bows down to worship Christ because of his heroic act on our behalf:

With your blood you purchased for God
    persons from every tribe and language and people and nation.
You have made them to be a kingdom and priests to serve our God,
    and they will reign on the earth.…
Worthy is the Lamb, who was slain,
    to receive power and wealth and wisdom and strength
    and honor and glory and praise! (Revelation 5:9–12)

As Christ's disciples, our calling is to join him in his rescue mission. It's extremely dangerous, and it may even require your life. But if you are walking in your Rabbi's dust, you are called to follow him into the ashes of our crumbling, burning world.

That's why Jesus spoke so often about our reward. At the end of Revelation, he promises, "Look, I am coming soon! My reward is with me, and I will give to each person according to what they have done" (Revelation 22:12). When you realize that your mission is inherently costly and hazardous, you see why the highest accolades will go to those for whom it has cost most. Those who served without any earthly recognition will experience great joy when Christ himself reveals their faithfulness. No one will feel jealous at another's reward — indeed, everyone will burst into applause when they hear what others have accomplished on Christ's behalf.

The ultimate reward for Christ's disciples, however, will be the praise of God himself, when he says, "Well done, good and faithful servant!" (Matthew 25:21, 23) for our willingness to serve his Son's mission of redeeming the Father's precious world.

Wisdom for the Walk

1. Which slip of paper do you need to read most often: "I am but dust and ashes," "The world was created for my sake," or "All of humanity is precious to God, not just me"?

2. When was the last time you saw the demeanor of Christ imprinted on the life of one of his disciples? What did it look like?

3. Read Genesis 1–4. What effect did sin and the fall have on the "image of God" in humans, as you see it?

4. Who are the most despicable people you know of? How does knowing that God formed them in his image affect your thinking about them?

5. How does thinking about your mission as a disciple change how you understand Jesus' words about "reward"? See, for instance, Luke 6:20–23 or 6:35.

Afterword

One of the cardinal rules of writing, as one person puts it, is to write an opening sentence that functions like "a gunshot — *blam!* — and you'll have your reader's attention immediately. Make it powerful enough and as the smoke of the gun clears the reader will read on with the shot still ringing in their ears."[1]

Consider a few memorable first lines:

- It was a bright cold day in April, and the clocks were striking thirteen. — *1984* by George Orwell
- We started dying before the snow, and like the snow, we continued to fall. — *Tracks* by Louise Erdrich
- Of all the things that drive men to sea, the most common disaster, I've come to learn, is women. — *Middle Passage* by Charles Johnson

The Bible, too, has its share of memorable opening lines. My favorite among them are these:

> In the beginning was the Word, and the Word was with God, and the Word was God. He was with God in the beginning. Through him all things were made; without him nothing was made that has been made. In him was life, and that life was the light of all mankind. — The Gospel of John

I like the way John pulls you in. Who, you wonder, is this mysterious Word, and why does John link him to God and the world's beginning? Curious minds want to know. And so you page back to the very beginning, to the opening lines of Genesis 1:

> In the beginning God created the heavens and the earth. Now the earth was formless and empty, darkness was over the

surface of the deep, and the Spirit of God was hovering over the waters.

And God said, "Let there be light," and there was light.

The links jump out at you as you compare the two passages.

In Genesis, God creates the world by simply speaking it into being. Light out of darkness. Something out of nothing.

Then it occurs to you that in the New Testament Jesus speaks words that prove uniquely powerful: "He got up, rebuked the wind and said to the waves, 'Quiet! Be still.' Then the wind died down and it was completely calm" (Mark 4:39). Or this: "Then he said to the paralytic, 'Get up, take your mat and go home.' And the man got up and went home" (Matthew 9:6b – 7). Jesus here speaks eloquently, persuasively, powerfully so that everything he says and does communicates God to us. As such, his words are uniquely endowed with the power to remake our broken world. No wonder he is called the Word.

Yet for all that, we don't always understand him. The difference in time and culture creeps like a cataract over the Gospels, obscuring their meaning and making it hard for us to grasp the full import of what he is saying. That's what makes *Walking in the Dust of Rabbi Jesus,* the sequel to *Sitting at the Feet of Rabbi Jesus,* which Lois and I wrote together, so remarkable and so uniquely helpful.

Despite how far removed we are from the era and culture in which Jesus lived, Lois has understood something vital — that we are living in a unique moment, one that provides an opportunity to peer into the first-century Jewish world more closely than ever before. This fortunate opportunity comes to us by way of the work of both Jewish and Christian scholars who have transformed our understanding of the culture in which Jesus lived and taught. Instead of squinting through the dust of history to catch a glimpse of early first-century Judaism, we are now offered a powerful telescope with which to probe the past, helping us to understand better the religious and cultural milieu in which Jesus lived and taught.

Until now, many of these discoveries have been buried in the scholarly literature. Fortunately for us, Lois has done the heavy lifting by excavating the literature in order to bring out key insights for readers who are serious about understanding Jesus in his Jewish context. Through her writing, we begin to see just how remarkable this Rabbi is, a man whose words are sometimes shocking but always insightful, penetrating, and powerful. Texts that we thought we knew suddenly spring to life. Passages that have puzzled us begin to make sense. Words that stirred crowds and ruffled religious feathers hit home with greater force. Through Lois's books, we can begin to understand more about Jesus and why his contemporaries responded to him the way they did.

With its balance and insight, Lois's work has incited in me a passion to learn more about the Jewishness of Jesus. I hope that this book will do for you what it has already done for me — whet your appetite for more.

ANN SPANGLER

The Shema

The *Shema* is not actually a prayer, but three Scriptures that are recited morning and evening each day as a commitment of loyalty to God's covenant. They remind people to keep God's Word in their thoughts at all times and to teach it to their children. They also promise that God will care for the material needs of his people if they will be faithful to him.

Hear, O Israel: The LORD our God, the LORD is one. Love the LORD your God with all your heart and with all your soul and with all your strength. These commandments that I give you today are to be on your hearts. Impress them on your children. Talk about them when you sit at home and when you walk along the road, when you lie down and when you get up. Tie them as symbols on your hands and bind them on your foreheads. Write them on the doorframes of your houses and on your gates. (Deuteronomy 6:4–9)

So if you faithfully obey the commands I am giving you today —to love the LORD your God and to serve him with all your heart and with all your soul—then I will send rain on your land in its season, both autumn and spring rains, so that you may gather in your grain, new wine and olive oil. I will provide grass in the fields for your cattle, and you will eat and be satisfied.

Be careful, or you will be enticed to turn away and worship other gods and bow down to them. Then the LORD's anger will burn against you, and he will shut the heavens so that it will not rain and the ground will yield no produce, and you will soon perish from the good land the LORD is giving you. Fix these words of mine in your hearts and minds; tie them as symbols on your hands and bind them on your foreheads. Teach them to your children, talking about them when you sit at home and when you walk along the road, when you lie down and when you get up. Write them on the doorframes of your houses and on your gates, so that your days and the days of your children may be many in the land the LORD swore to give your ancestors, as many as the days that the heavens are above the earth. (Deuteronomy 11:13–21)

The LORD said to Moses, "Speak to the Israelites and say to them: 'Throughout the generations to come you are to make tassels on the corners of your garments, with a blue cord on each tassel. You will have these tassels to look at and so you will remember all the commands of the LORD, that you may obey them and not prostitute yourselves by chasing after the lusts of your own hearts and eyes. Then you will remember to obey all my commands and will be consecrated to your God. I am the LORD your God, who brought you out of Egypt to be your God. I am the LORD your God.'" (Numbers 15:37–41)*

---

*Text from the New International Version. Note: The third section (Numbers 15:38–41) is recited only in the morning when the *tallit*, the garment that carries the tassels, is put on.

Acknowledgments

Mange tusen takk (many thousand thanks, as the Norwegians say), to all who walked alongside of me through the writing of this book. Two dear friends especially, Shirley Hoogeboom and Marylin Bright, prayed and brainstormed with me through every chapter, pouring their encouragement into the many months of writing. I can hardly express how much your faithful friendship has meant to me. Several others joined them in loving support, like Hillari Madison, Kathleen Coveny, Sandee Sjaarda, Elizabeth Claar, Stephanie Wiggins, Bill Boersma, and Mary and Bruce Okkema, as well my wonderful family, especially David and Lora Tverberg and, of course, my dear Mom.

Thanks also to all who gave their feedback on my writing, including David Bivin, Toby Gruppen, Lisa and Loren Vredevoogd, Deanna Thompson, and Travis West. Every time you pushed beyond Minnesota Nice to share your honest criticisms, you helped hone my thinking. And to Jana Reiss, I appreciated your thorough editorial hand and many excellent suggestions for polishing the book. Most of all, I'd like to thank Lori Vanden Bosch for her wisdom for refining each chapter and her delightful friendship. It was a joy to work with you!

I'm especially indebted to everyone at Zondervan who lent their professional expertise to this work, especially associate editor and executive publisher, Sandra Vander Zicht. My appreciation also goes to Verlyn Verbrugge, senior editor at large, for his amazing eye for historical and textual detail. Many thanks to Tom Dean, senior director of marketing, for your efforts to put this book into the hands of the public. To the many others at Zondervan who helped with this book, please accept my thanks.

As I started writing last year, I spent several weeks in Jerusalem brainstorming with scholarly friends about this book. My gracious hosts were Halvor and Mirja Ronning at the Home for Bible Translators and Scholars, who also shared their expertise on the Bible's cultural setting. Your expansive library on Bible translation was the perfect place to begin my research. And Imma Buth, thanks for being such a loving Mom to me there! To all who carved out some time with me to ruminate over my writing, including Randall and Margret Buth, David and Josa Bivin, Brian Kvasnica, David Pileggi, and Jonathan Miles, I appreciated our discussions so much. My sincere gratitude also goes to That the World May Know Ministries for helping support the trip financially.

Having Ray Vander Laan and Ann Spangler both contribute to this book touches me personally, since both were instrumental in turning my life in this direction. Fifteen years ago, Ray's passionate teaching opened a new world to me. Ray, your encouragement in recent years has been an enormous blessing. Many thanks for sharing your feedback on this manuscript too. Working with Ann as my agent, cowriter, and good friend has been a rare gift. Ann, I appreciate so much your expertise in the publishing world and honest guidance for the craft of writing. Thanks to both of you, Ray and Ann, for responding when the Lord placed you at these key moments in my life.

I'm humbled to have gleaned from the hard work of many scholars. Every day I appreciate their efforts more — their endless hours of sifting through scholarly papers and grappling with ancient texts. My study of the Jewish context of Jesus is especially indebted to David Bivin, Randall Buth, Steven Notley, Marvin Wilson, Dwight Pryor, and Brad Young, as well as others of the Jerusalem School of Synoptic Research.

The work of Jewish scholars like Abraham Heschel, Nahum Sarna, Jeffrey Tigay, and Jacob Milgrom has been life-changing for me. Their insights have opened the Hebrew Scriptures and revealed the tremendous *hesed* of the God of Israel. Joseph Telushkin's writing on ethics has been especially transformational. We Christians desperately need to learn from Rabbi Telushkin about the importance of judging favorably and avoiding *lashon hara*!

I join the rest of Christianity in expressing our enormous debt to the Jewish people. Despite centuries of persecution, God continues to bless the world through you.

Notes

CHAPTER 1: **Brushing Away the Dust of the Ages**

1. As quoted in James Patrick, *Renaissance and Reformation* (New York: Marshall Cavendish, 2007), 713.
2. Lorenzo Matteoli, "The Restoration of the Last Supper: Homage to Pinin Brambilla Barcilon," at http://members.iinet.net.au/~matteoli/html/Articles/Leonardo4.html (accessed Feb. 14, 2011). Many thanks also go to Dwight Pryor (1945–2011), gifted teacher and founder of the Center for Judaic-Christian Studies (www.jcstudies.com), for sharing the da Vinci illustration.
3. Hershel Shanks, "Where Jesus Cured the Blind Man," *Biblical Archeological Review* 35/5 (September/October 2005): 16–23. The pool has only been partially excavated, so the dimensions are an estimate.
4. Most scholars prefer the term "Hebrew Bible" to "Old Testament" because the name sounds as if these texts are now outmoded and replaced by the New Testament. They use a more neutral term for the Scriptures that Christians and Jews both read to show their respect for our shared biblical heritage. I use "Old Testament" here because of its familiarity.

    Ray Vander Laan is a dynamic speaker—"a lightning bolt with skin on," one friend called him. My first study trip to Israel in 1999 (including the terrifying Hezekiah's Tunnel) was with him. He's also the creator of the *Faith Lessons* DVD series. See FollowTheRabbi.com for more.
5. I'm indebted to the expertise of others, especially the scholarship of David Bivin (JerusalemPerspective.com), Randall Buth (BiblicalLanguageCenter.com), and Steven Notley (EmmausOnline.net). For six years I worked with Bruce and Mary Okkema to found a ministry called the "En-Gedi Resource Center" in Holland, Michigan. See www.egrc.net for more.
6. God had specified that Abraham make an *olah*, a "burnt offering," in which all of the animal's flesh is consumed in the fire.
7. All references to the Talmud are to the Babylonian Talmud.
8. John Varriano, *Tastes and Temptations: Food and Art in Renaissance Italy* (Berkeley, CA: Univ. of California Press, 2009), 102. The grilled eel dish apparently was a trendy favorite of Renaissance Italy at the time.
9. For more details, see Ann Spangler and Lois Tverberg, *Sitting at the Feet of Rabbi Jesus: How the Jewishness of Jesus Can Transform Your Faith* (Grand Rapids:

Zondervan, 2009), 101–12. Some have wondered if Jesus' final meal was not a Passover because John seems to date the event to the prior day. The other Gospels specifically call the meal the "Passover" (e.g., Luke 22:15). For a discussion of this debate, as well as strong evidence for the meal as a Passover, see Joachim Jeremias, *The Eucharistic Words of Jesus* (London: SCM, 1966), 15–88.

10. John MacArthur, *Grace to You*, "Understanding the Sabbath" (Sept. 20, 2009). Text available at www.gty.org/Resources/Sermons/90–379 (accessed Feb. 17, 2011).

11. The Essenes were an influential first-century sect that rejected pagan influence on Jewish ritual practice. Many moved to the community of Qumran in the Judean Desert, where they lived with great ceremonial purity. Their writings were found among the Dead Sea Scrolls.

12. Paula Fredriksen, "The Birth of Christianity and the Origins of Christian Anti-Judaism," in *Jesus, Judaism, and Christian Anti-Judaism: Reading the New Testament after the Holocaust* (Louisville: Westminster John Knox, 2002), 8–30.

13. See Luke Timothy Johnson, "The New Testament's Anti-Jewish Slander and the Conventions of Ancient Polemic," *Journal of Biblical Literature* 108 (1989): 419–41.

14. It's hard to overstate the persecution that Jews have suffered over the ages because of this attitude. Christians are largely unaware that the Spanish Inquisition, the Russian pogroms, and even the Holocaust were all outgrowths of Christian hostility toward Jews for not believing that Jesus was the Messiah. Unfortunately, as historian Edward Flannery has noted, "The pages Jews have memorized have been torn from our histories of the Christian era" (*The Anguish of the Jews* [New York: Macmillan, 1965], xi).

   This book is written by an evangelical Christian Gentile for a Christian audience. To any Jewish readers, I sincerely apologize for my neighbor's offensive comment.

15. Peter Jones, *Stolen Identity: The Conspiracy to Reinvent Jesus* (Colorado Springs: Cook, 2005), 10.

16. A helpful summary of the trends and excesses of scholarship on the historical Jesus is Craig A. Evans, *Fabricating Jesus: How Modern Scholars Distort the Gospels* (Downers Grove, IL: InterVarsity Press, 2006).

17. John 10:22 states that the Feast of Dedication was taking place. This celebration of Maccabean victory and restoration of the Temple was later called Hanukkah. (Bagels originated in Austria in the seventeenth century, and dreidels come from a European children's game.)

18. A few decades ago, scholars were skeptical that rabbinic documents could be used to study the New Testament period. More recently, confidence has grown. For more, see David Instone-Brewer, *Traditions of the Rabbis from the Era of the New Testament* (Grand Rapids: Eerdmans, 2004), 28–40; and the review article by idem, "The Use of Rabbinic Sources in Gospel Studies," *Tyndale Bulletin* 50

(1999): 281–98. In this book I've taken care to use early Jewish sources as often as possible. If quotes are from later centuries, I've included them as general wisdom, not as Jesus' worldview. Generally, scholars assume that Jesus knew the thinking of his day but that later rabbis didn't know Jesus' words. Parallels between them come from a common cultural background.

19. Kenneth Bailey, *Finding the Lost: Cultural Keys to Luke 15* (St. Louis, MO: Concordia, 1992), 28–29. Bailey points out that while some aspects of societies change rapidly, like economic and political realities, others last for many centuries, like worldviews and cultural assumptions and attitudes.

20. In one fascinating study, anthropologists looked at the cultural life of *shtetls*, traditional Jewish villages that have existed for the past millennium in Europe and Asia (think of *Fiddler on the Roof*). They were surprised at how similar religious traditions were from one end of the continent to the other and at how little change had occurred over the centuries. Because of strong persecution, Jewish communities had mostly walled off the larger world and clung tenaciously to tradition. See Mark Zborowski and Elizabeth Herzog, *Life Is with People: The Culture of the Shtetl* (New York: Schocken, 1952). The greatest change has occurred in the past century, as Jewish denominations have diverged widely from more liberal (Reform or Reconstructionist) to Conservative, Orthodox, and ultra-Orthodox (Hasidic) Jewish groups.

21. Eugene Nida, *Meaning Across Cultures* (Maryknoll, NY: Orbis, 1981), 29.

22. For a full discussion of how the kingdom of God relates to Jesus' messianic claims, see *Sitting at the Feet of Rabbi Jesus*, 180–95. Also, see Craig Evans, "Messianic Hopes and Messianic Figures in Late Antiquity," *Journal of Greco-Roman Christianity and Judaism* 3 (2006): 9–40. This is also available at www.craigaevans .com/studies.htm.

23. Some point out that it wasn't until a few decades later that "rabbi" was used as a formal title, after AD 70. For this reason, modern scholars refer to teachers of Jesus' era as "sages" rather than "rabbis." During his lifetime, "rabbi" was a respectful way to address a religious teacher, because it means "my master." Some of the places where Jesus was addressed as "rabbi" in the Gospels are Mark 9:5; 11:21; and John 1:37; 3:2; 4:31; 6:25; 11:8.

24. This saying, from Mishnah, *Avot* 1:4, is ascribed to Yose ben Yoezer, who lived in the second century BC. The Hebrew literally reads, "powder yourself with the dust of their feet." Often translated as "sit amidst the dust of their feet," it also could refer to the fact that disciples sat at the feet of their teacher, as Paul did for Gamaliel in Acts 22:3. However, noted Jewish scholar Shmuel Safrai asserts that it likely refers to walking along the dusty roads together. See his *The Jewish People in the First Century* (Amsterdam: Van Gorcum, 1976), 965. For more, see the article "Covered in the Dust of Your Rabbi: An Urban Legend?" at OurRabbiJesus.com.

CHAPTER 2: *Shema*: Living Out What You Hear

1. Rabbi Jonathan Sacks, *The Koren Sacks Siddur: A Hebrew/English Prayerbook* (Jerusalem: Koren, 2009), 96–98.

2. Slovie Jungreis-Wolff, *Raising a Child with Soul* (New York: Macmillan, 2009), 85.

3. The command to teach children the *Shema* as soon as they can speak is in the Talmud, *Sukkah* 42a (5th century). The New Testament and other sources also note that children began learning the Scriptures at a very young age. For instance, Paul remarked that Timothy knew the Scriptures from infancy (2 Timothy 3:15). Both the first-century Jewish historian Josephus and the Dead Sea Scrolls (200 BC–AD 68) mention the practice of repeating the *Shema* each morning and evening.

4. Geza Vermes, *The Religion of Jesus the Jew* (Minneapolis: Fortress, 1993), 37–45. For more explanation of the rabbinic discussion on summarizing the Scriptures, see *Sitting at the Feet of Rabbi Jesus*, 176–78.

5. Often Jesus is misunderstood to say that he's deliberately trying to hide his message. The very point of this parable is to say the opposite—the problem is not that his teaching is cryptic; it's that his audience is unwilling to respond. It's not his words—it's their ears. His parables, like thousands of other rabbinic parables, were intended to clarify, not to confuse.

6. For those reading this book who know Hebrew, I realize that "*shema*" is not the correctly parsed form of the Hebrew verb transliterated š-m-ᶜ . I continue to use the word "*shema*" as a rough equivalent because my goal is to help Christians incorporate a Hebrew word into their thinking, with all its wider associations, rather than distorting it by replacing it with an English (non)equivalent.

7. The 8,000 words of biblical Hebrew arise from only about 2,100 root words. The actual vocabulary of ancient Hebrew was larger, but biblical Hebrew only includes words used in the Old Testament.

8. Taken from *Searchlight on Bible Words*, compiled by James C. Hefley (Grand Rapids: Zondervan, 1972), 19–23.

9. The word "YHWH" transliterates the four Hebrew consonants of God's name that Moses received in Exodus 3:14. Out of reverence, Jews never say this name aloud, but commonly substitute *Adonai* ("my Lord") or HaShem ("the Name") instead. Most Bible translations respect this tradition by rendering this name as "the Lord."

10. *Tanakh: The Holy Scriptures: The New JPS Translation According to the Traditional Hebrew Text* (New York: Jewish Publication Society, 1985).

11. See Jeffrey Tigay, *The JPS Torah Commentary: Deuteronomy* (New York: Jewish Publication Society, 1996), 76. Tigay points out that only two chapters before the *Shema*, in Deuteronomy 4:35–39, we find one of the most explicit statements of monotheism. He also shares several pieces of evidence that point to the fact that the *Shema* was considered a covenantal oath in the first century.

The Essenes spoke of the act of reciting of the *Shema* as "entering the covenant of God." The liturgy that traditionally follows the *Shema* concludes with many terms used in validating legal agreements, as if the speakers were solemnly affirming an oath before God.

12. Scholars also note the parallels between the beginning of the *Shema* and the first of the Ten Commandments: "I am the LORD your God, who brought you out of Egypt, out of the land of slavery. You shall have no other gods before me" (Deuteronomy 5:6–7). Both include two sentences, where the first is a statement about God that provides the motivation for the command to follow. *Because* the Lord is your God and he rescued you from slavery, you will have no other gods before him.

CHAPTER 3: Loving God with Everything You've Got

1. Mishnah, *Avot* 5:20.
2. Victor Frankl, *Man's Search for Meaning* (Boston: Beacon, 1992 ed.), 48–50.
3. In Hebrew, the future (imperfect) form of a verb can be used as a command.
4. Maimonides, *Laws of Repentance* 10.3.
5. Jeffrey Spitzer, "Shema as a Love Story," at www.myjewishlearning.com (accessed August 11, 2010).
6. Brian McLaren and Tony Campolo, *Adventures in Missing the Point* (Grand Rapids: Zondervan, 2006), 236–38.
7. Chuck Warnock, "The Most Important Thing Jesus Said," www.ethicsdaily.com /the-most-important-thing-jesus-said-cms-13379 (accessed August 12, 2011).
8. Personal communications from R. Steven Notley and David Bivin about Shmuel Safrai, a professor of Jewish history at Hebrew University, who won the Israel Prize in 2002.
9. Nida, *Meaning Across Cultures*, 29.
10. Talmud, *Berakhot* 61b.
11. John Oswalt, *The Bible among the Myths* (Grand Rapids: Zondervan, 2009), 71.
12. Me'od occurs about three hundred times in the Hebrew Bible. The one other place you find it as a noun is in 2 Kings 23:25. "Neither before nor after Josiah was there a king like him who turned to the LORD as he did—with all his heart and with all his soul and with all his *strength* [me'od], in accordance with all the Law of Moses." The writer here is actually quoting the *Shema* to illustrate Josiah's commitment.
13. My original source is Randall Buth's paper, "A Four-fold *Shma* Between Qumran and the Gospels," presented at the Society for Biblical Literature Annual Meeting, November 23, 2003. See also, Serge Ruzer, "The Double Love Precept: Between Pharisees, Jesus, and Qumran Covenanters," in *Mapping the New Testament: Early Christian Writings as a Witness for Jewish Biblical Exegesis* (Leiden: Brill, 2003), 71–100. Note that even ancient manuscripts of Mark and Matthew

don't entirely agree on whether "love the Lord" has three parts or four. Some of the earliest copies of Mark only list three components, and some copies of Matthew list four.

14. Robert Harris, Gleason Archer, and Bruce Waltke, *Theological Wordbook of the Old Testament* (Chicago: Moody Press, 1980), 487.

15. See OurRabbiJesus.com for an audio file of the *Shema* in Hebrew.

CHAPTER 4: Meeting Myself Next Door

1. Rabbi Moses Cordovero (1522–1570), *The Palm Tree of Deborah* 5.

2. As retold in *Cliff Ellis: The Winning Edge* (Champaign, IL: Sports Publishing, 2000), 253–54.

3. Marvin Wilson, *Our Father Abraham: Jewish Roots of the Christian Faith* (Grand Rapids: Eerdmans, 1989), 185–90.

4. Ismar Schorsch, "You Can't Be Holy Alone," *Judaism: A Quarterly Journal of Jewish Life and Thought* 55 (Fall–Winter 2006): 73–83. In the first century, women were included in the count for a *minyan*, according to Shmuel Safrai. See "Were Women Segregated in the Ancient Synagogue?," *Jerusalem Perspective* 52 (July–Sept 1997): 24–36. Of course, requiring ten people doesn't limit God's presence, but the *minyan* rule has reinforced the obligation to be a community, causing Jews to live and worship together rather than be scattered as a people.

5. For the text of the *Amidah*, see *Sitting at the Feet of Rabbi Jesus*, 212–15.

6. In English we read "and" in one passage and "but" in the other. But Hebrew uses the conjunction *ve* to mean either "and" or "but."

7. Rabbinic teachers also emphasized the centrality of the second "great" commandment. About a century after Jesus' time, Rabbi Akiva declared, "'And you shall love your neighbor as yourself'—this is the great principle of the Torah" (Sifra, *Qedoshim* 4). The two love commands may have even become associated with each other prior to Jesus' ministry. Jesus' words about love reiterated and affirmed the best in Jewish tradition; they were not casting it aside and replacing it. See David Flusser, *Judaism and the Origins of Christianity* (Jerusalem: Magnes, 1988), 474.

8. James Kugel, *The Bible as It Was* (Cambridge: Belknap, 1997), 455–60.

9. Joseph Telushkin, *A Code of Jewish Ethics*, Volume 2, *Love Your Neighbor as Yourself* (New York: Bell Tower, 2009), 8–9.

10. *Jubilees* 36:4, as quoted in Kugel, *The Bible as It Was*, 455.

11. David Bivin, *New Light on the Difficult Words of Jesus* (Holland: En-Gedi Resource Center, 2004), 89–92. Quote from the Manual of Discipline, IQS 1:9–10.

12. Sirach 28:2–4 (NRSV; italics added). Ben Sira lived c. 180 BC. For more on this, see "Jesus' Jewish Command to Love" by R. Steven Notley, at www.jerusalem

perspective.com/default.aspx?&tabid=27&ArticleID=1776 (accessed Feb. 24, 2011). Also, see David Flusser, *Judaism and the Origins of Christianity* (Jerusalem: Magnes, 1988), 469–89.

13. Josephus, *Jewish Wars* 2.232–34.

14. The similarity of the good Samaritan parable to 2 Chronicles 28:1–15 has long been noted, but it has been debated whether Jesus was using the story to prove his point. Recently one well-known scholar asserted that this is indeed the case. See Craig Evans, "Luke's Good Samaritan and the Chronicler's Good Samaritans," in *Biblical Interpretation in Early Christian Gospels*, Volume 3, *The Gospel of Luke*, ed. Thomas R. Hatina (New York: T&T Clark, 2010), 32–42.

The Samaritans of Jesus' time were a mixed population of Jews and foreigners that resettled Samaria after the Assyrian invasion in 722 BC. To Jesus' listeners, connecting them with the idolatrous northern tribes in Oded's time posed little problem. The Samaritans themselves believed they were the descendants of the tribes of Israel too.

CHAPTER 5: Gaining a Good Eye

1. The Mishnah is the written record of rabbinic scholarship from between 200 BC to 200 AD. Most of it concerns legal interpretation, but one section, *Pirke Avot* ("Sayings of the Fathers") or simply *Avot* ("Fathers"), contains ethical and wisdom sayings from around the time of Jesus.

2. Elizabeth Clare Prophet, *The Lost Teachings of Jesus* (Gardiner, MO: Summit Univ. Press, 1986), 281; Ethan Walker, *The Mystic Christ* (Redmond, OR: Devi, 2003), 77–78.

3. Herbert Lockyer, *All the Parables of the Bible* (Grand Rapids: Zondervan, 1988), 149–50.

4. For more on Jesus' use of "good eye/bad eye," see Samuel Tobias Lachs, *A Rabbinic Commentary on the New Testament: The Gospels of Matthew, Mark and Luke* (Jersey City, NJ: KTAV, 1987), 127–29; Craig Keener, *A Commentary on the Gospel of Matthew* (Grand Rapids: Eerdmans, 1999), 232. Although Jesus could speak in Aramaic, he most likely taught in Hebrew, as did other Jewish teachers of his day. See Randall Buth, "The Language of Jesus' Teaching" (subsection of "Aramaic Language"), *Dictionary of New Testament Background*, ed. Craig Evans and Stanley Porter (Downers Grove, IL: InterVarsity Press, 2000), 86–91.

5. The Greek text of Matthew 6:22–23 literally contrasts an eye that is *haplous*, "single," with one that is *poneros*, "bad." Often people assume that Jesus was preaching about being single-minded or sincere. But a "single eye" is not an idiom in Hebrew for sincerity. More likely, since Matthew's Greek readers wouldn't have understood "good eye" any more than we do, he translated it using *haplous*, because in Greek, *haplous* was an idiom that meant "generous." In 2 Corinthians 9:11, Paul tells the Corinthians that God has enriched them

so that they can be *haplotes*—meaning generous (see also Romans 12:8, 2 Corinthians 8:2; 9:13). (David Bivin, personal communication.) Also, see Henry Cadbury, "The Single Eye," *Harvard Theological Review* 47 (1954): 69–74.

6. Having an *ayin ra'ah*, a "bad eye," a self-centered attitude, should not be confused with "the evil eye" (*ayin ha'ra*)—a superstition that a person can cast a spell through an envious gaze.

7. The mountain where Abraham said this was Mount Moriah, the future location of Jerusalem. It was there, centuries later, that Jesus offered himself as the sacrifice, where God ultimately provided the lamb. (If you've ever sung "Jehovah Jireh, My Provider" you're actually singing "God will see.")

8. Mishnah, *Avot* 2:10.

9. Storing one's "treasure in heaven" may sound like a general reference to having godly priorities, but it clearly refers to giving to the poor in Matthew 19:21; Mark 10:21; Luke 12:33; 18:22; and 1 Timothy 6:19 as well as other Jewish texts. The expression comes from Proverbs 19:17: "Whoever is kind to the poor lends to the LORD, and he will reward them for what they have done." Normally a person lends expecting to gain interest. When one gives to the poor, God himself takes on the loan. In the world to come, he'll repay the investment and add a bonus. See Joseph Frankovic, "Treasures in Heaven," www.jerusalemperspective.com (accessed June 15, 2010).

10. "Receive the Coming Supernatural Wealth Transfer," Benny Hinn email newsletter, May 21, 2010, www.bennyhinn.org/articles/articledesc.cfm?id=7052 (accessed June 17, 2010).

11. The early church did not expect people to donate everything they owned. When Ananias and Sapphira donated the profits from selling some property to the community, they lied about how much they were paid. Peter said that it was their choice to sell their land and how much money they'd give; their sin was that they lied about it (Acts 5:1–5).

12. Christian Smith and Michael Emerson, *Passing the Plate: Why American Christians Don't Give Away More Money* (Oxford: Oxford Univ. Press, 2008), 32–33. This figure is self-reported by survey participants, so results are likely more optimistic than actual data. In comparison to Christians, only 8 percent of practicing Jews do not give to charity.

13. Henry Assael and C. Samuel Craig, eds., *Printer's Ink: A Journal for Advertisers: Fifty Years: 1888–1938* (New York: Garland, 1986), 362.

14. *Madame Blueberry* (VeggieTales, Big Idea, Inc., 1998).

15. Smith and Emerson, *Passing the Plate*, 144.

16. With a thirty-year mortgage at 6.5 percent interest, a family will pay an extra $412,000 for the more expensive house. If they don't buy it, they'll have over $14,000 more each year to support whatever cause most impassions them for serving the Lord.

17. Adapted from Paul Forchheimer, *Living Judaism: Maimonides' Commentary on Pirkey Avoth* (New York: Feldheim, 1974), 101. Jesus didn't teach that poverty was inherently virtuous, but that wealth is a weed that can choke away fruitfulness (Matthew 13:22). He and his disciples likely carried little because of the hospitality extended to religious teachers, as in Luke 10:4–7. See Bivin, *New Light on the Difficult Words of Jesus*, 109–14.

18. Rabbi Shmelke of Nicholsberg (d. 1778), as quoted in *Jewish Wisdom*, ed. Rabbi Joseph Telushkin (New York: William Morrow, 1994), 15.

19. Zborowski and Herzog, *Life Is with People*, 193.

20. David L. Baker, *Tight Fists or Open Hands: Wealth and Poverty in Old Testament Law* (Grand Rapids: Eerdmans, 2009), 307–15.

21. See John Walton, *Ancient Israelite Literature in Its Cultural Context* (Grand Rapids: Zondervan, 1994), 229–47.

CHAPTER 6: The Mystery of the Name

1. As told in their unpublished memoir by Svein and Elise Tverberg, *From Farm to Mission Field*. This happened in about 1919.

2. One example of this is the Sacred Name Movement, which emerged in the 1930s and has published several Bible versions that contain the true names, as followers believe them to be.

3. Other spellings of Jesus' Hebrew name are possible, like *Y'shua* or *Yeshuah*, because English can only roughly approximate the sound of the Hebrew word. Some hear "Jesus" as a deliberate mispronunciation of *Yeshua*, but it simply comes from how the Hebrew sounds were transliterated into English. It is no more significant than in French, the name is pronounced "YAY-soo," and in Malagasy it is "zhe-SHOO-shee."

4. Yeshua, however, was actually a common name in the first century and occurs in the Old Testament too. There, the name is found in twenty-eight places, but is transliterated as "Jeshua."

5. Also, in the Babylonian creation epic, the *Enuma Elish*, the precreation period is described as "when on high the heaven had not [yet] been named, and below the firm ground had not [yet] been given a name." From Nahum M. Sarna, ed., *JPS Torah Commentary: Genesis* (New York: Jewish Publication Society, 1989), 7.

6. For more on Jesus' habit of hinting to the Scriptures and expecting his audience to know the rest, see *Sitting at the Feet of Rabbi Jesus*, 36–50. To learn more about the Hebraic sayings of Jesus, see Bivin, *New Light on the Difficult Words of Jesus*, and Bivin's many articles at *Jerusalem Perspective Online* (jerusalemperspective .com).

7. See Gregory K. Beale and D. A. Carson, *Commentary on the New Testament Use of the Old Testament* (Grand Rapids: Baker Academic, 2007), 35.

8. You wouldn't think that a Gentile prostitute would be known for righteousness, but James writes, "In the same way, was not even Rahab the prostitute considered righteous for what she did when she gave lodging to the spies and sent them off in a different direction?" (James 2:25). And Hebrews 11:31 says, "By faith the prostitute Rahab, because she welcomed the spies, was not killed with those who were disobedient." Early rabbinic literature also portrays her as a model proselyte. See Leila Bronner, *From Eve to Esther: Rabbinic Reconstructions of Biblical Women* (Louisville: Westminster John Knox, 1994), 148–50.

9. The phrase "*kiddush hashem*" is known from some of the earliest rabbinic literature. In contemporary usage, it often has the more specific meaning of dying a martyr's death for refusing to give up one's faith. Over the many centuries of Jewish persecution, from the Inquisition to the Holocaust, there have been numerous instances where such martyrdom has occurred. For more on how *kiddush hashem* and *hillul hashem* apply, see Joseph Telushkin, *A Code of Jewish Ethics*, Volume 1, *You Shall Be Holy* (New York: Bell Tower, 2006), 456–75.

10. For more information about the ministry of *Shevet Achim*, see www.shevet.org.

CHAPTER 7: How to Have a Kosher Mouth

1. Jim Casey and Phillip J. O'Connor, "Teacher's Nightmare Ends; False Sex Abuse Claims Found to Be a Plot by His Students," *Chicago Sun-Times*, May 17, 1994.

2. Most English translations, such as the NIV, invert the verbs so that instead of the literal reading, "desiring life" and "loving many days," they read, "loves life" and "desires many good days." But the Hebrew in the passage is *chafetz chaim*, which means, literally, "desiring life" (see next note).

3. The founder of this movement was the late nineteenth-century rabbi Yisrael Meir Kagan, who dedicated his life to ridding Jewish culture of *lashon hara*. He became so famous for his teaching that he's often just referred to as "Chafetz Chaim" (one who "desires life," from Psalm 34:12, also the name of his masterwork on the subject).

4. Dan Levin, "Weaning Teenagers off Gossip, for One Hour at a Time," *New York Times*, March 27, 2008 (www.nytimes.com/2008/03/27/nyregion/27gossip.html?ref=nyregion [accessed May 7, 2010]).

5. Although Jesus and James warned against evil speech, most of the ideas in this chapter come from later Judaism (after AD 400). I share them here as wise thinking for us today. An outstanding resource on the ethics of speech is Rabbi Joseph Telushkin, *Words That Hurt, Words That Heal* (New York: William Morrow, 1996).

6. Talmud, *Arachin* 15b. Some commentators make the parallel between *metzora* ("leper") and *motzi ra* ("one who speaks evil"). During the yearly Torah reading cycle, it's traditional to preach about sins of speech during the week that Leviticus 13–14, the regulations on leprosy and mildew, are read.

7. Sharing negative information is generally only permitted in situations where people may be adversely affected if they make a decision without it. For instance, if a friend is considering going into business with someone you know is dishonest, you should tell the friend. But even then, you should share only facts you know and not unfounded hearsay.

8. Based on a traditional Jewish story as told in Telushkin, *Words That Hurt, Words That Heal*, 3.

9. *Bereshit Rabbah* 98:23.

10. See Lori Palatnik with Bob Burg, "Evil Speech Is a Triple Murder Threat," in *Gossip: Ten Pathways to Eliminate It from Your Life and Transform Your Soul* (Deerfield Beach, FL: Simcha, 2002), 34–38.

11. Humor is all right as long as the object of the humor sees it as funny. But you can't use "I was only teasing" as an excuse for holding someone else up for ridicule.

12. Talmud, *Bava Metzia* 59a.

13. Edecio Martinez, "Alexis Pilkington Brutally Cyber Bullied, Even after Her Suicide," CBSNews.com, March 26, 2010 (www.cbsnews.com/8301–504083_162–20001181–504083.html [accessed May 7, 2010]).

14. Tosefta, *Bava Kama* 7:3.

15. Joseph Telushkin, *The Book of Jewish Ethics* (New York: Bell Tower, 2000), 40–41.

16. Mishnah, *Avot* 4:1.

CHAPTER 8: Taking My Thumb Off the Scale

1. Mishnah, *Avot* 1:6.

2. Scales were a well-known metaphor for judgment around the ancient world. Often in the Old Testament, God was said to "weigh" transgressions, as in Job 31:6: "Let God weigh me in honest scales and he will know that I am blameless." In Greek mythology, justice is represented as a blindfolded woman holding a scale. And in Egypt they pictured final judgment as one's heart being weighed on a scale, with a feather in the other pan.

3. Talmud, *Shabbat* 127a. Out of anger, the farmer had pronounced his belongings *korban* ("dedicated to God") to punish his son. At Yom Kippur, during the fall feasts, a person can be absolved of rash vows like this. (Jesus also talks about *korban* in Matthew 15:5 and Mark 7:11.)

4. Zelig Pliskin, *Love Your Neighbor* (New York: Aish Hatorah, 1977), 261.

5. Charles Swindoll, *The Grace Awakening* (Nashville: Nelson, 2006), 154.

6. Joseph Telushkin, *A Code of Jewish Ethics*, Volume 1, *You Shall Be Holy*, 92 (includes a quote from Rabbi Simcha Zissel Ziv); for a masterful treatment of the ethic of "judging favorably," see pp. 69–94. Telushkin's reasoning here illustrates Jewish pragmatism regarding human behavior and using "the other hand" to examine the limits of an idea.

7. Based on a quote from Moshe Chaim Luzzato (1707–1746) in *Orchot Tzaddikim* ("Ways of the Righteous") on page 71 of *You Shall Be Holy*.

8. See Malcolm Gladwell, *Blink: The Power of Thinking without Thinking* (New York: Little, Brown, 2005), 30.

9. John Gottman and Nan Silver, *The Seven Principles for Making Marriage Work* (London: Orion, 2004), 27.

10. Parallelism pervades Psalms and Proverbs, and many of the prophetic writings too. For more, see David Bivin, "Cataloging the New Testament's Hebraisms: Part 4 (Parallelism)," at www.JerusalemPerspective.com (accessed May 23, 2011).

11. Keener, *Commentary on the Gospel of Matthew*, 184.

12. Mishnah, *Avot* 2:4.

13. One of the major differences between Judaism and Christianity is, in fact, its assessment of humanity. Judaism believes that people can live fairly righteous lives, but Christians see humans as universally separated from God by sin. In my mind, the origin of this split comes from Jesus himself, who preached that God was extending a "new covenant for the forgiveness of sin" through his atoning death (Matthew 26:28). His kingdom was made up of those who realized they needed God's forgiveness and extended it to others. For more on the contrast between Jesus' theology and that of his Jewish contemporaries, see *Sitting at the Feet of Rabbi Jesus*, 188–92.

CHAPTER 9: **Praying with *Chutzpah***

1. Abraham Heschel, *Man's Quest for God* (Santa Fe, NM: Aurora, 1998), 87.

2. Everett Fox, *The Five Books of Moses: A New Translation* (New York: Schocken, 1995), 384.

3. Brad Young, *Jesus the Jewish Theologian* (Peabody, MA: Hendrickson, 1995), 172, 178. See the rest of the chapter "Faith as *Chutzpah*" (pp. 171–80) for his explanation of how the Greek term *anaideia* in Luke 11:8 likely translates as *chatzufo* (related to *chutzpah*), and for rabbinic parables that build on similar themes.

4. See Lou Silberman, "Boldness in the Service of Justice," in *Preaching Biblical Texts: Expositions by Jewish and Christian Scholars* (Grand Rapids: Eerdmans, 1995), 29–35.

5. Athol Dickson, *The Gospel according to Moses: What My Jewish Friends Taught Me about Jesus* (Grand Rapids: Brazos, 2003), 19, 21.

6. Nahum Sarna, *Understanding Genesis: The World of the Bible in the Light of History* (New York: Schocken, 1966), 146–48.

7. *Fiddler on the Roof* (Santa Monica: MGM Entertainment, 1998), originally released in 1971. Even though much of Jewish prayer is communal and liturgical, Tevye's personal prayer style is part of a traditional Hasidic practice called *hitboddadut*. Each day it is customary to talk aloud with God alone, to share one's prayers and problems in order to grow in a childlike, trusting faith.

8. Mishnah, *Taanit* 3:8.

9. Talmud, *Betsah* 32b. The language here makes a typically Hebraic assumption that descendents will be like their forefathers. The same kind of reasoning is found in Matthew 5:44–45, "But I tell you, love your enemies and pray for those who persecute you, that you may be children of your Father in heaven. He causes his sun to rise on the evil and the good, and sends rain on the righteous and the unrighteous."

10. A fascinating comment on God's words to Moses, "Let me alone, so that I may destroy them" (Exodus 32:10; Deuteronomy 9:14), is that they were, paradoxically, a hint that Moses actually *should* plead for the people. After all, God didn't need Moses' permission to punish them. Rather, he was letting Moses know what would happen if he didn't speak up. Moses took the hint and ignored God's command to be left alone, pleading for Israel instead. See the *JPS Torah Commentary* notes on Exodus 32:10; Numbers 14:12; and Deuteronomy 9:14.

11. Rabbinic commentators were troubled by Noah's lack of concern for the destruction of others. Some imaginatively suggested that Noah took a hundred and twenty years to build the ark (enough time to grow the timber from seed!) because he was working as slowly as possible, to give people more time to repent. Others wove stories that maybe Noah actually did warn others about the coming judgment, because a man called "righteous" could hardly do otherwise. In 2 Peter 2:5, Peter calls Noah a "preacher of righteousness," likely because of this tradition. See James Kugel, *The Bible As It Was* (Cambridge, MA: Belknap, 1997), 113–17.

12. Nahum Sarna, *JPS Torah Commentary: Genesis* (Philadelphia: Jewish Publication Society, 1989), 50, 132.

CHAPTER 10: Thinking with Both Hands

1. Marvin Wilson, *Our Father Abraham: The Jewish Roots of the Christian Faith* (Grand Rapids: Eerdmans, 1989), 150–51.

2. Mark Galli, "The Man Who Wouldn't Give Up," *Christian History* 11/4 (1992): 11.

3. Rabbi Akiva (second century AD), Mishnah, *Avot* 3:16. For more discussion, see Wilson, *Our Father Abraham*, 151.

4. Wilson, *Our Father Abraham*, 152.

5. Dickson, *The Gospel according to Moses*, 80.

6. Abraham Heschel, *God in Search of Man: A Philosophy of Judaism* (New York: Farrar, Straus and Giroux, 1976), 20.

7. Three laws cannot be waived because of *pikuach nephesh*: murder, idolatry, and sexual immorality. These were considered the most heinous of sins. David Bivin suggests that these were also the proscriptions given to the Gentiles in Acts 15:19–20, assuming that "blood" is more likely "bloodshed" (*shefichut damim*), an idiom for murder. See Bivin, *New Light on the Difficult Words of Jesus*, 141–44.

8. A. K. Singla et al., "Are Women Who Are Jehovah's Witnesses at Risk of Maternal Death?," *American Journal of Obstetric Gynecology* 185/4 (2001): 893–95. A related observation is that while traditional Jewish law has forbidden abortion since ancient times, if the pregnancy puts the woman's life at risk, abortion is not just permitted; it's recommended (Mishnah, *Ohalot* 7:6). This is because the woman's life takes precedence over that of the unborn baby.

9. That being said, yet another principle comes in, that in lying you may be risking your own life to save another. A person is never obligated by Jewish law to sacrifice his or her life for another, although obviously such a deed is heroic (see previous note).

10. Augustine (AD 354–430), "On Lying," in *Treatises on Various Subjects*, trans. Mary S. Muldowney, ed. Roy J. Deferrari (Washington, DC: Catholic Univ. of America Press, 2002), 67.

11. Immanuel Kant (1724–1804), *Critique of Practical Reason* (Chicago: Univ. of Chicago Press, 1949), 346–50. For more discussion on when lying is permitted, see Telushkin, *The Book of Jewish Values*, 100–105.

12. Telushkin, *The Book of Jewish Values*, 51–54.

13. As quoted by Telushkin, *The Book of Jewish Values*, 2.

14. Mishnah, *Avot* 2:21.

15. Dan Levin, "Weaning Teenagers Off Gossip, for One Hour at a Time," *New York Times*, March 27, 2008.

16. Markus Bockmuehl, *Jewish Law in Gentile Churches: Halakhah and the Beginning of Christian Public Ethics* (London: Continuum, 2000), 6–8.

17. Many have noted that praying for healing and simply laying on hands were not prohibited on the Sabbath. But grinding herbs and brewing potions for treatment of chronic illnesses were prohibited because they involved types of labor not permitted on that day.

18. Paul appeals in 1 Corinthians 9:9 in a similar way to the law of muzzling an ox when he's arguing that the believers should support the work their leaders do among them. If an ox can enjoy the benefits of its labor, how much more should a human be able to do so!

19. About a century later, Simeon ben Menasia made a similar declaration: "The Sabbath is given to you but you are not given to the Sabbath" (*Mechilta de-Rabbi Ishmael* on Exodus 31:13).

CHAPTER 11: **The Treasure of the Text**

1. Rabbi Dov Peretz Elkins, *Yom Kippur Readings: Inspiration, Information and Contemplation* (Woodstock, VT: Jewish Lights, 2010), 103.

2. For more details about Jesus' habit of quoting the Scriptures and the bold messianic claims he made this way, see *Sitting at the Feet of Rabbi Jesus*, 36–49.

3. See also Isaiah 26:19–21 and 61:1–2.

4. For more on the debate between Jesus and John (and others) on how the Messiah would fulfill prophecy to bring God's kingdom, see *Sitting at the Feet of Rabbi Jesus*, 180–96.

5. There are slight differences in what texts are read between Ashkenazi (European) Jews and Sephardic (Spanish and North African) Jews. Nowadays, most Conservative and Reform Jews read the Torah on a triennial cycle. They read from Genesis to Deuteronomy each year, but they read a third of each *parasha* each week, alternating by year. The Christian practice of reading through a *lectionary*, a scheduled set of texts throughout the year, comes from this tradition.

6. The practice in Jesus' time was different than today. Then, one person read both the Torah and the *haftarah*, and now seven readers each read part of it. Also, while the Torah portion was predetermined, the reader was free to choose the *haftarah* according to his message. In the modern era, the *haftarah* is now preassigned.

7. Quoted by Louis Jacobs, *The Book of Jewish Belief* (West Orange, NJ: Behrman House, 1984), 2–3. The original author was Rabbi Bahya Ibn Pakudah, who lived in the eleventh century.

8. Mishnah, *Avot* 2:8.

9. Talmud, *Shabbat* 127a.

10. Abraham Heschel, *God in Search of Man: A Philosophy of Judaism* (New York: Noonday, 1983), 242.

CHAPTER 12: **The Secrets That God Keeps**

1. Abraham Heschel, *God in Search of Man*, 74.

2. Nahum Sarna, *Understanding Genesis: The World of the Bible in the Light of History* (New York: Schocken, 1966), 10.

3. *Genesis Rabbah* 1:10.

4. Howard Schwartz, *Tree of Souls: The Mythology of Judaism* (New York: Oxford Univ. Press, 2004), 36, 509. Schwartz explains that the Jewish expectation that the Messiah will teach a new Torah comes from Isaiah 51:4, "A new torah will come forth from me ..." (522).

5. William Barrett, *Irrational Man* (New York: Anchor/Doubleday, 1962), 79.

6. Peter Kreeft, *Three Philosophies of Life* (San Francisco: Ignatius, 1989), 89.

CHAPTER 13: **Our Longing Father**

1. Oliver Sacks, *The Mind's Eye* (New York: Knopf, 2010), 111–42. A few percent of the population lacks stereoscopic vision for various reasons, including the loss of sight in one eye. Many people are hardly aware of their deficit. Susan Barry's case is remarkable in that she acquired stereovision as an adult. Usually if the brain doesn't develop this ability in infancy, retraining the vision centers isn't possible later on.

2. Susan Barry, *Fixing My Gaze: A Scientist's Journey into Seeing in Three Dimensions* (New York: Basic Books, 2009), xii–xiii.

3. Obviously, one might wonder where the Holy Spirit fits into this discussion, but the Trinity is simply beyond the scope of this chapter.

4. See Sidney Greidanus, *Preaching Christ from the Old Testament* (Grand Rapids: Eerdmans, 1999), 22–25, for several examples of theologians over the ages who adopted versions of Marcion's perspective. One of the most famous was Adolf von Harnack (1851–1930), who advocated that the Old Testament be demoted to historical literature rather than Scripture.

5. For more on Marcion and the Greco-Roman view of God's impassibility, see Abraham Heschel, *The Prophets* (New York: Harper, 2001), 318–92.

6. Karen Armstrong, *A History of God* (New York: Ballentine, 1994), 98.

7. For example, see Eduard Schweizer, *Jesus* (London: SCM, 1971), 28.

8. Henri Nouwen, *The Return of the Prodigal Son: A Story of Homecoming* (New York: Doubleday, 1994), 36.

9. Kenneth Bailey, *Poet and Peasant* and *Through Peasant Eyes: A Literary-Cultural Approach to the Gospel of Luke* (Grand Rapids: Eerdmans, 1983), 162.

10. Philip Yancey, *Disappointment with God* (Grand Rapids: Zondervan, 1988), 97.

11. As quoted by Brad Young, *The Parables: Jewish Tradition and Christian Interpretation* (Peabody, MA: Hendrickson, 1998), 148–49. It's ironic that Rabbi Meir (AD 80–120) and Marcion (AD 140) taught within only a few decades of each other. While Rabbi Meir read his Scriptures in a Jewish way and found a gracious, merciful God, Marcion read it through Greek eyes and saw a God of harsh condemnation.

12. Other details suggest that Jeremiah 3 and 31 form the backdrop of Jesus' parable. The prophet speaks of two sons, Israel and Judah. One of them has deserted God, and the other is not much more righteous (3:9–10). God gives Israel a beautiful "inheritance," the land, but they betray their father and squander his wealth by offering its fruits to worthless idols (3:24). Nevertheless, God promises to lead his children home from spiritual and physical exile if they'll only repent when he declares, "I am Israel's father, and Ephraim is my firstborn son" (31:9).

13. Heschel, *The Prophets*, 364–65.

14. Jürgen Moltman, *The Crucified God* (Minneapolis: Fortress, 1993), 222.

15. *Genesis Rabbah* 12:15.

16. The "process theology" movement embraces God's emotions, but then says that God can't truly empathize with us unless God is himself in "process," still growing toward his potential. God hopes everything will turn out all right, but he's not sovereign over eternity. To me, this sounds like the Greek assumption that the supreme God cannot show emotions, only reversed—God empathizes, therefore he must not be in control. Why not just embrace the paradox that God is sovereign, and yet he's grieved by human suffering and sin? Didn't Jesus weep

with Mary and Martha one moment before he raised Lazarus from the dead (see John 11:35–43)?

17. Walter Brueggemann, *Genesis* (Louisville: Westminster John Knox, 1982), 81.

18. Terence Fretheim, *The Suffering of God* (Philadelphia: Fortress, 1984), 112.

CHAPTER 14: God's Image Stamped in Dust

1. Ethelbert Stauffer, *Christ and the Caesars* (Philadelphia: Westminster, 1955), 122–28.

2. Randall Buth, "Your Money or Your Life," *Jerusalem Perspective* 24 (January–February 1990): 9–10.

3. Mishnah, *Sanhedrin* 4:5. This saying is early—it would have been dated within a century of Jesus' time.

4. For more on the rabbinic method of training disciples, see *Sitting at the Feet of Rabbi Jesus*, 21–34, 51–65.

5. Philip Yancey and Paul Brand, *In the Likeness of God* (Grand Rapids: Zondervan, 2004), 235–37.

6. Talmud, *Ta'anit* 20.

7. Young, *The Parables*, 9.

8. As quoted by Norman Wirzba, *The Paradise of God* (Cambridge, MA: Oxford Univ. Press, 2003), 128.

9. C. S. Lewis, *Prince Caspian: The Return to Narnia* (New York: HarperCollins, 2008), 218.

10. Homer, *Odyssey* 20.201–3; *Illiad* 26.388. See William K. C. Guthrie, *The Greeks and Their Gods* (Boston: Beacon, 1955), 121.

11. See Steven Pinker, "A History of Violence," at http://edge.org/conversation/a-history-of-violence (accessed February 28, 2011). Pinker notes that violence has declined by several orders of magnitude in past centuries, most notably in societies influenced by the West (and, I would add, Judeo-Christian ethics).

12. See Moshe Greenberg, "Some Postulates of Biblical Criminal Law," in *Essential Papers on Israel and the Ancient Near East*, ed. Frederick E. Greenspahn (New York: New York Univ. Press, 1991), 333–52.

13. The rabbis placed such an extreme value on human life, however, that they were reluctant to prosecute capital crimes and made the rules for proving guilt nearly impossible to fulfill (Mishnah, *Makkot* 1:10). See Greenberg, "Some Postulates of Biblical Criminal Law," 343.

14. Rabbi Simcha Bunam of Peshischa, contrasting Mishnah, *Sanhedrin* 4:5 and Genesis 18:27.

15. C. S. Lewis, *The Weight of Glory* (New York: HarperOne, 2001), 45–46.

16. Abraham Heschel, *The Insecurity of Freedom* (New York: Farrar, Straus and Giroux, 1963), 153.

17. Heschel, *God in Search of Man*, 367.

Afterword

1. Christopher Jackson, "The Most Important Sentence: How to Write a Killer Opening," posted on "Fuel Your Writing," www.fuelyourwriting.com/the-most-important-sentence-how-to-write-a-killer-opening (accessed Sept. 14, 2011).

Glossary

Many of these words have more than one accepted spelling because the English word is a transliteration, which is an approximation because of language differences.

Adonai (ah-doh-NIY) — Hebrew for "my Lord" — A term of respect used for God or a king.

Amidah (ah-mee-DAH or ah-MEE-dah; lit., "standing") — The central prayer in Jewish liturgy, repeated three times a day and said while standing. Also called the *shmoneh esreh* (SHMO-neh ES-reh), meaning "eighteen," because originally it was composed of eighteen benedictions. Now a nineteenth has been added.

Avak Lashon Hara (ah-VAHK lah-SHON ha-RAH; lit., "dust of an evil tongue") — Jewish expression for showing contempt for others without actually uttering malicious words out loud (*lashon hara*). Rolling one's eyes in disgust at someone you dislike, or passing on a Youtube video that humiliates someone, are both sins of *avak lashon hara* — the "dust" of *lashon hara*.

Echad (eh-HAHD) — Hebrew word that most often simply means "one," but can encompass related ideas like being single, alone, unique, or unified. Central to the statement about God in the first line of the *Shema*, its meaning has been debated by Christians and Jews for centuries.

Essenes — Reform group active in the first century BC and first century AD. With the Pharisees, Sadducees, and Zealots, it was one of the four most influential groups during the time of Christ. The Essenes deplored the corruption of Judaism by pagan elements. Some withdrew into the Judean wilderness, to live with great ceremonial purity, studying the Scriptures and preparing themselves for the final battle between the "Sons of Light" (themselves) and the "Sons of Darkness" (pretty much everyone else). The Dead Sea Scrolls contain many of their writings, along with dozens of copies of biblical texts.

Gemilut Hasadim (gem-i-LOOT hah-sa-DEEM; lit., "deeds of loving-kindness") — Actions that help others, like visiting the sick, feeding the hungry, comforting mourners, and burying the dead.

Gezerah Shavah (ge-ze-rah sha-VAH; lit., "a comparison of equals") — One of Hillel's "Seven Principles of Interpretation," which says that two biblical texts sharing the same word or phrase can be used to interpret each other.

Halakhah (hal-a-KHAH; lit., "walk") — A Hebrew word that is used for legal ordinances in Judaism. (Note that "Torah" is not understood this way, but as "instruction" or "teaching.") *Halakhah* defines how the Torah is applied to your "walk" in life — laws and ethics. Rabbis, including Jesus, taught both *halakhah* — ethics and law — and *haggadah* — stories to explain the Scriptures.

Hashem (hah-SHEM) — Hebrew for "the name." Commonly used by modern Jews as a substitute for God's name, out of reverence for God. *Adonai* (meaning "my lord") is another substitution for God's name. In the first century, "heaven" and "the Holy One" were other common substitutions.

Hasidic (hah-SIH-dic) — Adjective describing ultra-Orthodox Jews, often in reference to a Jewish movement that began in the 1800s that emphasized mysticism and piety.

Haver (ha-VAIR; lit., "friend"; masc. pl., *haverim*, ha-ver-EEM) — One who partners with another to study religious texts together. A female study partner is a *haverah* (ha-ver-AH; pl., *haverot*, ha-ver-OTE).

Hesed (HEH-sed) — Hebrew word referring to a faithful, enduring love that often results in gracious actions on behalf of even the least deserving. Usually rendered as "mercy," "kindness," or "love," the word's full meaning is often lost in translation.

Hillel (hill-LELL) — A famous Jewish teacher who was active between 30 BC and AD 10. He was known for his gentleness and moderation in interpreting the law. His school of disciples often debated the disciples of Shammai over their stricter interpretations of Jewish law.

Hillul Hashem (hi-LOOL ha-SHEM; lit., "profaning the name") — To cause those who don't know God to despise him by doing something evil publicly and associating God with it.

Kavanah (ka-vah-NAH or ka-VAHN-ah; lit., "intention") — To focus one's attention and concentration on being in the presence of God; to direct one's thoughts toward God.

Kiddush Hashem (ki-DOOSH ha-SHEM; lit., "sanctifying the name") — To bring God honor among those who don't know him by living a life of integrity or doing a heroic deed. In recent centuries of Jewish persecution, it often has referred to dying a martyr's death, refusing to give up one's faith in God.

Lashon Hara (la-SHON ha-RAH; lit., "an evil tongue") — Jewish idiom for all kinds of gossip and malicious speech. More specifically, *lashon hara* often refers to revealing negative (but true) information about others that is unnecessary and damaging.

Marcion (MAHR-shun or MAHR-see-on) — (AD 85 – 160) Early Christian in Turkey who believed the God of the Old Testament was a vengeful, inferior deity to the Christ he saw in the New Testament. He advocated removal of the Old Testament and some of the New from the Christian Scriptures.

Mashiach (mah-SHEE-akh; lit., "anointed") — Hebrew word for Messiah; Greek is *Christos*. It means literally "Anointed One" and refers to the fact that God promised that one would come who would be specially chosen and anointed as a great king and priest for his people.

Messianic Jew — A person who believes that Jesus is the Messiah, but retains his or her Jewish identity. Some Jews avoid using the term "Christian" because of the assumption that Christians are Gentiles.

Minyan (min-YAHN) — A gathering of a minimum of ten adult male Jews required for some public prayers. In the first century, women could be included in this number too.

Mishnah — The collection of rabbinic rulings and sayings compiled and committed to writing around AD 200. The Mishnah records the sayings of teachers who lived and taught during the previous four hundred years, both before and after the time of Jesus.

Mitzvah (MITS-vah; lit., "command"; pl., *mitzvot*, mits-VOTE) —

Hebrew word meaning "commandment," referring to a religious obligation, often to a "good deed."

Pharisees (lit., "the separated ones" or "separatists") — The roots of this sect can be traced to the second century BC. Unlike the aristocratic Sadducees, most were common laborers who devoted their spare time to study and teaching. Pondering the lessons of exile and persecution, they concluded that the best hope for the future lay in devotion to God. They carefully studied the Torah to discover how best to live according to the law. One of the most influential groups in the New Testament period, they determined the character of rabbinic Judaism after the fall of the Temple in AD 70.

Pikuach Nephesh (*pi-KOO-akh NEH-fesh*; lit., "preservation of life") — The rabbinic principle for interpreting the law that stated that if life was at stake, all laws except three (murder, idolatry, and sexual immorality) could be set aside.

Pirke Avot (*peer-KAY ah-VOTE*; lit., "Chapters of the Fathers," often simply called *Avot*) — A section of the Mishnah that contains rabbinic ethical and wisdom sayings from between 200 BC and AD 200. Many comment on the same topics that Jesus did, shedding light on how his words were understood in his time.

Rabbi (lit., "my master") — A term of respect that was used when speaking to teachers of the Scriptures in Jesus' day. After AD 70, "rabbi" became a formal title.

Rosh Hashanah (rosh ha-SHAH-nah; lit., "head of the year") — Jewish New Year, also called *Yom Teruah*, the "day of trumpeting."

Sadducees — Members of the Sadducees came primarily from the ruling priestly and aristocratic classes. They controlled the Temple worship. Many people resented them for fattening their purses and securing their position by collaborating with the Romans. Unlike the Pharisees, they did not believe in the resurrection of the dead, and they considered only the written Torah as binding. Their influence ceased with the destruction of the Temple in AD 70.

Shabbat (shah-BAHT) — Hebrew for "Sabbath," meaning "to cease." A time of ceasing from labor, according to the Bible. Jews observe Shabbat from Friday sunset until Saturday sunset.

Shammai (SHAM-mai) — Famous Jewish scholar of the first century BC who was known for his strict approach to interpreting the laws of the Torah. His school of disciples often debated the more moderate disciples of Hillel during the first century, and these debates shed light on the context of Jesus' sayings.

Shema (sheh-MAH or shmah; lit., "hear") — Three Bible passages recited morning and evening by Jews over the millennia, since before Jesus' time. They are Deuteronomy 6:4 – 9; 11:13 – 21; and Numbers 15:37 – 41. The first word of Deuteronomy 6:4, "Hear, O Israel; the Lord our God, the Lord is one." *Shema* means "hear," but it implies action, also meaning "take heed" and "obey." To pray the *Shema* is to commit one's self to loving God and obeying his laws. See pages 195 – 96 for text.

Sukkot (soo-KOTE; lit., "booths") — The Feast of Tabernacles, a harvest festival held in the fall, the last of the seven biblical feasts. For seven days, Jews are commanded to live in booths in order to remember dwelling in the wilderness for forty years after they left Egypt.

Synagogue (lit., "assembly") — A local community center that is the place of prayer and study of Scripture, which likely arose during the exile in Babylon when Jews were unable to worship at the Temple. In the first century, all kinds of meetings were held there — school during the week, and prayer and study of the Torah on the Sabbath.

Talmid (tahl-MEED; lit., "student"; pl., *talmidim*, tahl-me-DEEM) — A disciple or student of a rabbi, one who has dedicated himself to life together with a rabbi, humbly serving him and learning the rabbi's understanding of Scripture and his way of living it out.

Talmud — Large volume of commentary on the Mishnah. The commentary is printed section by section surrounding each verse of the Mishnah. There are two Talmuds: the Jerusalem (or Palestinian) Talmud, completed about AD 400; and the Babylonian Talmud, completed about a century later. The latter became authoritative.

Tanakh (TAH-nakh or tah-NAHK) — The Jewish term for the Bible. It includes the same books as in the Protestant "Old Testament." *Tanakh* is actually an acronym of the first letters that start each of the three main sections. These are the:

- **Torah** (Pentateuch): Five books of Moses — the covenant and laws
  - **Neviim** (neh-vee-YEEM; lit., "prophets"): Joshua, Judges, 1–2 Samuel, 1–2 Kings, Isaiah, Jeremiah, Ezekiel, and the Minor Prophets
    - **Ketuvim** (ket-u-VEEM; lit., "writings"): Psalms, Proverbs, Job, Ruth, and the other books not yet mentioned

Torah (TOR-ah) — Hebrew for "teaching, instruction." Refers to the first five books of the Bible, also called the Pentateuch. Christians often translate Torah as "law," while Jewish translations usually render it "teaching."

Tza'ar Baalei Hayim (TZA-ar bah-ah-LAY hi-YEEM; lit., "suffering of living things") — Rabbinic principle of law interpretation that prohibits cruelty toward animals.

Tzedakah (zeh-dah-KAH) — Hebrew word that literally means "righteousness," but has been an idiom for giving to charity since before Jesus' time.

Yeshua (yeh-SHU-ah) — Jesus' name as it would have been pronounced in Hebrew. It is a shortened form of *Yehoshua*, which in English is "Joshua." Both mean "God's salvation," which is why the angel said, "You are to give him the name Jesus, because he will save his people from their sins" (Matthew 1:21).

Yom Kippur (yome kih-PUHR; lit., "day of covering") — Day of Atonement. The most holy day of the year for the Jews, when they fast and pray for forgiveness of sins. In biblical times a scapegoat was sacrificed, and the high priest entered the Most Holy Place of the Temple to make atonement for the sins of the nation.

Zealots — The Zealots originated during the reign of Herod the Great. A political party with religious underpinnings, this group advocated the violent rebellion of Israel against Rome. The Galilee region where Jesus lived and taught was a Zealot stronghold. This movement came to the fore in the Jewish revolt against Rome in AD 66–70.

Recommended Resources

Books and DVDs

Bailey, Kenneth E. *Poet and Peasant* and *Through Peasant Eyes* (combined edition). Grand Rapids: Eerdmans, 1983. From his experience among traditional Middle Eastern peoples, Bailey shares a wealth of cultural insights on Jesus' parables.

Bivin, David. *New Light on the Difficult Words of Jesus: Insights from His Jewish Context.* Holland, MI: En-Gedi Resource Center, 2005. Excellent overview of Jesus' first-century life and teachings in their Jewish context.

Dickson, Athol. *The Gospel According to Moses: What My Jewish Friends Taught Me about Jesus.* Grand Rapids: Baker, 2003. A conservative Christian attends a Reform Jewish Torah study and uncovers rich wisdom for his own faith.

Evans, Craig. *Fabricating Jesus: How Modern Scholars Distort the Gospels.* Downers Grove, IL: InterVarsity Press, 2006. Excellent popular-level book by a respected scholar on recent theories about the historical Jesus.

Flusser, David, with R. Steven Notley. *The Sage from Galilee: Rediscovering Jesus' Genius.* Grand Rapids: Eerdmans, 2007. An academic study of the Jewish historical reality of Jesus by a renowned Jewish scholar.

Heschel, Abraham. *God in Search of Man: A Philosophy of Judaism.* New York: Farrar, Straus and Giroux, 1976. A comprehensive study of Judaism. Not light reading, but full of profound insights.

———. *The Prophets.* New York: Harper and Row, 1962. Another masterful book by Heschel that reveals the passionate God who spoke through the prophets.

Instone-Brewer, David. *Traditions of the Rabbis from the Era of the New*

Testament (vol. 1 of 6). Grand Rapids: Eerdmans, 2004. A scholarly study of rabbinic sayings that describe the Judaism of Jesus' day.

Kaiser, Walter, and Duane Garrett. *Archaeological Study Bible: An Illustrated Walk through Biblical History and Culture.* Grand Rapids: Zondervan, 2006. Colorfully illustrated NIV study Bible, full of articles on culture and archaeology that shed light on the biblical text.

Pearl, Chaim. *Theology in Rabbinic Stories.* Peabody, MA: Hendrickson, 1997. A delightful collection of rabbinic stories and discussion of the ideas within them.

Pryor, Dwight A. *Behold the Man.* Dayton, OH: Center for Judaic-Christian Studies, 2008. (DVD Series & Study guide.) Twelve sessions on the significance of Jesus' Jewishness for Christians today. Excellent for a group study.

———. *Unveiling the Kingdom of Heaven.* Dayton, OH: Center for Judaic-Christian Studies, 2008. (DVD Series & Study guide.) Excellent introduction to Jesus' teaching on the kingdom and its implications for our lives.

Safrai, Shmuel, and Menahem Stern, eds. *The Jewish People in the First Century.* (2 vols.) Philadelphia: Fortress, 1976. Scholarly and difficult to find, but an outstanding resource on first-century Jewish life and times.

Schechter, Solomon. *Aspects of Rabbinic Theology.* Peabody, MA: Hendrickson, 1998 (1909). An overview of the theology of Judaism by a conservative Jewish rabbi; older but very readable.

Spangler, Ann, and Lois Tverberg. *Sitting at the Feet of Rabbi Jesus: How the Jewishness of Jesus Can Transform Your Faith.* Grand Rapids: Zondervan, 2009. An introduction to first-century Jewish culture, prayers, and feasts that shed light on Jesus' life and words.

Stern, David H. *Jewish New Testament Commentary.* Baltimore: Messianic Jewish Resources International, 1992. In depth, verse-by-verse commentary on the New Testament by a Messianic Jewish scholar. Very good reference.

Telushkin, Joseph. *The Book of Jewish Values.* New York: Bell Tower, 2000. Daily readings on practical application of Jewish ethics. Very insightful—an outstanding book to discuss with a group.

————. *A Code of Jewish Ethics*. Vol. 1, *Love the Lord Your God*; Vol. 2., *Love Your Neighbor as Yourself*). New York: Random House, 2006, 2009. Comprehensive guide to biblical ethics from a Jewish perspective. An excellent guide to becoming more Christlike.

————. *Words That Hurt, Words That Heal: How to Choose Words Wisely and Well*. New York: Harper, 1998. Superb guide on how and how not to use your tongue.

Tverberg, Lois, with Bruce Okkema. *Listening to the Language of the Bible: Hearing It through Jesus' Ears*. Holland, MI: En-Gedi Resource Center, 2004. Dozens of brief reflections on Hebrew words and Jewish concepts that enrich Bible reading.

Tverberg, Lois. *Listening to the Language of the Bible: Companion Bible Study*. Holland, MI: En-Gedi Resource Center, 2005. A study guide for the previous book, for those who want to learn to read the Bible in light of its Hebraic context.

Vander Laan, Ray. *Faith Lessons Video Series*. Grand Rapids: Zondervan, 1998–2008. (DVDs and study guides.) Outstanding video series that shares insights on the land and culture of the Bible, exploring its implications for Christians today.

Wilson, Marvin. *Our Father Abraham: The Jewish Roots of the Christian Faith*. Grand Rapids: Eerdmans, 1989. A must-read introductory text for anyone wanting to learn more on this topic.

Young, Brad. *Jesus the Jewish Theologian*. Peabody, MA: Hendrickson, 1995. Excellent study of Jesus' life and teachings in their Jewish context.

————. *The Parables: Jewish Tradition and Christian Interpretation*. Peabody, MA: Hendrickson, 1998. A scholarly examination of Jesus' parables in light of rabbinic parable traditions.

Websites

OurRabbiJesus.com — Our Rabbi Jesus: His Jewish Life and Teaching. Lois Tverberg's blog, which features insights from a Hebraic perspective on faith and daily living.

Egrc.net — En-Gedi Resource Center. Educational ministry that teaches about the Jewish context of Christianity. Books and articles by Lois

Tverberg and other authors. Hundreds of links to other recommended sites for study.

FollowTheRabbi.com — Follow the Rabbi. Website of Ray Vander Laan, source of *Faith Lessons* video series, leads trips to Israel and Asia Minor. Many articles and resources available.

Hebrew4Christians.com — Hebrew for Christians. Very nice site for learning Hebrew and about Christianity's Jewish heritage.

JCStudies.com — Center for Judaic-Christian Studies. Material by Dwight Pryor and others. Excellent audio/video materials about applying Hebraic study to life today.

JerusalemPerspective.com — Jerusalem Perspective. A large number of excellent articles on Jesus' first-century Jewish context.

JewishEncyclopedia.com — Jewish Encyclopedia. Searchable online Jewish Encyclopedia in the public domain, published in 1905. Older, but has useful articles on Jewish traditions by outstanding scholars of its time.

Scripture Index

General Index

saving a life, 135–36
scales of judgment, 105–6
scientist, thinking as a, 131–33
scribes, 154
Scripture, studying, 145–53
scroll, sealed, 157–58
scrolls, writing, 154
second coming, 161–64
secrets, God's, 145, 154–64
secularism, 27, 48
"see," Hebraic meaning of, 71
self-therapy, 73
September 11, 190, 162–63
shakla v'tarya (give and take), 130
shaming others, 99–100, 113
Shammai, 25
Shechem, 150
Shema, 31–40, 42–53, 195–96
  hear/obey, 33–36, 40
  in *Hebrew*, 31, 33, 34, 53
  reciting, 48–49
  text of the, 195–96
  three- vs. fourfold, 51–52
Shevet Achim, 89–90
shmirat halashon (guarding the tongue), 95
shophet (judge, vindicator), 119
short-term love, 50–51
Silver, Rabbi Eliezer, 31
Simchat Torah (Joy of the Torah), 149
Simeon ben Shetach, 87
sin, 61–64, 104–5, 109–14, 128, 136–37
  problem of, 188–91
singing alone together, 57, 65
sitting at a rabbi's feet, 29
Sitting at the Feet of Rabbi Jesus, 11, 29, 58
slander, 23–24, 92–93, 95–97
slips of paper, 187, 188, 191
slow drip of study, 151
snowflakes, 166

"soap opera," biblical 150
Sodom, 122, 127–28, 163–64
soils, parable of the, 36
solitude, 56–57
soul, loving with, 48–49, 54
  toning up one's, 101–2
sovereignty, God's, 185
Spangler, Ann, 192–94
speculating, futility of, 156–57
speech, evil, 38, 92–103, 110, 137–38
stamping coins, 181
Star Trek, 167–68
steadfast love, 49–50
"stealing" someone's mind, 100–101
stinginess, 69–80
storybook Bibles, 150
strabismus, 165
strength, loving God with, 50
study, as worship, 153
  difficulty of, 151
  in heaven, 157
  love of, 10, 145–53
  rewards of, 151
suffering, of God, 174–78
  Christ's, 161
  innocent, 158–61, 173
Sukkot, feast of 17–18, 26
Swindoll, Charles, 108–9
synagogue, 146, 148
Syrophoenician woman, 118–9

Tabernacles, feast of, 17–19, 26
tabloids, supermarket, 155
talk, malicious, 92–103, 137–39
Talmud, 25
taxes, 180–81
teachers, traveling, 146
"teaching," Torah as, 145
Telushkin, Joseph, 58–59, 101, 109, 136–37
Temple, 17–18, 23
tenacious faith, 120–29

Share Your Thoughts

With the Author: Your comments will be forwarded to the author when you send them to *zauthor@zondervan.com*.

With Zondervan: Submit your review of this book by writing to *zreview@zondervan.com*.

Free Online Resources at
www.zondervan.com

Zondervan AuthorTracker: Be notified whenever your favorite authors publish new books, go on tour, or post an update about what's happening in their lives at www.zondervan.com/authortracker.

Daily Bible Verses and Devotions: Enrich your life with daily Bible verses or devotions that help you start every morning focused on God. Visit www.zondervan.com/newsletters.

Free Email Publications: Sign up for newsletters on Christian living, academic resources, church ministry, fiction, children's resources, and more. Visit www.zondervan.com/newsletters.

Zondervan Bible Search: Find and compare Bible passages in a variety of translations at www.zondervanbiblesearch.com.

Other Benefits: Register to receive online benefits like coupons and special offers, or to participate in research.

ZONDERVAN

ZONDERVAN.com/
AUTHORTRACKER
follow your favorite authors